Dear D.

Saint Stephens is a true blessing to our family! You are a wonderful leader and I appreciate your vision for character development in our rising generations.

Sincerely,

-Pete

2018

DEFINING THE TEACHABLE MOMENTS IN SPORTS

A GUIDEBOOK TO CHARACTER LITERACY DEVELOPMENT

by

PETE PACIOREK

Character Loves Company

P.O. Box 14983

Bradenton, FL 34280

www.characterlovescompany.org

Cover artwork by Amy Paciorek

Cover design by Jocelyn Greene, Green Girl Designs

Library of Congress Catalog Number: 2016915482

ISBN: 978-1-5375-2536-5

1. Sports 2. Ethics 3. Coaching 4. Mentoring 5. Parenting

First Edition

Printed in the United States of America

CONTENTS

List of Contributors to Guidebook..v

Foreword by Fred Claire..ix

Preface: Quote from Coach John Wooden Leads into Character Literacy Development (CLD)...xi

Part I: Where is Character Development in Youth Sports Today?

Chapter 1: The Plight of Youth Sports Today (An All Too Common Recurrence).........1

Chapter 2: The Lost "Potential" of Sports (The Need for Character Literacy Development **CLD** from Coach-Mentor)..7

Chapter 3: An Investigation into the Downward Plight of Sports—Micro-Level Perspective (What happened to the Pride and Honor of the Title of Coach?)..............17

Chapter 4: An Investigation into the Downward Plight of Sports—Macro-Level Perspective (The Two Vices That Are Holding Youth/Amateur Sports Hostage)........37

Chapter 5: My Research (What the Expert Coaches Think)...............................43

Part II: Character Literacy Development—25 Character Values & 25 Character Contributor Narratives..55

Chapter 6: Level 1: CLD—Foundational Level (5-7-Year-Old Range)

Character Values (1-5):

1. *Respect for Parents*...63
2. *Sportspersonship*..73
3. *Respect for Coaches, Opponents, Officials, Rules*...................................79

4. *Gratitude (Love of Sport/Fitness and Opportunity)*............................85

5. *Appreciation/Care for Others (Interdependence and Commitment)*............91

Chapter 7: Level 2: CLD—Post-Foundational Level (8-10-Year-Old Range)

<u>Character Values (6-10)</u>:

6. *Coachability (Willingness to Learn)*............................97

7. *Integrity & Honor*............................107

8. *Concept of Working to a Common Goal (Teamwork)*............................113

9. *Listening and Focus*............................119

10. *Understanding how to Compete (Honestly/Ethically)*............................125

Chapter 8: Level 3: CLD—Mid-level (11-14-Year-Old-Range)

<u>Character Values (11-16)</u>:

11. *Discipline*............................133

12. *Timeliness (Time Management)*............................139

13. *Humility*............................143

14. *Work Ethic/Sense of Accomplishment*............................149

15. *Leadership*............................155

16. *Confidence Without Being Cocky*............................165

Chapter 9: Level 4: CLD—Advancing Level (14-16-Year-Old-Range)

<u>Character Values (17-22)</u>:

17. *Sacrifice*............................173

18. *Handling Adversity/Resilience (Toughness/Grit)*............................179

19. *Process Oriented*............................191

20. *Body Language Awareness*............................199

21. *Community Service/Outreach*............................207

22. *Honest Evaluation (Self & Peers)*............................213

Chapter 10: Level 5: CLD—Advanced Mastery Level (16-19 & 19-23+ Year-Old-Range)

<u>Character Values (23-25)</u>:

23. *Winning (How to Win the Right Way)*............................219

24. *Servant Leadership*............................227

25. Legacy (Impact on Others Now and in the Future)..233

Part III: The Application, Retention, and Assessment of Character Literacy Development (CLD)

Appendix: Moving Forward: Three Essays on Important Topics for the Future of Youth Sports...247

    1) Bridging the Great Divide Between Parents and Coaches:
The Need to Unify a Common Message...249

    2) Coaching the Next Generation of Coaches: What Type of Behaviors and Values Are We Modeling?...253

    3) Cleaning up the "Locker Room" Talk: We Cannot Continue to Turn a Blind Eye...259

Supplemental Guide "CLD" Coach-Mentor Guide:.......................................263

✓ Team Activities & Assignments from **CLD** Guidebook for each of the **25 Character Values (CVs)**

✓ Important Tables, Charts, and Graphs

✓ Link to **C-SALT** (Student-athlete **CHARACTER** Literacy Test)

✓ Contact Information for Author—Coach Pete Paciorek (to share stories/ideas that I can use with future curricula)

Addendum: Contributing Research & Literature in the Field............................297

References...305

Acknowledgements..315

25 FEATURED CONTRIBUTORS TO
CHARACTER LOVES COMPANY GUIDEBOOK:

*(Contributors are listed in the order that they first appear, as well as the Character Value **CV** section[s] in which they are discussed)*

1. -Betsy Mitchell

Olympic Gold Medalist in Swimming for USA in 1984; Current College Athletic Director **[CV #1 Respect for Parents, CV #11 Discipline, CV#12 Timeliness, CV #17 Sacrifice]**

2. -Ryan Arcidiacono

2016 NCAA Final Four Men's National Champion & 4-year Captain of Villanova Wildcats **[CV#1 Respect for Parents, CV#4 Gratitude, CV#8 Teamwork, CV#20 Body Language]**

3. -Rafael Perez

Major League Baseball, Director for Dominican Republic; Son of 50-year youth Coach **[CV#1 Respect for Parents, CV#4 Gratitude, CV#5 Appreciation/Interdependence, CV#7 Integrity, CV#25 Legacy]**

4. -John Paciorek

Youth Coach/Mentor for 50 Years; MLB Record Holder for Highest Lifetime Batting Average **[CV#1 Respect for Parents, CV#7 Integrity, CV#17 Sacrifice, CV#25 Legacy]**

5. -BJ Bedford-Miller

Olympic Gold Medalist in Swimming for USA in 2000; Board Member for PCA **[CV#2 Sportspersonship, CV#3 Respect for Coaches/Rules, CV#6 Coachability, CV#10 How to Compete, CV#17 Sacrifice, CV#22 Honest Evaluation, CV#23 Winning, CV#24 Servant Leadership]**

6. -Beth Work

Assistant Director, Boys & Girls Clubs, Manatee County; long-time youth Mentor **[CV#2 Sportspersonship, CV#4 Gratitude]**

7. -Lee Ellis

College Athletic Director; Coach/Mentor; Character Educator **[CV#3 Respect for Coaches/Rules, CV#24 Servant Leadership]**

8. *-Addison Staples*

Tennis Expert; long-time youth Coach/Mentor, founder of non-profit "Aces in Action" for underserved youth [**CV#3 Respect for Coaches/Rules, CV#5 Appreciation/Interdependence, CV#21 Community Service, CV#22 Honest Evaluation**]

9. *-Ken Wasserman*

20-year MLB Physician; Current Physician, Baltimore Orioles [**CV#4 Gratitude**]

10. *-Dan Duquette*

Baltimore Orioles GM, Long-time MLB Executive [**CV#5 Appreciation/Interdependence**]

11. *-David Prince*

Track & Field World Record Holder in the 200M and 400M for Single Amputee in Paralympics; youth Mentor [**CV#6 Coachability, CV#18 Adversity/Grit, CV#19 Process Oriented, CV#23 Winning, CV#25 Servant Leadership**]

12. *-Jenna Marston*

Team USA Gold Medalist; 2-Time Team USA Sportswoman of the Year; NCAA Scholar-Athlete [**CV#6 Coachability, CV#9 Listening/Focus, CV#13 Humility, CV#18 Adversity/Grit**]

13. *-Ken Leavoy*

Team Canada Women's Softball Assistant Coach Gold Medalist in Pan Am Games; Professional & College Softball Coach/Mentor [**CV#6 Coachability, CV#11 Discipline, CV#15 Leadership**]

14. *-Fred Claire*

World Series Champion GM for the Los Angeles Dodgers and Expert on Leadership [**CV#1 Respect for Parents, CV#7 Integrity, CV#14 Work Ethic, CV#15 Leadership, CV#16 Confidence, CV#22 Confidence, CV#23 Winning**]

15. *-Amanda Butler*

Head Basketball Coach, University of Florida; Coach of the Year [**CV#8 Teamwork, CV#10 How to Compete, CV#12 Timeliness, CV#20 Body Language, CV#23 Winning**]

16. -David Ross

World Series Champion with Boston Red Sox; 15-Year MLB Veteran, Leader; former Teammate of author of this Guidebook [**CV#9 Listening/Focus, CV#11 Discipline, CV#15 Leadership**]

17. -Master Boon Brown

35-Year Youth Instructor/Mentor—Fifth degree Black Belt [**CV#11 Discipline, CV#13 Humility, CV#19 Process Oriented, CV#22 Honest Evaluation, CV#24 Servant Leadership**]

18. -David Santos

Second-year Cadet at West Point [**CV#11 Discipline, CV#23 Winning**]

19. -Chivonne Kiser

Veteran High School Volleyball and Track & Field Coach; previous NCAA DI student-athlete [**CV#15 Leadership, CV#22 Honest Evaluation**]

20. -Tribute to Scott Studenmund

Army Staff Sgt.; Green Beret [**CV#17 Sacrifice, CV#25 Legacy**]

21. -Malaika Underwood

2-Time Team USA Women's Baseball Gold Medalist and Captain; Youth Role Model, Former UNC Volleyball Standout [**CV#18 Adversity/Grit**]

22. -Jeremy Peterson

Former Army Ranger [Served Country During Gulf War]; current youth Coach/Mentor of Martial Arts for boys and girls [**CV#18 Adversity/Grit, CV#23 Winning, CV#25 Legacy**]

23. -Angus Mugford

Toronto Blue Jays, Special Assistant to General Manager; previous Director of Mental Conditioning at IMG Academy [**CV#20 Body Language Awareness**]

24. -Michael Sagas

Professor and Chair of Department of TRSM at UF; founder of Twinnor, non-profit organization for underserved youth [**CV#21 Community Service, CV#25 Legacy**]

25. -Alex Rivera 40-year youth Coach/Mentor [**CV#25 Legacy**],

　　-Glen Beattie High School Coach [**CV#25 Legacy**],

　　-Perry Skaggs High School Coach [**CV#25 Legacy**]

FOREWORD

Pete Paciorek was raised in a sports family that reaches back in time and continues with contributions that branch into the future and all areas of athletics.

There are many books and publications on the wonderful game of baseball with instruction offered in every conceivable area. One of the fascinating parts of the game involves the many facets that are required to be a successful player and a winning coach.

Quite often overlooked in all of the wisdom and instruction that is offered is perhaps the most important area: the "make-up" of the player. The term that really should be used is the term that Pete has chosen for his title: "**Character**."

When coaches and fans talk about players, there seems to be the emphasis on talent and that certainly isn't surprising. It takes talent to play the game and the need for talent advances as the level of play advances.

In my 30 years with the Los Angeles Dodgers, I had the chance to know and be involved with many talented players, in fact, Hall of Fame type of talent. It isn't just the talent that has defined the game's greatest players. It has been the **character** of the individual that has been the true trademark.

I saw many talented players who never reached the top level of success. And when I think back to those players who achieved at the highest level, I see the component of **character** that I would define as a combination of dedication, perseverance, a willingness to learn and think of the team first, and a refusal to give up.

At the end of a game, at the end of a career, a player has to ask himself only one question: *Did I give the very best of what I had to give at ALL times?* If the answer to that question is a resounding "yes," the player has found success.

After all, the only thing any of us can give to the game [or sport] we play and to our careers is the very best we have to give. And that is exactly what must be given for ultimate success—the very best. And to give the very best at all times is what **character** is all about.

My long-time baseball friend, Joey Amalfitano, has spent a lifetime in baseball and his words will forever be in my mind: *"Respect the game."* You show that respect through your approach in everything you do, on and off the field.

In a word: **Character**.

—***Fred Claire***, 1988 World Series Champion GM of the Los Angeles Dodgers and Author of: *Fred Claire: My 30 Years in Dodger Blue*

PREFACE

"What we emphasize gets improved upon."–John Wooden

In the world of sports, and equally in the world of business and leadership, Coach Wooden is regarded as one of the greatest coaches, mentors, and leaders of the 21st century. As Coach Wooden so clearly stated in the above quote, we need to be *intentional* and *deliberate* about what we emphasize to our youth concerning the values of sport participation. It is equally imperative that the nature and content of what we emphasize is appropriate for the age range of the children that we are teaching/mentoring. Character building needs to be advanced in the same way that reading literacy and other literacies are measured. This guidebook is designed for facilitating a building block approach for promoting and assessing character growth through athletics.

Too many coaches nowadays justify a singular and hyper-focused concern for winning and end results based on the fact that their favorite DI or professional head coach adheres to the same approach. I know this because youth and amateur coaches have in fact shared such sentiments with me over the past year and a half as I have traveled across the country giving community talks on the topic of this guidebook.

This book is a unique blend of the theoretical studies on youth and amateur sport, my own UF-IRB[1] research projects and surveys, and 25 powerful contributions from the likes of Olympic Gold Medalists, World and National Champions, and 40+ year veteran youth coaches. The triangulation and intersection of these three components add validity in support of the 25 character values that I present, as well as make for an inspiring and motivational read through personal narratives and real life defining moments in sports that translate into success in life after sports. The content of this guidebook is the foundation of my non-profit organization, **Character Loves**

---

[1] UF-IRB stands for University of Florida Institutional Review Board approved studies.

Company,[2] which I established as a means to mentoring junior high school and high school students through my eight-week Character Literacy Development **(CLD)** curriculum.

---

[2] My non-profit organization, "Character Loves Company," was created with the desire to continue to provide my free grassroots-level talks across the country to youth recreation centers and schools for coaches, parents, and children, as well as provide my eight-week Character Literacy **(CL)** curriculum for junior high school and high school aged children/students at local recreation centers. For more information go to: www.characterlovescompany.org

Part I:

Where is Character Development in Youth Sports Today?

CHAPTER 1—The Plight of Youth Sports Today

Allow me to take you inside the current world of youth sports. If you are new to recreational and amateur athletics in America, the picture I am going to paint for you will be unsettling. However, if you have spent much time around the playing fields, pool decks, or gymnasiums that house youth sports nowadays, the hypothetical scenario that I present below will most likely come as no surprise, but may turn your stomach in a way that sparks a desire to seek rectification.

As someone who has been involved in youth and amateur sports for the past three decades, I have witnessed an alarming trend at all levels of athletic involvement over the past few years. What was once a proud domain specializing in the character development of our youth has spiraled into a chaotic mess of unrecognizable madness. As the focal point of my academic research and graduate school studies over the past two years, I have closely tracked the news and media on youth and amateur athletics, and how it relates to character development. Not a single day has gone by where one or more of the involved constituents across our country (i.e. coaches, parents, administrators, or players) failed to find a way to disgrace the sanctity and true intent of athletics at all levels of sports participation.

I want you to imagine that you are the head baseball coach of an 11 and under summer Travel Ball team (11-U).[3] Your team is leading 8-1 on the scoreboard and the

---

[3] Competitive Travel Ball or Competitive Club participation has been around for the past two decades, but never in the way that it is today. Today there are competitive 4-U teams (yes, 4-years-old and under): http://www.usssa.com/baseball/Rank1/#/?gdSport=1, which seems over-the-top from every standpoint. They travel all over the country, and even world, in search of the supposed best "ranked"

game is in the final inning. You have a player named Paul on your team who works extremely hard, but he is just not very good. However, Paul has a passion for pitching and he has been putting in considerable time and effort working to improve. You have been waiting for the ideal situation to present itself, when the game is not on the line, in order to put Paul in to pitch.

With this large lead you decide that it is the time to reward your player for his commitment to improvement and to the team, so you enter him into the game. What seemed like the perfect situation for him to taste a little success on the mound quickly begins to backfire. He walks the leadoff batter of the inning. Then he hits the next batter with a pitch. No big deal, you are still up 8-1. After a barrage of wall-clanking hits, the score is now 8-5 with only one out. All of a sudden, you begin to hear it from your team's parents in the stands who are becoming restless and extremely nervous. I am not trying to downplay the importance of winning,[4] but keep in mind that this is an 11-U game.

You hear a dad scream, "Get him out of there, Coach, before it is too late." That comment incites another similar one, and then another that progressively get louder and more disconcerting. Your pitcher hears the peanut gallery in the stands, and now he becomes noticeably rattled by the runners on base and the fact that he could blow the game for his team.

You ask the umpire for timeout, and you jog out to the mound to relieve your deflated young pitcher. As you are making that 100-foot jaunt to the mound, the game starts to speed up on you a bit. You are now a little worried that your coaching decision could cost the team the game, but most importantly, you are concerned with the confidence and psyche of your 10-year-old pitcher, Paul. In a matter of two to three seconds - the time it took you to go from the dugout to the pitching mound - you have come up with a few words of encouragement to assure your pitcher that he will have another chance to get back out on the mound soon, and that you are going to have a teammate come in and relieve him to get the last few outs. As you extend your hand out

competition. This is a concept that I will talk more about regarding age-appropriate character development to go hand-in-hand with the age-appropriate physical development models.
[4] Winning is a very important value that I strongly believe needs to be preserved in American society. When you read about the number of professional athletes and high level collegiate student-athletes in my family, you will not doubt the passion that my family and I place on the value of winning. However, the key is "winning the right way."

for the ball from Paul, your star shortstop asserts himself and confidently states, "Leave Paulie in, Coach. We've got his back."[5] In shock by the pure act of leadership displayed by your 11-year-old shortstop in support of his struggling teammate, you decide to ride that character wave back to the dugout. After all, how could you take him out of the game following the courageously bold and considerate support of his teammate? As you turn to head off the field desperately trying to hold back the smile of joy and pride that has overtaken you, the moment is stolen out from underneath you as quickly and unexpectedly as it came.

The few disorderly parents who were shouting at you prior to your mound visit have now doubled your trouble to a collusion of horror. By the time you reach your post in the dugout, this group of parents is now hovering around the chain link dugout fence - a mere five feet behind you - like a pack of hungry dogs awaiting their next meal. They unequivocally let you know how they feel about your decision to leave the pitcher in. **Quick reminder: You are a volunteer coach and you are unpaid for the time that you commit to your team. You chose to coach the team because your son or daughter is on the team, and the other coaching option was one of the four screaming loudmouths behind you.** You sit there getting berated by the following statements: "Coach, you should be ashamed of yourself" and "You are doing a disservice to our kids." The worst that the coach heard was, "If we lose this game, YOU are teaching these kids to be losers!"

Though it seems like an eternity and the turmoil around you is overwhelming, you maintain your composure, at least externally. Your pitcher, Paul, makes a few more pitches, before inducing a game ending 4-6-3 double play. For many baseball enthusiasts, the game-ending 4-6-3[6] double play is poetry in motion, and one of the most beautiful displays of **teamwork** in all of sports. Late inning, game-threatening rally thwarted, all on one well-executed team play. However, for you as the coach of this 11-U team, the

---

[5] Whenever I share this true recount during community talks around the country, I always have to take a few seconds to pause and let that moment take root. I have shared this story on courage and teamwork close to 100 times and those eight words from an 11-year-old boy are an inspiring encouragement for the cause that I am fighting.

[6] The pitcher has to execute the pitch (maybe a two-seamer on the black of the plate that dives away from the left-handed hitter), the second baseman has to field the ball cleanly before gracefully pivoting his body and delivering a chest high dart to his shortstop. The shortstop then has to receive the throw, while simultaneously swiping his right foot across the back edge of the base, avoid the incoming baserunner, and release his best fastball across the diamond to first base to end the game.

character values on display of **teamwork, overcoming adversity, leadership, winning the right way, learning how to compete, humility, confidence, focus, sense of accomplishment,** and **respect and appreciation for others on the field** boiled down to nothing more than a sigh of relief that your team won. By allowing your perspective of the value of the game to be measured solely by the end result on the scoreboard, you have just allowed yourself to actively accept and proliferate the current "win-at-all-costs"[7] or "zero-sum game"[8] traps that I discuss in this book.

The sad truth of the scenario that I present above is that this situation was not a hypothetical. Rather, it is one of hundreds, if not thousands, of similar displays of unethical behavior from parents, coaches, players, or sport managers across our country each year. What is equally disturbing to me about such frequent occurrences is that the true acts of character that take place on that field are often unrecognized and unappreciated for the sake of the almighty "win." Is that the sole focus of what youth and amateur sports have become in our society?

For the coach who had to live through that unfortunate and disgusting lack of character by his team's parents, his answer was "yes" and he was ready to throw in the towel on sportsmanship and the other values of sports. This coach shared his story with me one month after it happened, and the after effect was still fresh in his mind. He heard me talking to a group of 80 baseball campers about the concept of being coachable and open to the teachable learning moments that day at IMG Academy in Bradenton, Florida where, at the time, I was the head baseball instructor and summer baseball camp coordinator. After he recounted the above scenario to me one-on-one, he told me that he vowed never to volunteer his services as a coach again after the season's conclusion. What bothered him the most about the situation was how he had missed out on what was one of the most courageous and pure acts of heroism from an 11-year-old, as well as the 10-year-old pitcher, that he could have ever imagined. Not only was his joy in the moment immediately stripped away, but more disturbing to him was that he failed to capitalize on the teaching moment for all of the young participants on his team. This

---

[7] The "win-at-all-costs" mentality is exactly what it says it is and is also synonymous with the "zero-sum game."

[8] The "zero-sum game" or product is a concept that is used to shed light on the many flaws to the win-at-all-costs mentality that permeates our current youth/amateur sports landscape. The zero-sum game and win-at-all-cost traps are the concepts that I will discuss in more detail in Chapters 3 and 4.

guidebook was formulated for the sole purpose of seeking out and seizing opportunities such as these to infuse character in our youth today.

The aforementioned narrative, as well as other similar recounts, was the impetus for this guidebook on the concept of **Character Literacy** or **(CL)** and the need for an appropriate curriculum in **Character Literacy Development** or **(CLD)** in youth sports. Through first-person narratives from business men and women, World Series Champions, youth coaches, high-level college coaches, Olympic Champions, World Champions, Major League general managers, athletic directors, and recreation center directors, this guidebook on character building will blend the empirically-driven research with real life stories of the negative and positive in youth and amateur athletics.

In this book, I not only uncover but specifically pinpoint the two major vices that are currently holding youth sports hostage and keeping our kids from rising to their full potential as positive leaders and people of character. The first and greatest culprit is the blatant (or for some, latent) fallacy that emphasizing character in sports is a sign of weakness. The second disconcerting problem is the "win-at-all-costs" mentality that trumps all other character values potentially learned through athletics.

After unpacking and elucidating why the above two vices have created a path to nowhere, I will spend the remainder of this guidebook presenting a new paradigm, or way of thinking, based around my research and the inception of the concept of Character Literacy **(CL)** and Character Literacy Development **(CLD)**.

The fact that some coaches and parents have point blank told me as I have traveled across the country that emphasizing character in sports is "a sign of weakness" or "lack of toughness" is absurd. Couple this sentiment with the equally alarming "win-at-all-costs" mentality of many involved in sports even in the lowest levels of youth and amateur athletics, and we need to recognize that this is becoming an endemic problem.

This book provides a resource guide which lays out the foundation of a progressive age-specific curriculum based on the 25 most commonly noted character values from 125+ of our country's veteran-expert coaches. These 25 character values create a foundational framework for the coach at all levels of youth and amateur sports to follow in order to effectively and consistently **identify**, **promote**, **develop**, and **assess** for comprehension and retention of the immeasurable value of character literacy development **(CLD)** in our youth.

CHAPTER 2—The Lost "Potential" of Sports

For the past 20 years, dating back to my career as a professional athlete,[9] I have been contemplating and studying the many character values that athletic participation has the potential[10] of developing. In life, as well as in the world of sports, the word "potential" has a powerful significance. I use the word in the subsequent sentence to express the importance of the delivery mechanism. Sports, if delivered in the appropriate manner by administrators, coaches, parents, and participants, have the *potential* to invoke positive lifelong influence in the lives of our children and society. This book is a guide to anyone who shares a passion for effectuating positive change in our youth through the vehicle of athletics.

I love sports. I have a passion for helping young athletes (student-athletes)[11] continue to work their way up the ladder of success in life through their involvement in sports. The term "student-athlete" requires that all participants in athletics, whether individual or team sport, must fulfill the first responsibility before being granted the privilege of the second. We need to be *deliberate* about our messages to our youth, and I believe that all of our children need to learn at the earliest of ages that academics always

---

[9] I was a member of the San Diego Padres and Los Angeles Dodgers organizations for nine years, and I come from a family that has produced eight professional athletes.

[10] "Potential" in sports is a loaded word—you either live up to it or you do not. If potential is not developed and fully tapped into, it is said to have been wasted. People would argue that Peyton Manning (who never won a Heisman) has lived up to his potential, while Heisman trophy winner Johnny Manziel has squandered or wasted his talents. The verdict is still not out on recent Heisman trophy winner, Jameis Winston. A focus on successful Heisman trophy winners will be a topic of focus in Chapter 4.

[11] I refer to all youth and amateur athletes who are not professionals as student-athletes (SAs) because of what that term symbolizes. Irrespective of whether I was in my role as an NCAA head coach at Principia College, a head coach at IMG Academy, or I am teaching a 5-7-year-old group of young boys and girls at a local recreation center, I always refer to them as student-athletes because academics must be their priority.

come before athletics. While it is true that athletic participation can have transformational power and influence over young student-athletes in ways that the walls of a classroom cannot, education will always continue to be the most influential player in the game of life.

While a significant portion of the research in the field of youth and amateur athletics will support the fact that sports, if delivered correctly by those involved, have the *potential* to positively shape our society's future generations, the inverse is also true. A great deal of research vehemently depicts that when sports are not delivered appropriately, they can drive our youth away and leave a lasting scar (literally and figuratively).

The next two chapters of this guidebook on **CLD** will juxtapose the research that is split down the middle on the highly contested debate as to whether sports build positive or negative character in our youth all the way up through adulthood. Though my philosophy is grounded in an unshakeable love and appreciation for the countless lifelong values that sports participation has summoned in me, I do not believe that athletics build positive or negative values in and of the sport itself. However, I cannot imagine where life would have taken me without what I have learned through the many wonderful coaches, parents, and mentors that I was fortunate to have had in athletics. Over the past two decades, I have learned that the good and the bad in sports are directly correlated to their delivery.

My family namesake (Paciorek) attaches a great deal of pride in the endless values that can be built through athletics. In total, my family name carries a genetic predestination to excel in sports. In the last two generations, the Paciorek family has produced more than 10 college athletes and eight professional baseball players (which is the second most of any family since the turn of the 21st century). With this inclination for athletic achievement and the pursuit of excellence through competitive sports, I learned many life lessons through the daily teaching moments from my dad, a coach for the past five decades, and many of my coaches growing up. A significant portion of my character was shaped through this athletic inheritance.

As a young boy, I dreamed of becoming a professional football player (like Walter Payton), then an Olympic sprinter in the 100-meter dash (like Carl Lewis), then a professional basketball player (of course, growing up in the 80's and 90's, I wanted to be like Mike—Michael Jordan, that is), before I finally embraced my dream of becoming a professional baseball player (like my dad, John, and uncles Tom, Mike, Si, and Jim). Or maybe it was baseball that chose me. I was fortunate to be a professional baseball player for nine years in the Los Angeles Dodgers and San Diego Padres organizations. With an entire previous family generation of males who were members of Major League Baseball (MLB) organizations, I followed suit. I chased this passion for athletic competition and achievement as long as I was able to garner a uniform, falling just short of the Major Leagues.

In my family, we joke that my brother Mack and I (sons of John, owner of MLB's lifetime highest batting average of 1.000), my two cousins Tommy (son of Tom, 18-year MLB player and 15-year MLB announcer) and Joey (son of Jim, MLB player and Batting Champion in Japan in 1990) let the family down as we were not able to reach the Major League level. However, if you ask anyone, they will tell you that we played the game **the right way**[12] during an era when a lot of people were not. In doing so, we all enjoyed the ride and learned a lot about life along the way.

Upon transitioning out of being a professional athlete for almost a decade, I finished my undergraduate studies and immediately chose to follow my dad's footsteps in becoming a coach. I guess you could say that my dad had been grooming me to be a coach ever since I was 15-years-old and a freshman in high school. He has been a youth coach for the past 50+ years. Currently, he is in his 41st year at the same school as an elementary and junior high school Physical Education teacher and coach in Southern California. A few years back, a *Los Angeles Times* writer learned about my dad's life and he wrote a book about his influence on tens of thousands of children as a youth coach.[13] If you do not know the story of my dad, John Paciorek, he played the most perfect single game in the history of Major League Baseball as an 18-year-old rookie. A serious back injury never allowed him to play in the Major Leagues again. His career on the biggest stage was stunted, but his story of influence is both inspiring and motivating.

---

[12] The 1990's and early 2000's are known as the "Steroid Era" for a reason. Despite being right on the edge of accomplishing my dream of playing in the Major Leagues, I am proud that I never succumbed to the pressures to take steroids. If I had cheated to enhance my performance, I would not be able to write this book on character, as well as stand before thousands of young aspiring student-athletes and look them in the eye in discussing the importance of having integrity and strong character.

[13] *Perfect: The Rise and Fall of John Paciorek, Baseball's Greatest One-Game Wonder*, by Steven K. Wagner (2015). While my dad is a very humble person, though he was honored to have a book written on him, he did tell me that the title should have been *The Rise and Fall and Resurgence*, because he feels that his coaching career was a resurgence for him.

My dad is 71-years-old and I would not be surprised if he continues to coach well into his 80's. He is an inspiration to me and my family, as well as the countless young lives that he has motivated and encouraged over the past five decades. I know that my passion and energy to positively influence youth as well as my "kids first" approach were derived and modeled by him. When I see him coach, I am never amazed, but always motivated by how fun he makes sports for the kids. He has a nickname for every young boy or girl whom he ever coached, and he was doing this long before ESPN's Chris Berman became notorious for it.

What is most fascinating and representative of my topic on **CLD** in youth sports is what my dad has done ever since his *potential* - there is that word again - as an MLB superstar came to a screeching halt back in 1963. He could have sulked in despair, but instead he chose to **battle through adversity** and persevere despite his misfortunes. I have no doubt that the 25 character values that I discuss in this book all played a role in how and why my dad *deliberately* and *intentionally* chose to make the impact on so many young lives as a coach.

During the near decade of my life as a professional baseball player, I always saw role modeling and mentoring for the youth in the stands as a part of my job description. I believe this was due to the fact that I began coaching for my dad at such a young age.[14] However, it took me some time to become *active, deliberate,* and *intentional* in this role of youth coach/mentor.[15] The title of youth coach/mentor is one that I wear with an immense amount of pride, taking a backseat only to being a husband, father, and family man. The combined term of coach/mentor needs to be seen as non-negotiable in the world of youth and amateur athletics.

For the past 10 years, I have become much more *intentional* about my role as coach/mentor of youth and amateur student athletes. The platform that I had as an NCAA college head coach at Principia College in Illinois allowed me to begin to see the influence for good that I could have on those whom I coached, and even coached against. Principia College is a leader in the domain and space of character education in higher education. For five wonderful years, I grew in my own character and morals,

---

[14] My first coaching opportunity was in 1991 when I was 15-years-old. I coached the following sports at the junior high school level: flag football, soccer, basketball, track and field, volleyball, and baseball.
[15] To specify, throughout the remainder of this book, as well as during all of my community talks around the country, the title of youth or amateur coach also carries the imperative and integral duty of being a mentor in word and action. You cannot be one without also being the other.

alongside the student-athletes and my colleagues. I then became a head coach and lead instructor at perhaps the most prestigious multi-sport training facility in the world, IMG Academy, in Bradenton, Florida.

While at IMG, I realized how much more important my role as a positive mentor trumped my role as the lead coach. IMG has thousands of young aspiring student-athletes come to its campus each year (not counting professional athletes), and I quickly realized that a strong mentor was much more vital than someone who simply taught them how to hit, field, or throw. This heightened realization of the role or duty that all coaches have to serve as positive mentors was formed through many years of training.

For 20 years of my life, my paid occupation has been split down the middle as a professional athlete and a professional instructor/coach. My passion during this time has been making a positive difference in the lives of youth. Over the past few years, I have stepped outside of my comfort zone by actively and assertively reaching out to the outside community as a youth mentor.

For a year and a half now, I have been giving talks and seminars on character development through sports to coaches, athletic administrators, parents, and young student-athletes. I do not plan to slow down in my delivery of my vitally important message. The turnouts to my volunteer, grassroots outreach talks have been as few as 10 coaches in attendance and as large as 200 community members. I have presented my **CLD** curriculum mostly in Florida, where I live, but also in New Jersey, Illinois, Missouri, and California. I have spoken at numerous schools and recreation centers with groups of students to share my **CLD** curriculum.

I often meet with coaches, parents, and administrators to share ways that they can better infuse character development into their daily practice and game routines. I have found that the most effective delivery for my 30-minute outreach presentations is at local recreation centers or schools during their pre-season parent, coach, official, and player orientation meetings. These are typically meetings when all constituents are required by the centers, or at least expected, to attend. As witnessed by the trend of unethical acts in youth athletics nowadays, it would be safe to say that my talks on character literacy development would not attract the biggest turnouts if completely mandatory.

However, I embrace speaking to these grassroots groups about the many values of sports participation when delivered appropriately, for the simple fact that the current research shows that volunteer coaches comprise more than half of our country's youth coaches.[16] This has been an excellent way to apply my Master's degree in Public Speaking and Leadership.[17] These community talks also provide me with a forum and audience for the focus of my Master's degree in Sport Management from the University of Florida (UF). My M.S. from UF is specifically geared around an emphasis on my topic of **CLD**. I have conducted two research studies on character development and the establishment of an age-appropriate progression for **CLD** in youth and amateur athletics, both were fully supported by the research sanctioning body at UF. These integral research studies (presented further in Chapter 5) along with a snapshot of the relevant review of the literature in youth sports provide an empirically-driven theoretical lens from which I derived **CL** and **CLD.**

What is Character Literacy? **CL** is a concept that I coined along with the Chair of the Department of Tourism, Recreation, and Sport Management at the University of Florida, Dr. Michael Sagas. **CL** is demonstrable proof that one has learned the requisite character values in order to understand how to morally and ethically respond to a given situation. More importantly, an advanced-level of **CL** will assure that one's actions are in accordance with these learned character values. Character Literacy Development **CLD** posits a progressively developmental process for youth character enrichment and unfoldment that needs to be *deliberately* and *intentionally* emphasized. The character values of **CLD** need to be formulaically taught as a vital life skills component to developing our youth with an equal emphasis to "reading literacy" and "health literacy." **CLD** is an integral subset and corollary support to the foundation for the Athlete Development Literacy (ADL) model that UF's Lab for Athlete & Athletics Development and Research (LAADR) has created.

---

[16] According to research, there are more than 2.5 million volunteer youth coaches across America each year: http://opinionator.blogs.nytimes.com/2011/10/20/the-power-of-positive-coaching/
[17] My 184-page master's thesis dissertation on leadership (DODGER BLUES: A CASE STUDY INVESTIGATING HOW CHANGES TO MANAGEMENT AND LEADERSHIP STYLES AFFECTED THE ORGANIZATIONAL CULTURE OF THE LOS ANGELES DODGERS: 1958-2006) was nominated by the college and recognized by CSULA as one of the University's top thesis dissertations in 2006.

There is a difference between intelligence, expertise, and being literate on a topic. Merriam-Webster's Dictionary defines intelligence as "the ability to learn or understand things or to deal with new or difficult situations," while expertise is stated as "special skill or knowledge" (2015). According to UF's LAADR, "Literacy is the ability to meet challenges, obstacles, and take advantage of opportunities" (2015). These are the life skills in our domain of athletic development. It is one thing to know the correct answer or "right way" of doing something, but it takes literacy to act in accordance with one's knowledge and expertise.

My **CLD** curriculum provides stage by stage assessments or measurement outcomes for our youth involved in sports. These testing grounds, so to speak, will lay the foundation that will inevitably guide our children through the rigors of life in order to make a positive impact in society. **CLD** is focused on the lifespan approach for character unfoldment. **CLD** provides the core building blocks, or the road map, for young student-athletes, as well as our society as a whole, to follow in order to develop high levels of character literacy.

CL is integral to the continued success of youth and amateur sports, as well as the morals and ethics of our society. I believe that those committing unethical acts need to be called out. If a coach, parent, student-athlete, or any member of our society is going to act in a manner opposed to ethical values, then that individual does not have any business or right to coach, teach, or be in a position of influence with our youth. We would never consent to having someone who is reading illiterate in the classroom teaching our children. So, why do we continue to allow coaches who are "character illiterate" around our children in the athletic classrooms?[18]

As parents, coaches, mentors, and people of character, we have to demand that individuals who are character illiterate are kept out of coaching. Why can a coach throw chairs during a game, scream profanities, and demonstrate all of the negative qualities of someone who is "character illiterate," and yet still be called a good coach? At times, such character illiterate coaches are even put on a pedestal simply because they win championships.

As coaches of high character, we have to bring that sense of pride back into the title of "coach." With the title and prestige of the term "coach" comes the role of

---

[18] The athletic classrooms are our fields, swimming pools, gymnasiums, or other athletic arenas.

mentor, and we need to get back to where that title is rightfully recognized as a badge of honor.

As parents, we should not have to choose between a coach with a high level of knowledge of a sport and their level of **CL**, as we need to seek them both for the development of our children. However, if we had to choose one quality over the other, we need to prioritize character, in order to weed out all of the character illiterate coaches across our country. Coaches who know the sport and have played it at a high level of college or professionally are a dime a dozen. Becoming a youth coach/mentor who can seamlessly teach character alongside the physical development should be the ultimate goal of any coach, man or woman, who picks up a whistle and clipboard to help develop our youth. This type of coach will become much more the norm once we all stop supporting the character illiterate coaches.

What I have done in this guidebook is present the empirically-driven data and research on the topic, while at the same time intertwining the findings with real-life stories to better connect the theoretical dots of academic research. I grant the reader inside access to the treasured stories of character unfoldment, and the lack thereof, that have been told to me primarily in the privacy of homes around our country's dinner tables. Through personal narratives, I relay some of the most vivid memories and insightful recollections on the topic of character in sports gathered from 25 contributor interviews, all who have had a significant impact on their communities as well as our country, inside and outside of the athletic arena. The contributors to this guidebook all speak to the importance of these character values during their pursuits of athletic excellence. Not one of these accomplishments would have made the cut if not for the strong and enduring values that were nourished and refined through the test of sports.

This guidebook will help the reader identity, promote, develop, and assess the 25 character values of **CL** though a *systematic* and *deliberately* progressive character curriculum. These values need to be developed through sports participation from youth through early adulthood, where they should all crystalize to form the connecting tissues of lifetime **character literacy**. Regarding the 25 character values that I analyze throughout this guidebook (Chapters 5-10), it is important to note that no single character value has any enduring power on its own, but rather, it is the connection, or link, from one value to another that forms not only a way of thinking, but a way of living. Such noted character proof has exponential power through the process of **CLD** for this generation of youth and beyond. That is why coaches, parents, and administrators involved in youth and amateur athletics need to own their role as mentors and be *systematic* and *deliberate* about how they shape the character of their student-athletes.

In the next two chapters (3 and 4), I dissect the "what" and the "why" that has lowered our societal standards of ethics in sports below the moral minimum.[19] From Chapter 5 through the final page of this guidebook, I unravel a systematic curriculum for the reader (parent, coach, or administrator) to follow in order to progressively **identify**, **promote**, **develop**, and **assess** the **CL** growth in our youth through sports.

---

[19] This concept of moral minimum and the need to raise the bar on character in youth and amateur athletics was the focus of an article written by Sagas and Wigley (2014) entitled: *Gray Area Ethical Leadership in the NCAA: The Ethics of Doing the Wrong Things Right.*

CHAPTER 3—An Investigation into the Downward Plight of Sports—Micro-Level Perspective

The stories and staggering statistics in the next two chapters will appall you and leave you with a bitter taste in your mouth, or at least I hope they will. With that being said, my gut tells me that most of you were drawn to the title of this guidebook on character because you, like me, see the *potential* that sports participation can play in the lives of our youth. My guess is that you had favorable and impactful experiences in youth sports, and you want to see your daughters and/or sons have the opportunity to do the same.

Undoubtedly, you place a high premium on the value of youth sports participation, in the same way that I do. I would be honored if you would join me in my desire to identify with, promote, develop, and assess the retention and advancement of the following character values in our youth through sport involvement:[20] **integrity, discipline, timeliness, humility, sacrifice, work ethic/sense of accomplishment, the concept of working to a common goal/teamwork, handling adversity/resilience, respect for parents, respect and appreciation for others (commitment and interdependence), respect for opponents/officials/rules, listening and focus, gratitude (love of sport/fitness and opportunity), sportsmanship, leadership, coachability, learning how to compete (honestly and ethically), confidence without being cocky, process oriented, body language**

---

[20] As you have seen in the first few chapters, any mention of these most highly desired 25 character values in this guidebook will always be highlighted in **bold**. I will expand on how these character values made the Top 25 list in Chapter 5, when I present the findings of my two research studies, as well as what the current literature in the field of youth/amateur athletics says about building morals and stronger values through sports participation.

awareness, community service/outreach, honest evaluation (of self and of peers), how to win the right way, servant leadership, and **legacy**.

I firmly believe that the above 25 character values were what Nelson Mandela had at heart when he made the following statement about the potential for sports in his speech at the Laureus Lifetime Achievement Award in Monaco, *"Sport has the power to change the world...it has the power to inspire. It has the power to unite people in a way that little else does. It speaks to youth in a language they understand. Sport can create hope where once there was only despair"* (2000). The head of the Roman Catholic Church at the Vatican, Pope Francis, also sees the great impact that sports have on the world as a whole. According to Ourand (2016) featured in <u>Street and Smith's SportsBusiness Journal</u>, *"Pope Francis will make sports a focus of his papacy's third global initiative on education...The three-day event will examine the role sports can play in society, from establishing relationships to helping promote health and wellness."*

For those of us who have witnessed the many benefits of athletic endeavor, we share and embrace the optimistic vision for the value of sports that the late President Mandela and current Pope Francis share with much of the world. One would think that such a stance on the importance of sports and the aforementioned 25 character values (referred to as **CVs** from now on) would seem to be the normal and natural byproduct of sports participation. Yet, this utopia for youth and amateur sports has drifted further and further away from reality across America today.

This is not to say that many wonderful coaches and parents are not delivering character to our youth. However, it is simply not a common enough practice. I know that there are extraordinary coaches out in our communities paving the way for character growth. I am certain of this because I have seen it first-hand during my nearly 20 years as a youth coach, and more specifically during my travels around the country giving grassroots-level talks in youth recreation centers and schools. However, these occurrences are not in the overwhelming majority as should be the case. Our great challenge is to root out the two aforementioned evils that have taken the current youth sports world hostage.

In this chapter, as well as the subsequent chapter, I bring a heightened awareness to the problem, and why we need to work together to make simple but profound adjustments to the delivery system of youth sports. This chapter will look at the problem from a micro-level,[21] while Chapter 4 will focus the lens outward toward the effects on society from a macro-level.[22]

I would be the first to admit that I have not been flawless in my delivery as a coach/mentor, but my intent has always been to teach life lessons even when those lessons are not received favorably by the student-athletes or their parents at that particular time. In my role as a mentor/coach for the past 15 years, I have been speaking about and attempting to model behavior reflective of positive character development with my teams and student-athletes.

After giving more than 25 community talks around the country on character development, I gradually began to notice discernable patterns in the feedback, both directly and indirectly. A percentage of parents, coaches, administrators, and even the student-athletes themselves would approach me afterwards to thank me for what they referred to as a "much-needed message" on the values of character development and importance of modeling the appropriate behaviors for youth. Others, however, would show noticeable disagreement with my overarching focus on character building. In a few smaller settings for my talks, some parents or coaches have even openly challenged my approach, stating, in essence, that too much emphasis on my 25 character traits would lead to overly sensitive and "soft" players. Though I am always taken aback by such statements, these individuals were not alone in feeling the way they did, as they tended to have a small following of shared perspectives.

At most, if not all, of my recreation center grassroots talks or smaller group meetings, I would inevitably face dissention, whether through body language, scoffs, or comments mentioned above. This tends to be accompanied by the statement or attitude that such an emphasis on character development would negate the toughness and competitive drive that many parents and coaches value about athletics. These instances of uncomfortable division became my light-bulb moments, as I realized that here lies the great divide and the deepest root to the problems facing youth sports.

---

[21] The micro-level will look at the more individual issues taking place in communities and countries across the country.

[22] The macro-level will look at how the byproduct of all of the small communal and recreational leagues and sports clubs across the country have contributed to a nation-wide epidemic in youth and amateur sports.

I am working diligently to dispel the negative sentiment towards the term "character building." Now, I always preface my community talks with the fact that I am as competitive as anyone in the room, and my family background in professional athletics can attest to that. With a family of seven growing up, it was competitive just blocking out your own plate at the dinner table. I make it very clear that winning, or learning how to win the right way, is highly important in our society, and that I do not want to downplay the significance of competition and winning.

Despite the fact that I clearly include winning the right way as a highly important and prized character value, close to 50% of some of my audiences are on the defensive trying to justify winning as the end all value. Based on the feedback that I have received, I have summed up the following pattern: 25% of the attendees love the message and they tell me they wish there was more of it, and another 25% are on the other side, and as I mentioned previously, they believe this character stuff is for "sissies" and will create "soft" or weakened individuals. Okay, so perhaps my message may never resonate with this bottom 25%.[23] I will never tire in my relentless quest to get all coaches and parents to put **CLD** first and foremost. However, 50% of my audience is positioned somewhere in the middle, and if I (we) can get this 50% to join forces with the top 25% who eat it up already, then we will start to move that "character needle." If I (we) can at least get them to think about my message of **CLD** on their drive home, and to have a little bit better perspective on the true character values of sports, then we can begin to make a dent. After all, it takes only one follower to create a movement.[24] If that middle 50% began to swing toward the side of true character development, that would predictably have influence on the bottom 25%, as character truly does love company, much in the same way that misery does.

The pie chart below depicts this generalized breakdown of the audience response to my emphasis on **CL** and **CLD** from my 25+ community talks over the past

---

[23] The people in the bottom 25% are character illiterate and hold deeply entrenched views that winning the game or competition at all costs is likened to surviving to live another day. We may never be able to get through to such a rigid mindset, but over time, as my concept of character literacy takes root, that lower percentile will not want to be stigmatized as "character illiterate." However, in order for this to happen, our society of youth sports needs to take a stand and stop endorsing such illiteracy in coaches.

[24] There is a terrific TED Talk by Derek Sivers from February, 2010 that discusses leadership, and what it takes to create a movement. While this is a humorous video demonstrating the importance of the leaders and the first follower, who in essence becomes a leader, to start a dancing movement. This TED Talk is entitled "How to Start a Movement," and can be found on YouTube.

year. The pie chart on the top right reflects the current crowd sentiment from the perspective of those who accept or reject my prioritizing character development in sports. The shaded portion showing 25% is the group that I label as the "character illiterate." As you can see in the other three pie charts, this percentage will either grow more and more out of control, or we can choose to do something about it and work to shrink the shaded portion that is lacking character.

Figure 1: Response from audience attendees regarding Character Illiteracy

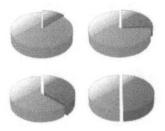

As coaches, parents, and administrators of character, we have to be willing to take this cause directly to the source.[25] I am fully aware that at times and in certain environments my "character first" approach will not be in line with the majority perspective. I am proud to be in the minority in these moments, especially when it comes to my overflowing value of character development over winning-at-all-costs. It is never easy going against the grain, but sports, delivered correctly, teach us not to back down to the challenge of being the underdog. I have learned to step up to the plate with confidence in my message for the good of **CLD** in our children and future generations.

Imagine walking in to a meeting with 12 football coaches of a local recreational football league, asking them for 20 minutes during their busy schedules to present a talk on my character literacy program. The first few such coaches' talks on **CLD** that I presented felt like I was walking directly into the lion's den. I knew that I would get some rolling of the eyes from some who were not used to hearing someone speak so

[25] In this case, the source is every youth and amateur sports and recreation training center in our country. We need school athletic directors and directors at our local recreation centers to hold coaches, young student-athletes, and parents accountable, as many recreational and athletic directors across the country are doing.

passionately on the character values that need to be more *deliberately* and *intentionally* emphasized in youth sports. I was, and am, well aware of the looming argument from the character illiterate coaches across our country who hold the view that such overemphasis on character would "soften the boys [or girls]." In one such talk, the league's draft of the players was directly following my talk, and a few coaches openly made it clear that they were not necessarily looking for the most compassionate souls on their teams. They did not want the "chicken soup for the soul" kind of kids. These coaches, and any others who share such misguided sentiment, are missing the point completely. Compassion and dedicated commitment to someone other than one's self is not, in fact, a sign of weakness. Rather, it is quite the contrary and a sign of great strength and courage, except in the eyes of those who are character illiterate. Until we change that mindset, we should not be surprised with the Johnny Manziels of the world, and the frequency of Ray Rice type incidents. We should also not be surprised with the alarming statistic from the National Fatherhood Initiative that more than one-quarter of American households are without a consistent or committed father figure,[26] or supportive male role model.

The troubling responses mentioned above from coaches, parents, and administrators who themselves lack character literacy, and whose priorities are misaligned, are definitely not the overwhelming majority. Most are vacillating somewhere in the middle and they will be influenced by the wind, or any other push or magnetic pull to either side of the spectrum.

I will never forget a character literacy talk that I gave at the recreation center on Anna Maria Island in Florida to a small group of football coaches as part of their tryout day, orientation, and player draft. Though there were only eight coaches in the room, I had a very clear sense when I introduced the topic of my 20-25-minute presentation that some of them were fine with tuning me out and possibly taking a short *siesta*. This was not my first talk on character with football coaches, and though I do not want to stereotype any group of coaches, I knew going in that some can be hardwired with the old school authoritarian style of coaching by intimidation and fear. I specifically focused

---

[26] http://www.fatherhood.org/fatherhood-data-statistics This reality will be discussed in the next chapter on macro-results of the current effect of youth sports on our society, as well as in an essay in the Appendix.

my message on how the qualities of toughness, perseverance, commitment, grit,[27] determination, and the never quit mentality need to be taught and demonstrated to our youth through sports such as football. After all, this would transfer over to effective parenthood, business practices, and positive relationships after the transition out of sports. I included the previously noted statistic that one in every four households in America is without a consistent father figure in the picture. I stated that if we, as coaches in the room, could see sports participation as a platform for developing life skills and habits in our youth, we would naturally place higher emphasis on the values in this guidebook. In turn, we would begin to develop more young men with a better understanding of what it means and takes to be a true father and mentor, or someone who will be there through thick and thin for their children and families.

As I neared the conclusion of the short talk, I started to notice more open and receptive body language from the group of coaches. Just as I was getting to the PowerPoint slide where I discuss some of the methods in which they could more *intentionally* and *deliberately* incorporate **character moments** into their daily practice and game planning, the coach who seemed to be the alpha male, or in sports terms, "the vet" of the group, put his hand up to interject a question. In my mind, I figured, *"Well, at least I came this far with my message before the onslaught of faults or unrealistic expectations of my focus on infusing more character in youth."* To my surprise, the coach simply remarked how he loved the message, and how he completely agreed that character had to play more of a *deliberate* role in the way he coached and influenced his athletes. His question was simple, *"But, how do we do this on a daily basis?"*

What I shared with the group of coaches that day is what I am going to share with you in this guidebook. It is about being *deliberate* and *intentional* in identifying with, promoting, developing, and assessing the developmental values that make up character literacy for student-athletes across their lifespan. But, before I do that, it is important that I give you an accurate portrayal of the ugliness that has disfigured the youth sports landscape. The two central causes for the current downward spiral are: 1. the myth that character emphasis is a sign of weakness, and 2. the "win-at-all-costs" mentality. These

---

[27] There is a terrific book written by Paul G. Stoltz, Ph.D. entitled: *Grit: The Science of What It Takes to Persevere, Flourish, Succeed* (2015). Stoltz discusses how "grit" is the number one character value for success.

two separate but convergent topics need to be "uprooted" and overturned in order to effectuate positive change to the existing paradigm of youth sports in America.

Let's now drill down on the myth that talking character is a sign of weakness. Can placing such a high premium on character make it impossible to instill that competitive instinct or edge that it takes to accomplish great feats?[28] From a more academic or scientific standpoint: Is there an inverse relationship between the value of character taught and the ability to achieve elite levels of athletic performance? These are concerns that have been raised after my talks from parents, coaches, and administrators. The fact that these beliefs or reservations exist sends a resounding need for a **CLD** wake up call to build more awareness to what is gradually becoming a character-numb[29] society. If we have a society of adults who do not recognize the value of character in sports, and who lack the correct perspective on the many values of sports aside from solely winning, we are going to see the trend repeating itself in coming generations.

Through my curriculum on **CLD**, I point to candid interviews with some of the most highly successful, competitive, and decorated individuals in the world of sports over the past four decades. Their stories are testaments to the fact that it is possible, and actually mandatory, to display the highest levels of character in order to maximize one's ultimate potential and success. For anyone who thinks that an emphasis on character diminishes one's edge, you need to keep reading.

In today's society of sports, people are ranked or granted elevated status according to the number of championships that they have won, along with their national ranking.[30] Take Peyton Manning, for instance, who is one of the most decorated athletes

---

[28] This is a real concern to some people whom I speak with about the importance of character. Their hesitation is that too much talk on character might stunt the competitive edge that it takes to be an elite athlete or performer. To this, I simply share the scores of interviews and conversations that I have had with some of the most elite athletes in the world that discredit such a fallacy in reasoning. Even if it were true, which it absolutely is not, the percentage of amateur athletes who will actually make a living playing their sport of focus is so miniscule that it has to be more about long-term development than short-term results.

[29] Character numb is a nicer way of saying character illiterate. No one likes to be labeled as "illiterate," but we should not shy away from using the term to describe coaches, parents, administrators, or student-athletes who fit the bill.

[30] There are many different companies in the showcase market of amateur baseball, and all sports for that matter, who have devised a ranking system to codify all baseball players across the country based on their graduation class overall, state rank, and rank by position. Over the years, I have had players come up to me with excitement because their ranking status had recently improved in the category of LHP or the category of Outfielder in their grade level. Though I am not sure exactly what that means for anything aside from an inflated ego, I do know that when one's ranking goes up, another person's ranking must go down.

over the last 20 years in America, and for whom I hold a great deal of respect. Until his Denver Broncos team won the 2016 Super Bowl, the media was incessantly talking about how Manning was not a lock for the illustrious NFL Hall of Fame because he had only won one Super Bowl prior. The media made it seem as if his entire 18-year career, his **legacy**,[31] would be predicated on one big game. In the eyes of much of the media, it was make or break for Manning, or their minds, a win-at-all-costs zero-sum game.

What I found meaningful was that Manning's focus seemed to be quite the contrary to the media's narrow scope. He showed no concern for his own accomplishments on Super Bowl Sunday, but rather, he spoke about his **love** and **gratitude** for his teammates, coaches, family, friends, and fans. During his brief on-field, post-game interview (with confetti and noise all around him), he mentioned being **grateful** and he used words of **appreciation** seven times in less than one minute. However, this message of **gratitude** went unnoticed by much of the media, who decided to highlight a different message.[32]

Manning's expressions of care, compassion, and gratitude for those whom he competed with and against during his career are not the norm in our current society. The societal sentiment in youth and amateur athletics today is that if you show concern for other people and put other's needs above your own, you will be left behind. The thought by many is that those around you will get the glory, the big contract, the scholarships, etc. Sacrificing for others goes against the nature of the ego-oriented student-athletes that our youth sports society has raised.

I refer to the above mentioned student-athletes as the "*à la carte* showcase culture" kids. These young children are pressed so hard to become the next sports

---

[31] **Legacy** is one of the top 25 character values that I have identified in this guidebook. Whether Peyton Manning won the 2016 Super Bowl in his final season should have had no bearing on whether he would be voted into the Hall of Fame. After all, Manning was known as one of the greatest field generals or **leaders** on the football field of his time. He won five league MVPs, an NFL record 14 Pro Bowls, and numerous career and single season records.

[32] The media's message was more on the fact that the Super Bowl 50 victory was his entry ticket into the Hall of Fame. There was also a focus on a message about the company Budweiser, which Manning referred to multiple times. Though Manning has been a terrific role model for youth during his brilliant career, this brings up a point that more professional athletes need to be very cautious and aware of what they say because of the fact that they are role models and looked up to by our youth. However, this appreciation of the civic duty of professional athletes will only be fully realized when we are teaching them character literacy from youth levels on up.

superstar (sometimes from the age of 3-years-old).[33] There now exist supposed "elite-level" travel ball teams in all sports and in all states across the country with entry ages beginning as early as 7- or 8-years-old. While the field of sports performance is exploding in a positive way and we have seen tremendous growth in productivity and breaking through performance barriers, we have also seen its exploitation adversely infect our youth. Elite-level performance development techniques have seeped down deeper into the youngest levels of sports[34] as parents and coaches are searching for every advantage to give their children the edge who, in their minds, are destined for stardom. What worked for Michael Jordan, Tiger Woods, and even Peyton Manning with their physical and mental capacities as elite level athletes, most likely will not translate for more than 99.9% of the rest of the population. The most important point of emphasis, when it comes to elite-level athletes, that deserves highlighting is that they became great leaders (many of whom ended up winning championships) when they began to focus less on themselves and more on how to make those around them better.

Most coaches, teachers, and parents would agree with the quote at the very beginning of this guidebook from the great Coach John Wooden who preached that what one emphasizes most improves the most. However, looking at how our society trains our athletes from the youngest of youth up through college, it is ever apparent by the length of time spent on character development that it is simply a box to check off, as if to say, "Done that." It is the same way in the study of sports in academia. We take our one class in Sports Ethics and then we are moved on to the more important areas, the areas where the money is to be made (i.e. Sports Marketing and Sports Finance, which should include a stronger emphasis in character in business practices).

Now, if our society of youth sports is not collectively emphasizing character, then just what is it emphasizing? The exact opposite. For the overwhelming majority of coaches and sports management professionals today, it is about the wins and the money. Talking character does not currently put people in the seats, and some individuals involved in sports, even at the lowest levels, feel that the emphasis on higher ethics

---

[33] Tom Farrey, author of *Game On: The All-American Race to Make Champions of our Children* (2008), discusses in the early portion of his book how parents and coaches are pushing our youth into highly competitive sports as early as 3- and 4-years-old in order to gain the competitive advantage.
[34] The concepts of early sampling and deliberate play vs. deliberate practice will be discussed further in the next chapter. Basically, parents are skipping right past vitally important stages of fun in youth sport development, in order to get the edge on the competition. This is causing more of our youth than ever before to leave sports.

would "soften" the culture and detract from athletic success, which is viewed primarily by wins and losses.

What are the effects of winning-at-all-costs? Have we ever truly sat back and pondered the connotation and meaning of that message? Take a few seconds and deliberate over what that message means to an 8-year-old boy, or an 11-year-old girl, or an 18-year-old college student-athlete. To win-at-all-costs means to do whatever it takes to score more runs, more goals, more points, to swim faster, run faster, and jump and throw farther. Well, what happens when a child is a late bloomer[35] and everyone else passes him or her by because of it? The common response from kids has been that they quit the sport they love forever. What happens if the opposing team is cheating? Most often they feel that it is necessary to also cheat in order to win. What happens when the opposition is superior and one feels that he or she cannot stop or defeat them fairly? Quite frequently, one attempts to physically or emotionally injure others in an effort to increase their chances of winning. What happens when someone is naturally or unnaturally stronger than your child? Your child turns to steroids and other performance enhancing drugs (PEDs)[36] in order to win and feel worthy.

You may think that these responses are vastly overstated. However, these byproducts of the win-at-all-costs or zero-sum game are not exaggerated. **Fact check:** These are very real negative end results that are supported by research. By breaking down the win-at-all-costs and zero-sum game effect, we should not be shocked by the results that we are producing in our youth. The fact of the matter is that today's youth are being taught that there are no other values that exist outside of winning. This trend does not just apply to the pressures put on youth and amateur student-athletes. It applies equally to their coaches, and could be a valid explanation for why coaches are motivated by the incessant need to bring home the victories and the championships.

In my mind, one of the most recognized character coaches in all of college athletics, Mark Richt, was recently relieved of his duties as a head coach in the ultra-

---

[35] The term "late bloomer" describes the young boy or girl who is undersized physically due to the fact that he or she may have hit puberty at a later time than his or her peers. In the world of youth and amateur athletics, the unfortunate late bloomer is often left behind or skipped over by coaches because they are not as physically developed early on in their teens.
[36] Performance enhancing drugs (PEDs) were rampant in the 1990's and early 2000's in professional and collegiate sports in America. PEDs almost up-ended the foundation of Major League Baseball. The use of PEDs has trickled down into amateur and even youth sports in order to gain an unfair advantage in the cut-throat world of sports in America.

competitive Southeastern Conference (SEC),[37] most likely because he did not win the "Big Game." Despite an impressive 145-51 overall record at the University of Georgia, the zero-sum game effect, which oftentimes means winning the national title, had eluded him for too long. The University and the fans were most likely tired of seeing SEC rivals hoisting that National Champion trophy, so it was time to part ways with Richt, who was quickly swept up by Miami University to lead the Hurricane Football Program.[38]

From all that I have read and researched about Coach Richt over the years, he prioritized, first and foremost, that his players learned to be men of character on and off the field. The most unfortunate circumstance is not that Richt had to uproot his family and move,[39] but the fact that the student-athletes in the Georgia Bulldog program were losing access to a quality role model and life-mentor.[40] Sadly, the winning-at-all-costs justification for hiring and firing has been going on for decades at both the collegiate and high school levels, and the NCAA and other governing bodies continue to do nothing about it. This promotes the ongoing proliferation of the zero-sum game, where winning or losing becomes a literal life or death event.

This numbness to character development endorsed by the win-at-all-costs mentality (zero-sum game) has infiltrated our communities and towns across the country. As evidenced by daily occurrences of unethical behavior as well as the current research and literature in the field, youth and amateur sports coaches and participants are in dire need of this **CLD** curriculum.

Highly esteemed professors and PhD's in the study of sport management, Shields & Bredemeier (2007) and Shields, et al., (2007), challenge the very foundation on which youth sports stand. They present findings from their research that sometimes sports participation creates and promotes negative consequences in our society's youth. The above noted articles depict the negative effects from sports participation such as high levels of developed and pent up aggression, blatant cheating and foul play in an

---

[37] The SEC is perhaps the toughest conference in all of NCAA college football. Of late, powerhouses such as Alabama, Auburn, LSU, and Florida have gone on to win the national title in eight of the last ten years.

[38] Miami University Football Program (aka "The U") has been one of the most storied major college football programs in the country. However, "The U" has also been known for unethical behavior by its coaches, administration, and its players, both on and off the field.

[39] Uprooting one's family, belongings, and having to leave one's friends and neighbors is a normal and accepted part of being a highly paid DI NCAA coach, especially in football.

[40] The title of positive mentor is one that Coach Mark Richt has worn with great pride. He is beloved by his players (both past and present).

effort to win by any means necessary, as well as a lack of respect for opposition and officials.

Renowned sport sociologist Eric Anderson (2010) furthers the position of theorists such as Shields and Bredemeier as he raises the ante and after-effect in his book *Sport, Theory, and Social Problems: A Critical Introduction.* Anderson makes no effort to conceal the intention of his book, which is to help all sports lovers to divorce themselves from such love. He vehemently states that sports in America today are "socio-negative," or inherently bad, in most aspects. He posits that sports, as they are currently practiced, have more of a negative effect than a positive one, and thus should be removed from our society. He feels there are much better uses of our time that would net greater benefits than the current activity of sports (2010). Though his overly-critical lens presents some very eye opening perspectives and truths, his posturing that sports are an inherent evil is hard for even the harshest of sports critics to fully support. Though Anderson's views rest as far to the left as conceivable, many other sport sociologists and theorists are stuck somewhere in the middle between his take on the ethical implications of youth sports and my positive vantage point on the effects of youth sports when delivered appropriately. The issue that needs to be addressed in order to save the sanctity of youth sports is not whether or not sports are inherently good or bad, but rather, the heart of the matter lies in the delivery mechanism.

The current literature on the plight of youth sports clearly points out that participation and overall satisfaction is trending rapidly in the wrong direction. According to Beatty & Fawyer (2014) in the research brief for Aspen Institute's *Project Play*, "…[out of] *millions of youth participating in sport each year, approximately one-third choose to quit organized sport activities because they are not having fun, change interests, lack the appropriate skill level, feel burned out, are bored, or do not like the coach.*" It has been my intent over the past few years to carry out an extensive study that aims to identify possible solutions to rejuvenate youth sports, and it will continue to be my driving force.

I believe that at the core of this youth sports participation decline is a need for more focus by coaches and parents toward a "kids first" **CLD** approach to converge and coincide with the physical development approach. I believe that children want to know that their efforts in athletics transcend winning on each particular day by building for lifetime success.

I am absolutely convinced that the primary reason why children and teenagers are opting out of sports more frequently now than ever before is tied to high ethical implications. Youth and amateur sports have strayed so far away from what they used to be when I was growing up in the 80s and early 90s. Even in a family that produced eight professional baseball players who played in Major League organizations, I never had to experience the extreme pressures, overspecialization, overtraining, burnout, social isolation, and inflated expectations that many children deal with nowadays (Côté, et al., 2009; Burgess & Naughton, 2010; Subotnik, Olszewski-Kubilius, & Worrell, 2011, Horton, 2012). Back in my youth, and long before, when youth sports seemed much purer, we did not need a coach or official to mediate all forms of competition and practice like kids do now. We knew what was right and wrong, what a foul was and was not, and we played within the rules. We were self-governed much of the time and that led to a better comprehension of, and appreciation for, fair play. This also kept a normal flow of the games and a proper amount of focused practice time because we were playing more for fun and a love of sports.

The harmful effects on youth of early specialization and overspecialization, as well as taking away the concept of "deliberate play"[41] from the lowest levels of development, are driving kids away from sport participation in hordes (Côté, et al., 2007 & 2009; Burgess & Naughton, 2010; Subotnik, Olszewski-Kubilius, & Worrell, 2011, Horton, 2012). The current inclination towards the win-at-all-costs approach and the ego-driven rush to "10,000 hours" of individual training has displaced the quest to build character through the challenge and enjoyment of sport participation. Many kids are walking away from sports prematurely due to the heavy pressures from parents and coaches and the excessive overtraining, which strip sports of their fun and enjoyment (Côté & Fraser-Thomas, 2008; & Jayanthi, 2012).

Overtraining and overspecialization can lead to burnout, where athletes become physically and emotionally exhausted from their sport and quit never to return (Gould, et al., 1996). I have seen this unfortunate occurrence repeatedly over the past decade in working with young athletes in numerous sports. Oftentimes, these are high school athletes who never take a break from their sport for fear of someone else surpassing

---

[41] The term "deliberate play" is credited to Jean Côté (PhD and a lead theorist in field of sports) as a way to categorize the age of development during the youngest years of youth sports (the 5-8-year-old range) where the emphasis should be on fun and creativity.

them and taking their scholarship or professional draft position. These young high school athletes (and sometimes junior high school athletes) are nowhere near their full growth physically or mentally, yet they are training longer and harder than professional athletes. Why? It is because the priorities of youth and amateur sport managers and parents have lost touch with the true value of developing stronger character through the vehicle of sports.

The adverse effects of overspecialization and overtraining in relation to social development and social isolation have been thoroughly studied and analyzed (Wiersma, 2000; Côté, et al., 2009; & Branta, 2010). I cannot help but think of how some of the elite athletes in our society over the years have been so completely focused and driven towards one singular goal that they often find it difficult to associate well with others. Some do not have an ounce of **concern** or **appreciation** for others whom they compete with or against because they are so consumed by their own ego-driven success and quest for the college scholarships or professional contract.

ESPN Reporter Tom Farrey authored a book called *Game On: The All-American Race to Make Champions of our Children* (2008). Farrey's book relies on more than 20 years of reporting on the field of sports across the country in order to depict many of the problems with youth and amateur athletics today. He takes his reader on a wild ride across the landscape of America in search of the "silver bullet" or "golden nugget" that is sure to produce the next "LeBron" or "Serena" or "Manning" boy. Along the way, he brings to light that, more often than not, the end result is not the desired one. With the constant pressures, overtraining, burnout, and lack of fun for children that this quest for athletic dominance creates, the highest number of youth participants than ever before are quitting sports for good (2008). If these young boys and girls were not constantly pressured by the zero-sum game effect, would they not better appreciate the countless values, along with winning, to be learned through sports and thus be more prone to stick with it?

Fraser-Thomas, et al., (2005) present an excellent article about coaching programs focusing on the concept of retention in youth sports. The authors here are looking for ways to keep youth involved in athletics, which should indeed be the goal. It is great that the leading scholars/researchers in the field of youth and amateur sports are looking at ways to improve retention. However, it is my belief and hypothesis that until character is riding front and center in the driver's seat, instead of being an afterthought, the lifelong values of one's involvement in youth sports will never be fully appreciated. I am certain that the only way to maximize physical performance it is to *deliberately* and *systematically* blend it with **CLD**.

While a more expansive development of coaching excellence and effective instructional delivery are vital, an emphasis on **CLD** is the backbone for youth sports development. Deep down, perhaps far below the surface level, youth and amateur athletes want to know that what they are investing in and learning through sports participation translates into other areas of life (family, business, etc.). The age group that is most highly scrutinized is the 11-14 range. This is when most children drop out of sports for a variety of reasons, and why, more than ever before, a credible expert-coach is deeply in need. This coach should not only know the sport inside and out, but he or she should also understand how to teach and motivate players on and off the field. A coach with these requisite abilities (credibility and ability to teach) can truly be a transformational leader[42] (Kuhnert & Lewis, 1987; Conger, 1999, Bass & Riggio, 2006; Hall, et al., 2002) because he or she has earned the players' respect and attention. Only then can a coach understand when and how to recognize the "teaching moments" that can develop positive character growth in our youth to the fullest potential (Borland, et al., 2014). It takes just one transformational coach to change the moral complexion of many lives. Imagine if we could help develop a trend toward such transformational coaches?

There are two types of leaders: the transactional leader and the transformational leader. With the transactional leader, every interaction involves a clear transaction. The same holds true for the transactional coach. At the earliest ages of sports, the child who can swim the fastest, jump the highest, or throw the hardest will be given preferential treatment and attention. But, as soon as that child's performance drops, so does the access to the top instruction and royal treatment. In my years as a youth coach, I have seen and heard horror stories of young student-athletes being flown across the country to pitch one game to win a 15-U travel ball tournament (all expenses paid for the entire family). What happens when that young prized pitcher hurts his arm due to overuse or misuse? He is out of a job, so to speak, because he no longer brings value to the

---

[42] The transformational leader is juxtaposed in the next few paragraphs with the far too common transactional leader. Ex-NFL star Joe Ehrmann wrote a book entitled *Inside Out Coaching: How Sports Can Transform Lives* (2011), which is a great read on this topic.

transaction. The transactional model of coaching is grossly ineffective to the development of our young boys and girls.

On the other hand, the transformational coach/mentor, is more actively engaged in the development of his or her student-athletes as a whole. This coach does not see student-athletes as a means to an end, but rather as the end in itself. In other words, this coach sees value in all of the players on his or her team. Now, do not get me wrong, I am not about everyone getting equal playing time and everyone getting a trophy[43] simply because they participated. The transformational coach and mentor is going to get the most out of each player on the team. Certain players may rarely play, but if you (as the coach) make them feel valued, they may actually surprise you with what they are capable of and how hard they are willing to work. Anyone can coach the elite player, but the players at the bottom end of the talent pool are the ones who can be the true testament to your ability to teach and instruct the sport.

I challenge you as a coach or parent of a student-athlete to adhere to the criteria of a transformational leader or coach. With the 25 character values of my **CLD** curriculum, you can help your student-athletes come up with and articulate a realistic game plan or vision each season. As their leader and mentor, they are going to be watching your every move and hanging on your every word. Be certain that you are modeling the behaviors that you wish to see in your student-athletes or children. This is the only way that you will get buy-in towards the select **character values** that you choose to focus on each season with your team(s). Now, whether you are at the bottom of the dogpile at the end of the season (preferably watching from the side), or scratching to finish with a .500 record, you will know that the season was a successful endeavor. Once you make the conscientious choice to be a transformational coach, the heavy burdens that are tied to the transactional coach will disappear. Only then will you be able to earn the title of coach and wear it like a badge of honor.

More than ever before, our country needs transformational coaches to rise up and lead our next generation out of the ashes of unethical despair. Looking back over the past five to ten years in the media, the youth and amateur sports world has been dragged through the mud. The hideous actions and defective leadership from coaches across the

---

[43] We live in a trophy generation. As a few of my contributors mention, some of whom have medaled in the Olympics, the medal is nothing but a reflection of their hard work. Why is our society so concerned with giving trophies bigger than the children themselves for fifth place?

country lend overwhelming support to the research that I provide regarding the tattered and beaten down foundation of youth sports. No sport has been immune, as if to say any sport in and of itself is above immoral acts. We have seen and read about the atrocious acts from within the athletic arenas of football, baseball, soccer, USA swimming,[44] USA gymnastics,[45] lacrosse, and the list goes on. I am fighting desperately (scratching and clawing like a bobcat in a phone booth)[46] to dispute what many research studies, including those cited above, on youth sports are finding: There are more negative effects of youth sports than positive effects. As I have noted, my argument is very simple: It is not the sport that is inherently good or bad, but rather the delivery mechanism of all involved in the management and facilitation of youth sports. For this reason, the *deliberate* and *intentional* emphasis on **CLD** is the absolute necessity of all coaches, parents, and administrators involved in youth and amateur sports.

Coaches used to be regarded as the model citizens, and the title of coach used to mean something. Growing up with a dad[47] whom I looked up to, the term "coach" was synonymous with the reverence of a doctor, a captain, a pilot, an officer, or a firefighter.[48] Now, we have coaches who are ordering their football players to "take out"[49] the official when he is not watching because the coach feels that the official's calls are not favoring his team. We have coaches who are physically, verbally, and even sexually abusing young athletes, as the footnoted articles on USA Swimming and USA Gymnastics attest to. It is no wonder that youth sports have reached such a low point.

What has happened to our coaches who, in the past, had been some of most positively influential role models? How have they fallen from such esteemed regard? I feel that the answer lies in the fact that our society has truncated its value on character development. It seems that most people, even those in the sports world, who we assume

---

[44] See K. Whiteside's article (2014) in *USA TODAY Sports* entitled: "Citing sex abuse cases, swimmers protest Hall of Fame induction."

[45] See M. Rosenberg's article (2016) in *Sports Illustrated* entitled: "It's Time for USOC to Step up after USA Gymnastics Sex Abuse Scandal."

[46] "Scratching and clawing like a bobcat in a phone booth" is a quote from one of my favorite coaches going back to my playing days with the San Diego Padres. My Single-A manager, Tom Levasseur, used to tell our team that sports teach you how to fight through adversity and never back down or give in to a challenge. His analogy of a bobcat in a phone booth has stuck with me over the years.

[47] As previously mentioned, my dad has been a youth coach for the past 50 years.

[48] These titles are associated with positions of influence and trust, and those with such titles are all people to whom society would entrust their children's well-being.

[49] See article by McLaughlin, E. & Lett, C. (2015). *CNN.* "Texas coach accused of ordering player to hit referee resigns."

have a "kids first" approach, would rather pick another topic to discuss aside from character development. My grassroots-level focus in our communities has been to work to infuse more **CLD** into these youth sports programs.

CHARACTER
LOVES
COMPANY

CHAPTER 4—An Investigation into the

Downward Plight of Sports—Macro-Level Perspective

"Know a culture by how it plays its games." –Marshall McLuhan[50]

I would be remiss not to draw a correlation between the microcosm of youth and amateur sports to the bigger picture of our nation as a whole. While I am certainly not trying to place the ethical and moral woes that plague our great nation on the backs of youth sports coaches across America, I do see a vital role to be played in the long-term development of our children and society through sports participation.

In case you have forgotten, allow me to provide you with a reminder of a few of the heinous and intolerable actions by our country's coaches that made the front page news over the past decade or so. The acts of sexual misconduct and abuse toward young campers by Penn State assistant coach Jerry Sandusky[51] are now being mirrored exponentially by male swim and gymnastics coaches across the country toward young female student-athletes. One article that I read recently claimed over 100 elite swimming coaches have been banned from the pool deck[52] in the past few years after numerous

---

[50] Marshall McLuhan was a highly regarded media theorist who contributed a great deal to the field of media studies over the past century. In his 1967 book, *The Medium is the Massage,* he coined the phrase "Global Village" and other forward thinking concepts for his time that are still applicable to our global world on a macro-level.

[51] In the 2015 article linked below, NBC reports, "The university settled with 26 victims of Sandusky, 71, a longtime assistant to legendary head football coach Joe Paterno, for about $60 million in October 2013. Sandusky was sentenced to 30 to 60 years in prison in October 2012 for having abused 10 boys he met over 15 years through his charity for troubled children." http://www.nbcnews.com/news/us-news/penn-state-could-face-claims-six-more-alleged-jerry-sandusky-n469766

[52] In this *USA Today* article, more than 100 US swim coaches have been banned from pool decks: http://www.usatoday.com/story/sports/olympics/2014/05/29/swimming-hall-of-fame-induction-protest/9738737/

claims and evidence of sexual misconduct towards those whom they have been granted the privilege of coaching and mentoring. These horrendous acts are being committed from city to city and county to county and should put all citizens of America on high alert, whether they have children or not. These glaring evils, along with other dreadful examples that we are seeing in towns across America, are framing the national identity of our entire country.

The micro-level problems in our small towns and local recreation centers and sports leagues are overflowing and thus flooding what McLuhan coined as the "Global Village." The reference to the term "global village" infers that there is always an after-effect of what our young student-athletes are learning at the community level. This bigger picture expands into a national paradigm or lens through which to view the world. What boys and girls learn at young ages through sports participation begins to formulate habits, or ways of doing things. As Aristotle said, *"Excellence is not an act, but a habit."* As coaches and parents involved in youth and amateur athletics, we need to ask ourselves what kind of habits are we instilling in our youth?[53]

From a macro-level perspective, it is with hardly an ounce of pride that we can look back on the last two decades filled with wrongdoings both in the athletic arena and throughout society as a whole. I am not here to join forces with previously mentioned sociologists such as Eric Anderson (2010) in a way that attempts to state that sports have a negative effect on society. However, I do see a correlative link between what we are teaching our youth through the vehicle of sports, and the undesirable and destructive actions and habits of such generations as they grow into adulthood, and thus pass down to future generations.

The many images of horrendous acts across our country over the past decade are still fresh in our hearts and minds. We need to find a way to eradicate the trend of evil that this vicious cycle continues to produce. Rather than attempt to replay all the recent atrocities in detail, I have listed a sample of the troublesome ills that undoubtedly echo in our minds: We have been witness to bullying at its highest levels and extreme violence

---

[53] In response to the question concerning the habits that we are building in our youth through sports, I wrote an essay included in the Appendix discussing an important message on how we, as coaches, need to clean up the language in the locker rooms, and realize that our words and our modeled behaviors will have an effect on the formative years of our rising generations.

inside and outside of our schools, rampant steroid use at all levels of sport, dishonesty in the financial sector, rising domestic violence, and sexual abuse and assault.

I am not trying to scapegoat youth and amateur sports for the deterioration of the morals and ethics in our society. Indeed, I am highly optimistic of the positive power of the change agent of sports. As I quoted in my introductory chapter from Nelson Mandela, Noble Peace Prize recipient and one of our history's most influential humanitarians, *"Sport has the power to change the world...it has the power to inspire. It has the power to unite people in a way that little else does. It speaks to youth in a language they understand"* (2000). Coaches, parents, and sports administrators involved with our youth have the influential responsibility to develop strong character and effectuate positive change in the habits and perspectives of our rising generations. Mandela's words echo the idea that sports have the power to change, inspire, and unite our world. What he is saying, in essence, is that the entity of sports can positively change the world if, and only if, administered appropriately by all those involved in its participation.

How can we assure that we are administering sports appropriately? As John Wooden responded time and time again when asked about which of his 10 NCAA National Championship teams was the best, or even who was his best player, he would state that he would not know for 20-30 years. The test of time will always be the judge of one's character. We have the character results from the data over the past few decades at our fingertips. From both the micro- and macro-level perspectives, it is apparent that we need to be more *deliberate* and *intentional* about how and what we emphasize through youth and amateur sports. We cannot wait another 20-30 years.

I have interviewed world-class Olympians, collegiate and professional athletes, managers of sports at all levels, and business men and women for this guidebook, all who have been, and continue to be, supremely successful because of their foundation in character. In my mind, the two-time "Sportswoman of the Year" on my panel of contributors is more impressive than someone who has won the highly prestigious Heisman Trophy. Our society should desire the balance of excellence, reliability, grit, and commitment in our "Sportswomen" or "Sportsmen." Do not get me wrong, the overwhelming majority of Heisman trophy winners have been phenomenal people, both on and off the field. However, there have been occasions where blatant lack of character in a Heisman candidate has been overlooked, simply because that individual won ballgames and tallied impressive on field accolades. This is a shame because this occurrence has tarnished the sanctity of what many feel is the most recognized and prominent award in all of amateur sports. I used to think **strong character** and **sportsmanship** were essential criteria in order to win the Heisman Trophy. However, some of the recipients of this award over the past decade have proven that **high character** and **sportsmanship** are no longer required criteria.

What does this message tell our up-and-coming generations about what it means to be successful? Crush out your opponent and anyone who gets in your way. It is okay to be a pompous fool and stand up on your desk in a college classroom (or public place, for that matter) and spout out profanities and use demeaning language to the opposite gender if you have superior athletic talent.[54] In the end, this approach will catch up to these superior athletes who were rarely held accountable and taught real life lessons through the vehicle of sports. As long as winning-at-all-costs is rewarded and the zero-sum game continues, the transactional coaches at all levels will continue to reign as they will trade the teachable moments for the price of a win any day.

Is the price of victory worth all that some coaches, parents, and student-athletes have been willing to sacrifice of late: **dignity**, **respect**, **discipline**, and **integrity**, etc.? No! As the data shows, it equates to cheating through PEDs and other means, corruption and greed, violence against others, and sexual abuse. None of these indefensible trends that we are seeing are worth the price of championships in the athletic arena, let alone a singular victory.

To take a page out of Coach Wooden's playbook, or from the late great Coach Pat Summit,[55] as coaches and others involved in youth and amateur athletics, our true gauge of how effective and proficient we are should not be measured by our trophy cases, but rather by the lasting impact of our influence on the lives of our student-athletes. Only through the test of time will we truly know. As Wooden stated, *"Be more*

---

[54] See article in *Huffington Post*: http://www.huffingtonpost.com/2014/09/17/florida-state-jameis-winston-obscenity_n_5836616.html. According to numerous news stories, FSU star quarterback Jameis Winston, actually stood up on a desk in class and made demeaning and derogatory comments to students in his class. For this appalling act, Winston was granted a one-half game suspension, which is hardly a slap on the wrist. Such a weak punishment oftentimes does more harm than good because it reinforces a "mightier than thou" mentality of many cocky and brash young athletes. The character moment was not only missed for these character illiterate individuals, but also the greater community as a whole.

[55] The late Coach Pat Summit was a legendary women's NCAA basketball coach whose tenure spanned three decades. Her influence on women's sports, and coaching and leadership, in general, continue to be a guiding light in the field of sports.

concerned with your character than your reputation, because your character is what you really are, while your reputation is merely what others think you are." The win-loss record and the number of championships that a coach accrues will undeniably form his or her reputation in the win-at-all-costs culture that we live in, and that will most likely never change. It is a coach's true character, however, that will have the power to effectuate positive change and influence on those whom he or she coaches.

As coaches and mentors of our youth, we should be most concerned with the type of husbands, wives, fathers, mothers, friends, and business men and women that the participants on our teams become. That is where the long lost pride in the title "coach" will return to its past reverence. My hat goes off to the youth coach who teaches discipline and hard work to his or her team of 7- and 8-year-olds. Then to be able to watch them graduate from high school, and hopefully go on to college as a student or as a student-athlete; that is when that coaching badge of honor is worn with great pride.

In order to renew the noble reverence of the term "coach," we need an enhanced accountability system. In the same manner that our young student-athletes need to be held accountable for their actions, so do coaches. Coaches cannot simply continue to turn a blind eye to the negative actions and poor behavior of their players simply because they are talented. There is too much at stake.

Accountability is a two-way street that must be administered on a consistent basis. As citizens, sports fans, and athletic administrators, we need to back-track in time with some of these athletes who are committing terrible crimes and offenses. Obviously, the individual who commits the egregious act needs to be held accountable and responsible. However, as coaches, we need to have the power and influence to dole out the tough love and discipline that many of these young people need when we have the teachable moments right in front of us. Many coaches are afraid to discipline their star athletes out of fear of losing them or fear of not being liked. With that title of coach comes the needed courage to stand up for what is right. As many of my contributors shared with me during my one-on-one interviews with them, it was their coaches and teammates, or more importantly, their parents, whom they held the most enduring respect and admiration for in the long run because they held them accountable for their actions. They may not have liked it at the time, but those mentors were the game-changers who made lasting impressions.

In the same light that the student-athletes need to be held to a higher standard of accountability, so do our coaches at all levels of amateur and recreational sports. If our coaches could grasp the expansive impact and influence that they have on our youth, they would inevitably be more conscientious toward the content of their character and their overall message to their players. However, as I have seen, and as you have read about in the last few chapters, it is just not registering for many of our coaches. We need to hold these character illiterate coaches to the fire as if their livelihood and legacy depend on it. Coach and mentor are synonymous terms and we cannot accept one without the other. When players come through a program, they should not just be better athletes but better and more balanced individuals in society.

For each and every one of the superstar first-round draft choices in all of sports over the past decade who ended up in prison or on the streets, I think we need to start backtracking and do some investigatory work. You see, the behaviors of the Johnny Manziels[56] of the world do not just pop up out of nowhere. Most criminals have a rap sheet, and that rap sheet continues to grow and the trend becomes more vicious if they are not held accountable and disciplined appropriately. The string of Heisman Trophy candidates must have inevitably had some coaches who cowardly turned a blind eye because of such players' elite athletic abilities. All individuals in a productive society need to be held accountable, but when it is all about the "almighty win" as it relates to sports, many coaches compromise the value of character. The message to these coaches needs to be loud and clear: **If you will not hold the student-athletes accountable and teach them life lessons, then your reputation and your legacy as a coach will be forever tarnished.** Looking at the lives and testaments of the greatest coaches, mentors, and leaders of the last century, they all emphasized character as the ultimate victory. This all ties back to Coach Wooden's quote about how what we emphasize gets improved upon.

---

[56] Johnny Manziel is another recent Heisman Trophy winner who, in my opinion, made the Hall of Shame list. In a recent article, his father made it publicly known that the college team captain and All-American turned NFL first-round pick's life had spiraled so badly out of control that he is now in prison and on the brink of losing his life: http://www.foxsports.com/nfl/story/johnny-manziel-dad-my-son-is-a-druggie-and-he-needs-help-062416

CHAPTER 5—My Pivotal Research Studies
from 125 Top Expert Coaches & Beyond

How and why are my two studies important to the advancement of character development in the field of youth/amateur athletics and the creation of my **CLD** curriculum? Throughout the past two years of study, I have completed an exhaustive review, literally scouring the literature relevant to my focus on character development in youth sports. Though there have been some key theoretical advances in this field, a glaring void still exists in the consistent application and delivery of character development in the athletic arena. In order to better connect the dots between theory and application, I conducted two salient research studies supported by the University of Florida IRB.[57] Both studies rely on the vantage point of seasoned expert[58] coaches at all levels of athletics in order to navigate through this rocky and troublesome terrain of youth and amateur sports.

For the sake of not disrupting the fluidity and readability of this book, I have deferred the inclusion of additional pertinent literature that prompted my two studies to the Addendum of this book. This final section is a condensed version of a 40-page review of the literature that I completed for graduate school, chock-full of books, scholarly journal articles, websites, and organizations focused on the topic of character development through sports, or the lack thereof.

---

[57] "IRB" stands for Institutional Review Board which is the governing body that oversees the validity and credibility of all educational research studies.
[58] My definition of an expert coach here is someone who has been coaching and mentoring youth for a minimum of five years. Many of the current studies on coaching efficacy have used data gathered from the perspective of undergraduate level students, graduate students, or from surveys gathered from student-athletes or children.

The ultimate priority of my ongoing research is to lean heavily on the perspective of expert coaches who have been in the field of coaching and mentoring for a minimum of five years. As the previous footnote indicates, much of the prior research had been conducted on undergraduate students, graduate students, and the youth participants themselves. I do not want to downplay the important progress that has been made from these studies such as YSVQ 1 and 2[59] (which asked youth participants to rank 18 values in sports), but I find it imperative to see through the eyes of some of our nation's top expert coaches and mentors in the field.

I am all for keeping the interests of those who are playing youth sports (i.e. the children) front and center. But does the medical field look to the patients in order to create the community of best practices? Would we ask the patient how to perform surgery in the operating room? The answer is a resounding "no." Why then would we do so with matters of moral and ethical implications? Children and undergraduate or graduate students lacking a requisite minimum of five years of coaching experience have yet to be put to the true test. They simply have not accrued enough life experience in the athletic arena as coach and mentor, and their theoretical approaches, though sound and logical in the classroom, have not been fully, or even partially, vetted. My need to justify this point is expressly the reason why character development has failed to elevate off the theoretical runway, despite the vast well of knowledge and research on character development in youth sports from which to draw.

Teaching character through the vehicle of sports is not easy! For the past 30 years, the coach who has been willing and able to effectively seize the defining moments for character growth in our youth is oftentimes under-appreciated. It is time to take a closer look at what the experts have to say in this area. With a minimum threshold of five years, I am in no way stating that simply because a coach has been "at it" for that length of time that they are inherently an expert. The years of experience simply provide these coaches with the opportunities to put their theoretical coaching game plans to the test. However, my major study found that 70% of the coaches surveyed had been coaching for 11+ years, while 30% had been working on their craft for 15+ years, and a significant number of contributors had 40+ years of coaching expertise. To my knowledge, there

---

[59] YSVQ (Youth Survey Value Questionnaire) 1 and 2 are studies that draw a breadth of feedback from children ranging in age from 8-17. The focus of these questionnaires was to see what qualities children valued from sports.

has not been a study on youth sports that has gained the feedback of such a wealth of coaching acumen and experience.

My research was based on two questions: 1. Could a panel of expert coaches identify and rank the 25 most important character values *potentially* learned through sports? and 2. Could a panel of expert coaches then take this list of 25 character values and organize them into appropriate age-specific categories, or **CLD** building blocks?

My first research study began as a pilot study for the larger focus of my second research study. However, the findings of this first study were very revealing, as the feedback provided some clearly needed character values that I had originally omitted. The study asked the 60 expert coaches polled to rate each of the 25 character values **(CVs)** based on a 7-point Likert Scale.[60] There was also a line for coaches to type in any additional character values that they strongly felt should be included in my major study.

Similar to the YSVQ survey, I found that winning and end results were the least desirable, while the concepts of **respect, toughness, sportspersonship,**[61] and **appreciation** proved to be the most desirable. As you can see below from Paciorek UF-IRB Study 1 on Character Literacy, Figure 2, Figure 3, and Figure 4 all give a clear portrayal of what expert coaches value the most.

Paciorek UF-IRB Study 1--Character Lit

Figure 2 (Low-Rated CVs from Coach Respondents-Line Chart 1)

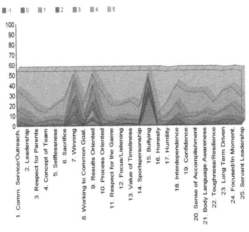

---

[60] The 7-point Likert Scale that I used ranges from -1 all the way up to 5. A negative or low score represented a character value that was not highly prized by coaches, while scores of 3s, 4s, and 5s meant that coaches placed a great deal of worth on that particular value.

[61] "Sportspersonship" is synonymous with "sportsmanship," but more appropriate as it is gender neutral.

Figure 2—Line Chart 1 depicts the drastic spikes like mountaintops for the values that coaches rated in the low or negative range: winning (#7), results oriented (#9), and bullying (#15). This chart and others from my research studies can be viewed in full color at: **characterlovescompany.org** under "Research."

Paciorek UF-IRB Study 1--Character Lit

Figure 3 (High-Rated CVs from Coach Respondents-Line Chart 2)

Figure 3—Line Chart 2 depicts the opposite data that Line Chart 1 did in Figure 2. You can see that the most important values involve respect (#3 & 11), concept of team (#4), process oriented (#10), sportspersonship (#14), honesty (#16), confidence (#19), sense of accomplishment (#20), toughness (#22), and focus (#24). These values cast the broadest web, as depicted by the shaded areas.

Figure 4 (High-Rated CVs from Coach Respondents-Bar Chart 1)

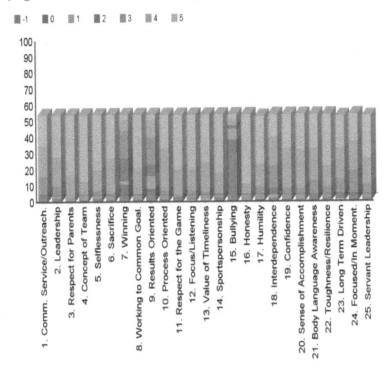

Figure 4—Bar Chart 1 presents a bar chart with all 25 values stacked side-by-side. The **character values** that demand the highest esteem and emphasis from the expert coaches polled have the largest amounts of shading coming down from the top. The three concepts that stand out as low-rated values are winning (which is the "winning-at-all-costs" mentality and not the "winning-the-right-way" mentality), results oriented, and bullying. What I labeled as bullying in this pilot survey was meant to indicate the idea or teaching concept of anti-bullying. However, the overwhelming majority of coaches polled rated this extremely low and in the negative range. This serendipitous oversight on my part ended up being a fortuitous eye opener when you analyze Bar Chart 1, because the dark shaded area from the bottom on bullying was the only category that reported more -1 and 0 ratings than the value and emphasis on winning. The message here speaks to the fact that many coaches who have been coaching for a while tend to shed much of the incessant need to adhere to the mantra of winning-at-all-costs over time.

The results from my pilot study are not entirely new or novel as there has been an ample amount of research focused on the most important values learned through sports. In fact, much of this data is organized into 18, 20, or 25 categories of emphasis. However, the data collection respondents have primarily been less experienced coaches, graduate students, or student-athletes. My pilot study, drawing from the experience of seasoned coaches, both supported and validated previous research in the field, as well as shed new light on important focal points in youth character development through sports. **Paciorek UF-IRB Study 1—Character Lit.** provided me with a current update in terminology of the 25 most relevant and essential **CVs** for my major research study: **Paciorek UF-IRB Study 2—Character Literacy Age Appropriate Curriculum**.

For the main research study, my guiding question was whether expert coaches could agree on a delivery of the 25 **CVs** in an age specific manner or developmentally progressive building block approach. After all, for decades, we have preached 18 or 20 or 25 similar character values to the ones on my list as Coach Wooden's "Pyramid of Success" will attest. So why is it that we continue to see rises in unethical behavior in youth athletics? Where is the disconnect between the theory of what we have known for decades and the application, retention, and proof of **character literacy development** in our youth through sports?

My "aha moment"[62] in response to the above question came as I was cross-researching the previously referenced works of Coach Wooden with the ideas of Istvan Balyi (renowned expert in sport performance). While Coach Wooden is often regarded as the guru of character and leadership development in the sports world, Balyi is considered by many as the founding father of the Long-Term Athlete Development Model (LTAD). The LTAD was originally created with the intent of maximizing the performance of elite-level athletes. Over the past decade, LTAD has sparked a whole new field of study in academia at American universities in Kinesiology, Sport Management, and Human Performance Development programs. Leading experts in this field of performance development in sports, Balyi and Hamilton (2004) and Côté et al., (2009), provide evidence that physical performance and growth can be maximized through age and ability-specific training regimens. If this is indeed the case with performance

---

[62] According to the Merriam-Webster dictionary, an "aha" moment is defined as, "A moment of sudden realization, inspiration, insight, recognition, or comprehension" (2015).

enhancement, then my hypothesis was that the disconnect has to be rooted in the delivery mechanism of character development in sports.

Similar to developmental reading literacy programs, I set out to construct a viable systematic and incremental approach to character development based on my 25 character values. However, I needed to see proof of concept in the numbers from other experts. After six months of gathering data from what ended up being 125+ expert coaches, the findings presented some very insightful takeaways about the need for emphasizing foundational values prior to ascending up the ladder of character. I had many coaches, some of whom had been coaching our youth for 40+ years, who went out of their way to express to me how much they enjoyed and appreciated the **CLD** curriculum that I was working to develop. It was then that I had a feeling that I was on to something, and the findings pouring in supported this hunch.

Before I get into the nitty gritty of the study's findings, I want to first discuss the methodology and intent to gain a representative sample of male and female coaches, as well as a balance of responses from coaches at all levels of youth and amateur athletics. In the field of youth sports, there are close to 70% men and 30% women (some studies will show it is close to 80:20%). I made it a priority to gain a representative sample of perspectives from female coaches or even exceed that 30%. I also visited many recreation centers and gathered the contact information of expert coaches working with youth at the youngest of ages in order to gain access to a full spectrum of vantage points from coaches at all levels of youth and amateur sports.

I have provided this demographic information of my survey respondents on the next few pages. This is an ongoing research survey and I continue to gain responses from expert coaches all over the country. If you are a coach and would like to contribute to this study, my contact information can be found at the end of the supplemental coaches' guide at the end of the book.

Paciorek UF-IRB Study 2--Character Lit Age Appropriate Curriculum Demographic Information from study

Figure 5 Gender of Coach Respondents—Bar Chart 2

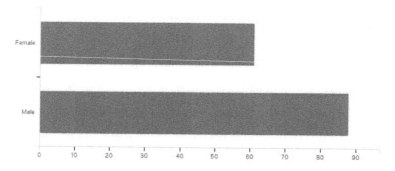

Figure 5—Bar Chart 2 presents the gender amongst the coaches who completed my survey which demonstrates a representative sample ratio of female: male coaches in the world of sports.

Figure 6 Range of ages that Respondents have coached—Bar Chart 3

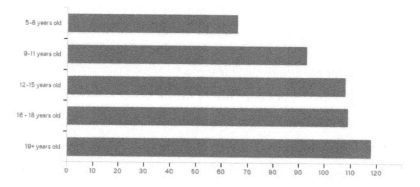

Figure 6—Bar Chart 3 illustrates that the sample of coaches who completed my survey had a broad range of coaching experience at each of the five noted levels.

Figure 7 Number of Years Coaching from Respondents—Bar Chart 4

Y-Axis=Number of Years Coaching/X-Axis=Number of Respondents

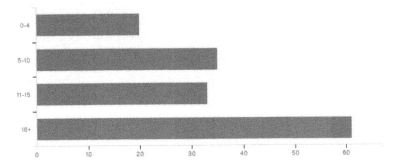

As noted in **Figure 7**—Bar Chart 4, more than 62% of the respondents to my study have been coaching for 11 years or more. Over 40% have been coaching for 16+ years while 20% have been in the field for over 40 years.

Paciorek UF-IRB Study 2--Character Lit Age Appropriate Curriculum

Figures 8-12 (25 Character Values Developed Through Sports—Best Age to Initiate Emphasis on Character Value—The Line Charts provided below show a noticeable bell curve that develops around the age grouping of CVs)

Y-Axis=Number of Respondents/X-Axis=Age Range to Best Initiate CVs

Figure 8

Highest Character Values for the 5-7-Year-Old Range (Line Chart 2)

<u>CVs</u>: *Respect for Parents, Interdependence (Care for Others), Sportspersonship, Respect for Coaches & Rules, Gratitude (Joy)*

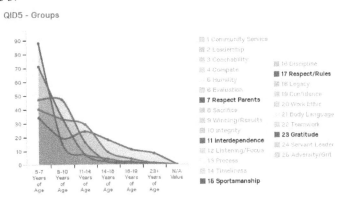

Figure 9

Highest Character Values for the 8-10-Year-Old Range (Line Chart 3)

CVs: *Coachability, Competition (Honest & Ethical), Integrity & Honor, Listening/Focus, Teamwork*

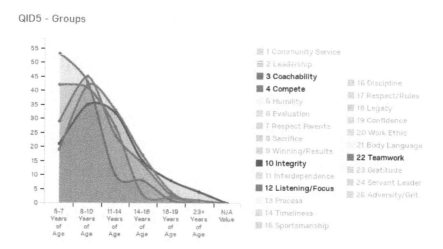

Figure 10

Highest Character Values for the 11-14-Year-Old Range (Line Chart 4)

CVs: *Leadership, Humility, Timeliness, Discipline, Confidence not Cockiness, Work Ethic/Sense of Accomplishment*

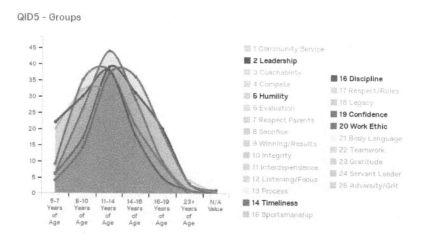

Figure 11

Highest Character Values for the 14-16-Year-Old Range (Line Chart 5)

<u>CVs:</u> *Community Service/Outreach, Honest Evaluation (Self & Peers), Sacrifice, Process Oriented, Body Language, Handling Adversity/Grit*

Figure 12

Highest Character Values for the 16-19 & 19-23+ Year-Old Range (Line Chart 6)

<u>CVs:</u> *Winning (The Right Way), Legacy (Impact on Others Now and in the Future), Servant Leadership*

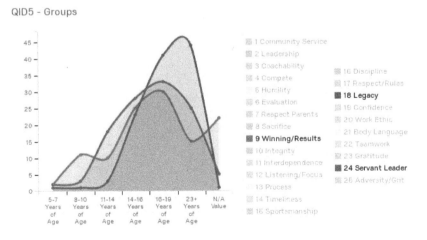

Along with conducting these integral studies, I have dedicated the past two years to investigating how coaches, parents, administrators, and student-athletes can improve character development in our youth. My research helped frame the constructs of the **CLD** curriculum. The 25 **CVs** that I discuss in the remainder of this book create the foundational framework and building-block approach for the coach at all levels of youth and amateur sports to follow in order to effectively and consistently identify, promote, develop, and assess for the comprehension and retention of the immeasurable value that character literacy development can play in our youth.

Part II:

Character Literacy Development—

Character Values &

25 Character Contributor Narratives

CHARACTER
LOVES
COMPANY

In the next few chapters, I highlight each of the **25 character values** and bring them to life with inspiring, motivating, and heartfelt testimonials. These narratives will speak to the soul of sports beginning at the foundational level of **CLD** with values such as **respect** and **appreciation**, and then they will progress upward to the advanced-mastery level values of **servant leadership** and **legacy**. These stories were shared with me primarily through powerful face-to-face or phone interviews, although a few of my contributors did choose to respond to my inquiry for defining moments in sports through written reflections. These narratives are evidence of the defining life lessons that can be enhanced through a *deliberate* and *intentional* character development emphasis on the part of both coaches and parents. My **CLD** curriculum provides the first systematic building-block approach to assure that character through youth and amateur sports is delivered appropriately.

Perhaps the toughest challenge in writing this book came after I had secured all 25 of my contributor interviews. The interconnectedness and overlapping virtues derived from striving for excellence through sports participation from all of my contributors made it difficult to select only three to four personal testimonies for each of the 25 **CVs.** The vivid reflections and demonstrations of these 25 **CVs** will be a reassuring echo of what sports once were, and certainly can be again one day. I take you into the living rooms or dining room tables of some real-life sports heroes and mentors to provide you with behind-the-scenes insights from their character defining moments.

At the conclusion of each of the 25 **CV** sections, I provide a series of suggested drills and activities that are well-suited for that particular level of **CLD.** These drills will aid the coach in helping student-athletes better identify with, comprehend, and retain the 25 **CVs** and vitally important character life skills. These developmental drills from each **CV** section are then collaborated in my supplemental **CLD** Coaches' Guide at the end of this book. Each of these drills has been proven time and time again, either through my own coaching experience or that of one of my many other expert coach contributors.

The supplemental guide also presents important figures and charts for reference, as well as a link for access to my C-SALT Test (Student-Athlete **Character** Literacy Test).

25 Character Values—Building-Block Levels of Development:

Level 1: CLD—Foundational Level (5-7-Year-Old Range)

Character Values (1-5):

1.   *Respect for Parents*
2.   *Sportspersonship*
3.   *Respect for Coaches, Opponents, Officials, Rules*
4.   *Gratitude (Love of Sport/Fitness and Opportunity)*
5.   *Appreciation/Care for Others (Interdependence and Commitment)*

Level 2: CLD—Post-Foundational Level (8-10-Year-Old Range)

Character Values (6-10):

6.   *Coachability (Willingness to Learn)*
7.   *Integrity & Honor*
8.   *Concept of Working to a Common Goal (Teamwork)*
9.   *Listening and Focus*
10. *Understanding how to Compete (Honestly & Ethically)*

Level 3: CLD—Mid-Level (11-14-Year-Old-Range)

Character Values (11-16):

11. *Discipline*
12. *Timeliness (Time Management)*
13. *Humility*
14. *Work Ethic/Sense of Accomplishment*
15. *Leadership*
16. *Confidence Without Being Cocky*

Level 4: CLD—Advancing Level (14-16-Year-Old-Range)

Character Values (17-22):

17. *Sacrifice*

18. *Handling Adversity/Resilience (Toughness & Grit)*

19. *Process Oriented*

20. *Body Language Awareness*

21. *Community Service/Outreach*

22. *Honest Evaluation (Self & Peers)*

Level 5: CLD—Advanced Mastery Levels (16-19 & 19-23+ Year-Old-Range)

Character Values (23-25):

23. *Winning (How to Win the Right Way)*

24. *Servant Leadership*

25. *Legacy (Impact on Others Now and in the Future)*

CHAPTER 6—Level I: CLD—Foundational Level
(5-7-Year-Old Range)

Plain and simple, this foundational level of youth sports participation needs to be about making it FUN. At this initial stage, our biggest focus as coaches, parents, and administrators of youth sports should be on the concepts of early sampling and deliberate play (approaches centered on fun and creativity discussed previously by Jean Côté et al, 2007 & 2009).

We want to attach fun with athletic activity and physical exercise. The most obvious reason for this is to get our youth involved in sports, as well as keep them interested and engaged. This, in turn, will inevitably combat the ever-growing obesity endemic caused by a sedentary lifestyle. Over the past few decades, even the lowest levels of youth sports have seen a trend toward bypassing deliberate play in order to skip ahead to deliberate practice, or even more advanced levels. The research has proven this to be deleterious to the foundational level of development from all vantage points (physical, psychological, sociological, and my biggest emphasis, the character development standpoint).

In this chapter, I lay out the "Big Five," which are the first five primary building blocks to **CLD**. It is vital that these five foundational **CVs** are learned prior to advancing on to successive levels of sports development. If our young student-athletes do not first learn to enjoy and appreciate athletic opportunities, as well as respect for others involved, they will be less receptive to the **CVs** that are vitally important to nurture at this earliest stage.

CHARACTER
LOVES
COMPANY

<u>Character Values (1-5):</u>

1. ***Respect for Parents***

2. *Sportspersonship*

3. *Respect for Coaches, Opponents, Officials, Rules*

4. *Gratitude (Love of Sport/Fitness and Opportunity)*

5. *Appreciation/Care for Others (Interdependence and Commitment)*

BUILDING BLOCK #1: **Respect for Parents**

"My father gave me the greatest gift that anyone could give another person, he believed in me."

-Coach Jimmy Valvano

Respect for parents is a vitally important foundational character value. If I were given a nickel every time a parent complained about how their children would not listen to them, or that they were lashing out towards them, I would have millions, and I would give all of it to charity. Some of this is attributed to the normal cycle of adolescence into adulthood and a child's rebellion and desire to chart his or her own course. However, today's youth are edgier (in a negative way) and more agitated and stressed out than ever before. This brings validation to the recent studies depicting a 6% decrease in athletic participation over the past six years. Our kids are getting so beaten down by their parents and coaches in the athletic arena that it is driving them away from sports in droves. The 2014 "Project Play" study by The Aspen Institute that I presented in Chapter 3 depicts that youth sports participation is at an all-time low.[63]

---

[63] http://www.aspenprojectplay.org/

My first contributor sheds some excellent insight on how we, as parents and coaches, can work together to reverse this trend. This concept of "Bridging the Great Divide Between Parents and Coaches" is the focus of my first essay on additional topics from the Appendix. We all need to work together for the sake of our youth to make sports fun and relevant again.

-Betsy Mitchell *(U.S. Olympic Gold and Silver Medalist in Swimming 1984 & 1988; U.S. Rowing World Championship team in 1994; first Female Athletic Director at California Institute of Technology in Pasadena, California; Role Model in her community):*

If you have ever had the pleasure to speak with, learn from, or be in the presence of Betsy Mitchell like I have, even for a short period of time, you will see most, if not all, of the **CVs** that I discuss in this book exuding out of her. She portrays that unique balance of humility, confidence, and resolve that can only be developed from a love of learning and willingness to grow as an athlete, and more importantly, as a person.

Betsy is a key community figure in Pasadena, California, where I grew up, as well as where my family started a youth, multi-sport development company, BAT1000.[64] Because of her significant outreach in the community, I spoke with Betsy and invited her to be the keynote speaker in the fall of 2015 for a panel of character-based talks held at Clairbourn School in San Gabriel, CA. Based on the studies that I have discussed in the early part of this book, the purpose of these talks was to highlight the effectiveness of a woman's approach to coaching and mentoring in youth athletics and juxtapose it with the often male-dominated, win-at-all-costs approach that has engulfed the youth sports landscape. Betsy agreed to come talk with our small group of coaches and parents, and her message resonated with everyone in attendance. She emphasized the caring and nurturing approach utilized by her parents, which gracefully blended supportiveness with a hands-off approach that empowered Betsy as a child to take ownership in her development and future goals through sports.

Betsy, along with another mentor of mine, Fred Claire (World Series Champion General Manager for the Los Angeles Dodgers in 1988 and expert on leadership in sport

---

[64] BAT1000 is named after my dad's short career in the Major Leagues that I discussed in the introductory chapter. With BAT1000, the 3-for-3 model is based on developing the following three pillars for lifelong success: academics, athletics, character/leadership. All three of these areas are emphasized side-by-side during the BAT1000 programs.

and business), was one of the first individuals whom I reached out to about the project of this guidebook on character development. During Betsy's address on that autumn afternoon to our small group of coaches and parents, I was moved and inspired by the immense amount of respect and appreciation that she displayed for her parents during her upbringing. I asked Betsy if she would be willing to provide the content of her message in written form that I could include in my guidebook. I chose Betsy's piece to lead the way because she masterfully crafted just how vitally important a parent or parents (as well as guardians, coaches, and mentors) can be in the developmental process of their children, if their support is provided in an appropriate manner. Here is what Betsy had to say about her parents' footprint on her:

I am often asked about the role of my parents in my swimming success. I usually shrug my shoulders and say, simultaneously, nothing special and I owe them everything…. a bit of a juxtaposition. Let me explain.

I owe them everything. An organism is the result of both forces of nature and nurture. In my case, my parents got an A+ in both. My athletic genes must be very good—my dad, a star basketball and track athlete in high school and mom, a synchronized swimmer, lifeguard, and horsewoman growing up. So, somewhere along the line, I inherited the potential for my massive VO2 max, sturdy but flexible skeleton, and strong musculature. My body readily accepted the progressive training that I loved, coaches provided, and my parents did nothing to mess up!

But, the environment in which I was raised, the nurture, was everything. It was special. I think I knew it then, and I definitely know it now. My parents absolutely let my experience be mine, not theirs, mine. This developed in me a humility, a confidence, a resiliency, and most of all internal motivation. They were involved, of course, and definitely supportive, present, encouraging, but they did a couple of key things that let the experience be truly mine.

First, they allowed me to stand on my own feet. I decided what sport and how much practice. I happened to love everything involved with my team so that part was easy, but I never felt pressure to go to practice, or a meet, or to swim a particular event. I got to make all those decisions. In fact, when it came time to consider starting morning workouts, I was too young to drive. So, in discussing the opportunity with my parents, I said I wanted to try morning practices a couple times per week. My dad immediately said that he would do anything to support me including driving me at 4:30 in the morning before work, but I had to get him up. He would not get me up. So, that is what we did. I set my alarm, I woke him up, and we went. (Thank heavens, this lasted only until my teammate could drive, then I just got myself up and he was able to sleep in.)

Likewise, my mom was completely supportive. She would volunteer in the bullpen,[65] at the concession stand, or awards desk. But, she never knew my times or places. She would just ask, 'how did you do?' or 'how did it feel?' These open-ended questions let me shape my feelings and opinions about my races and experience, rather than frame them in objective terms. This produced a striving and a satisfaction all my own.

My parents did shape my environment on one occasion. It was my eighth grade year and I wanted to go to some dance, not on the run from practice with wet hair, but dry and picked up by my date in a proper way. I asked my coach to miss practice, and he didn't want me to, but I decided I wanted to. We got into a bit of a stubborn way which ended with me crying in the upstairs hallway and my parents uncertain of what to do. When I said I was going to quit, my dad stepped off the sidelines and into the fray. He said he didn't care whether I went to practice or to the dance, either was fine. But, I was not going to quit in the middle of something. Evaluation was for the end of the season, not the middle. They, of course, left it up to me. The following week, I had a good talk with my coach and we didn't miss a beat after that. It emphasized good communication with my coach and expressing what I needed, not just following randomly assigned rules and roles.

I often think that I had nothing special because I had a very protected but 'average' upbringing. It gave me a tremendous sense of confidence. I did chores, we took family vacations on our schedule, not around swimming, I did other things with friends. It was not a specialized childhood—it was a personalized one. My parents gave me every opportunity, but they insisted in their own hands-off manner that I make and take from the opportunity, they did not do it for me.

My mom and I have an inside joke. She says that even from very young I used to say 'I can do it myself, Mom.' The trick is, she let me.

Betsy pinpointed the role of parents in their children's sports development, which can lead to higher amounts of respect from children. Most parents have the right intentions with their children in sports from the outset. However, after a few years of invested time, money, and energy into the developmental process of their children as athletes, many fall into the same trap that unfortunately occurs more often than not. I have witnessed

---

[65] The bullpen in swimming is the area where the swimmers get warmed up. It is similar to the bullpen in baseball, where the pitchers warm up before entering a ballgame.

hundreds, if not thousands, of parents who make the same mistakes over and over again when it comes to their role in their child's sports development journey. Far too many of them want to "live vicariously" through their kids and that is a recipe for disaster. It inevitably leads to burnout, high stress, low self-esteem, lack of perspective, and decreased motivation. Eventually, it results in what we have seen over the past six years, the dramatic 6% decrease in youth sports participation at the tune of 2.4 million kids per years dropping out completely, never to return to sports. If we truly want children to love and learn from sports, then we need to follow the example laid forth by Betsy Mitchell's parents.

Of the 25 highly successful contributors represented in this book, only one of them did not directly express a sincere and utmost gratitude for their parents' support in their journey to excellence. This particular individual (an ex-United States Army Ranger) was fortunate to have a wonderful grandmother as well as some terrific coaches and mentors in his life while growing up. This heroic individual, whose story is shared under character values #18 **Handling Adversity**, #23 **Winning the Right Way**, and #25 **Legacy**, still found a way to express appreciation for how his "rough" upbringing from his parents made him the person of character that he is today.

Along with Betsy's depiction of the invaluable role that her parents played in her unfoldment as a person, I had numerous other testimonies expressing the utmost respect for their parents. It was tough to narrow the contributions for **CV #1** down to only a few other powerful stories that I have gathered through my behind-the-scenes interviews, as well as the following poignant remarks from **Ryan Arcidiacono**, 4-year Team Captain and Leader of the 2016 NCAA March Madness Final Four Champion Villanova University Wildcats. In watching Arcidiacono's leadership and respect on the court and hearing about these qualities and more off the court, I reached out to Ryan to get his personal perspective on the integral role that his parents played in his development as a basketball player but, more importantly, as a person. This is what Ryan Arcidiacono shared with me:

> *The family values my parents instilled in me and my siblings not only helped me develop as a man but also improved my basketball game. The values they taught me growing up made me a better leader on the court; specifically teaching how to play together towards one*

common goal which helped our teams become successful and eventually win a National Championship my senior year.

Ryan's respect for his parents and others who have contributed to his life are ever-apparent in how he lives his life and how he treats others.

-Rafael O. Perez *(Major League Baseball, Director, Dominican Operations; Son of Legendary 50-Year Youth Coach/Mentor in Santo Domingo, Dominican Republic):*

I met Rafael Perez a few years back when I was in the Dominican Republic for community service work in conjunction with a project seeking ways to blend the power of the sport of baseball and the need for an increased emphasis on academics and education in the Dominican Republic. The highlight of my trip was definitely the two full days of youth baseball camps that I helped facilitate along with a few other IMG baseball coaches for 120-150 Dominican children on one single field. Witnessing first-hand the passion and enthusiasm that youth in the D.R. have for the sport of baseball was life-altering. It was during this trip that I was introduced to Rafael, as well as his father, Oscar, along with hundreds of young children and their parents who had the greatest respect and admiration for the Perez family's influence.

In continuing the importance of CV #1 **Respect for Parents**, Rafael pays his utmost respect to his father, Oscar. He told how his father moved from a small town called Moca to Santo Domingo when he was 12-years-old. Oscar did not have a father figure and he basically had to raise himself. Baseball became his father's refuge and passion and kept him on track. Baseball was the connection that Oscar used to keep the family together. Oscar had been coaching the local children in Santo Domingo, along with Rafael and his siblings, for many years prior to creating his own youth league, some 36 years ago. Here is what Rafael revealed to me about his father:

> *After more than 10 years of coaching, he decided in 1980 to create his own league which carried his name, "The Oscar Perez League" (ages 6-18-years-old). I actually spent my teenage years playing in my father's league. The last three years that I played in his league had the greatest impact on my character through sports.*

> *Growing up, baseball was really the only way he [Oscar] knew how to communicate with me or my siblings. He never had the opportunity to learn from his father, or anyone else for that matter, how to communicate with his own kids. It was after I graduated from college;*

that's when my father and I really established open communication about anything and everything without having to bring sports into each conversation.

I am who I am today thanks to how my father used sports to develop all the traits that have been instrumental in the success that I have obtained thus far in my life. The main traits he taught which shaped my character were: **discipline, passion for the game, hard work, learning how to deal with failure, caring for others, honesty, and integrity.**

Rafael shares multiple impactful life lessons learned from his father in the subsequent chapters.

-John Paciorek *(My father; 50-year Coach/Mentor; MLB Record Holder for Lifetime Highest Batting Average):*

Similar to Rafael's story and strong relationship and admiration for his father, my dad had a relationship with his father that was rooted in life lessons learned in the sporting arena, which were then passed down to my siblings. Below, my father shares his respect and adoration for his parents, and specifically his dad (my grandfather), in molding who he is today:

My dad [Grandpa] *should have had sainthood bestowed on him for all the self-sacrifice and virtue he displayed while providing for his family of ten. (But, nevertheless, because of the manner in which we related to each other, it wasn't so much respect, but rather FEAR that got my undivided attention.) He worked from early adulthood on the assembly-line at the Plymouth/Chrysler Plant on Mt. Elliot Road, about two and a half miles from where we lived. He didn't always have a car to get to work, but he never missed a day of work when he was sick (there were no "sick-leave" or vacation days then). The health and well-being of his family were too important to miss work for any reason. I remember him walking the two and a half miles on repeated occasions in blistering, snowy conditions because the car wasn't functional and no bus routes were available to him.*

My dad shares examples of his father's (my grandfather's) **legacy** through many different character values presented in this book such as **honesty, sacrifice,** and **work ethic**.

Many of these shared stories are legendary tales within my family, but a few were new even to me.

The respect for parents oftentimes comes from a balance between leading our youth by word and demonstration while, at the same time, empowering them to take ownership of their own experiences. The example that we set forth through our daily words and actions as parents and coaches are closely analyzed and mimicked by our children. This is how a sense of respect and trust is built.

CV #1 Respect for Parents: Activities and Drills to increase Retention/Assessment:
*Though my original intent was to provide drills that were applicable to the age-specific range of focus, some of these coach-initiated activities that I have provided at the end of each **CV** section (and in the **Supplemental Coaches' Guide** at the end of the book) may be a little advanced. This is deliberate on my part as I realize that coaches will be utilizing these **foundational level CVs** as character starting points for all levels from youth up through the amateur levels of collegiate athletics. The 8-week **CLD** curriculum that I facilitated this past summer in Pasadena, California was with high school students and we started at this foundational level. Please modify any and all of these drills to the age-range that you are working with.

- o The best way to get respect is to show respect and care for others. The best way to teach your players at this young age to respect and value their parents is to constantly make it a point of emphasis.
- o Have your players think about all of the sacrifices that their parents/guardians make for them to be out there playing the sports that they love. Remind your young players to thank their parents on the car ride home from practices or games, as well as at various moments each week. A simple "thank you" goes a long way and our players are never too young to learn this important gesture of gratitude.
- o Within the first few weeks of practice and the season, bring a notepad of paper, enough pens or pencils for all of your players, along with stamps and envelopes. Have your players brainstorm a bit on the topic of respect for parents and what they are appreciative of. Then, have them take 10 minutes at the end of practice on their own to write a handwritten note to mom or dad, or to their guardian. When they are finished, give them each an envelope with a stamp on it and have

them address and seal it with the letter inside. Gather up all of the letters and on your way home after that practice or game, simply drop the letters in the mail.

o   Depending on the age of your players, another great team activity is to have them stand up for 30 seconds and talk about someone who has been influential in their life (such as a parent or guardian). This not only works on their public speaking skills, but it also enhances the activity's effectiveness by having them articulate their respect and appreciation for the influential people in their lives.

CHARACTER LOVES COMPANY

<u>Character Values (1-5):</u>

1. *Respect for Parents*

2. ***Sportspersonship***

3. *Respect for Coaches, Opponents, Officials, Rules*

4. *Gratitude (Love of Sport/Fitness and Opportunity)*

5. *Appreciation/Care for Others (Interdependence and Commitment)*

BUILDING BLOCK #2: **Sportspersonship**

In discussing this concept of **sportspersonship**, *"It is thus proposed that through their interactions with their peers, parents, coaches, and other sport participants, children come to learn what sportspersonship is and what it is not. An important implication of this proposition is that athletes should be in a prime position to identify the nature of the concept of sportspersonship"* (Vallerand et al 1997). My first contributor to this section on **sportspersonship** is BJ Bedford-Miller.

-BJ Bedford-Miller *(U.S. Olympic Gold Medalist in Swimming & previous World Record Holder in the Medley Relay in 2000 Olympic Games in Sydney, Australia; NCAA All-American at University of Texas; Board Member of Advisors for Positive Coaching Alliance (PCA) in Colorado):*
        During our interview, BJ shared a story of influence in sportsmanship, or what is more appropriately referred to as **sportspersonship**. During her freshman year at the University of Texas, BJ and her team (comprised of many All-Americans and future Olympians) shattered the NCAA points scored record in a season en route to the National Championship title. It was a dream team, so to speak, and they literally "smoked teams," and blew them out of the water. Well, they lost a few key swimmers after that year, and BJ shared an awesome lesson in leadership and character that has resonated

with her ever since and helped define who she is today. As if it happened yesterday, BJ recalled back to 1991 and the life lesson that her team captains taught her:

> Going into the final day of the National Championship meet with Stanford, our captains [Katy Arris and Dorsey Tierney] called for a meeting with our team prior to going out for the final day of competition. They told us, 'We are not going to win tonight.' Mathematically, it had already been determined that Stanford's team had already accrued a large enough lead to determine that the final stage of the meet could not change the final outcome.

> [The captains continued:] 'There are going to be a whole lot of cameras out there. We, as a collective whole, are going to show class and dignity. We are not going to cry on national television. We are going to get up and clap for Stanford, as painful as it will be. When we won [last year], they clapped and were gracious to us.'

> Our captains showed great leadership for our team, and I learned a lesson that day. We did not want to be the agony of defeat. That lesson has stuck with me still today.

Fast forward close to 10 years later. BJ had earned her way onto the Olympic team representing the USA in 2000. She had just placed sixth in her individual race and quite possibly the biggest race of her life, the 100 Meter Backstroke Olympic Finals. She recalls, "After the race, I saw that the winner [Gold Medalist from Romania] was so nonchalant about just winning the Gold. I swam over to her and hoisted her arm in the air. I was proud to stand shoulder-to-shoulder with all of these women—we had worked so hard to accomplish our dreams."

I love this commentary from BJ, because it was proof that she was not only able to identify with the teachable moment from her teammates and captains while in college, but she was actually able to transfer it down the road in another competitive arena. This is the true demonstration of her retention of lessons in class, dignity, and **sportspersonship** towards others. While most athletes are wallowing in their successes or disappointments and focused on themselves, BJ was able to seize the moment.

BJ's narrative conjured up recollections of a similar act of **sportspersonship** and goodwill on display more recently during the heat of battle in a highly contested NCAA competition. The character moment took place during a pivotal softball game between rival teams, Central Washington and Western Oregon, to determine which team would advance to the regional playoffs. Two Central Washington players, Mallory Holtman and Liz Wallace, volunteered to carry their injured opponent, Sara Tucholsky from Western

Oregon, around the bases in order to complete the three-run homerun that she had hit prior to a leg injury that kept her from advancing on her own. Holtman and Wallace's act was 100% supported by their team and coaches, and though it contributed to their team's eventual season-ending loss, their act of character has become a guiding light and billboard for current and future generations of aspiring NCAA student-athletes to come.[66]

-Beth Work *(Vice President of Operations, Boys & Girls Clubs of Manatee County, Florida; Long-time Youth Mentor)*

Beth Work has been involved in youth sports for more than 30 years and she is highly involved in her local community as a leader. I met Beth at a community talk on the need for increased character development in youth sports that I presented for a local Rotary Club group where she was the president. During my recent interview with Beth, I specifically asked her about the value of sportsmanship or sportspersonship:

> *It is not just the Boys & Girls Clubs across America, but all of the great youth organizations out there providing for our youth. We can, and do, have such a lasting impact in developing this concept* [of sportspersonship].

> *With many sports teams across the country, there is a philosophy or tradition of shaking hands with the other team at the end of the game. I think that is such an important component. However, oftentimes, the true intent of gratitude and this expression of interdependence and appreciation for others involved is lost. I have seen both players and their coaches express poor sportsmanship and a complete lack of respect for the other team during this time of shaking hands. At certain times, players and coaches actually refuse to shake the hands of their opponents, which is the ultimate sign of disrespect in the world of sports. When players and coaches lose perspective and they are simply shaking hands out of lip service to a societal tradition of respect, that is extremely discouraging to see for someone in my position. This speaks to the fact that our children are missing the point or significance. My hope is that our youth participating in sports can be grateful that the other team came to their house to play…because without them, they could not have played the game that they love.*

---

[66] For more from this altruistic act of character, visit: www.values.com and search for the billboard: "Helped injured opponent win. SPORTSMANSHIP: Pass it on."

It is all about the camaraderie, respect, and humbleness (or humility), as well as many of the characteristics that are developed irrespective of whether they won or lost.

Our children need to learn that sometimes they are going to have a bad day, and that is okay and actually a part of life. It is not realistic for coaches and parents to think and expect our children to win every game. More importantly, we need to get rid of the misconception that we are giving kids that if they do not win, then there is nothing to be learned.

These remarks from Beth are congruent with what I am positing on the need for **CLD** and specifically sportspersonship and the desire to break away from the zero-sum mentality. Indeed, there is so much to be learned from the adversity of losing, and our children need to learn how to win with grace and how to lose with dignity.

CV #2 Sportspersonship: Activities and Drills to increase Retention/Assessment:

- o Share with your team the story above from www.values.com where Mallory Holtman and Liz Wallace demonstrated great sportspersonship to their opponent in the NCAA softball regional game. Go over the rules stating that her own teammate could not help her around the bases. What are your players' thoughts on this gesture of carrying a seriously injured opponent around the bases for a homerun? Help guide them to the side of sportsmanship vs. what many coaches/parents are teaching, the idea of gamesmanship. When it comes down to winning or losing, I know many coaches who would not have endorsed such a gesture. What is fair and right within the rules may not necessarily be correct as sportspersonship goes beyond doing what the rules dictate to what is actually the right thing to do.
- o Have your players work in groups of two or three. Ask each group to think about a recent event in the media where an individual or team demonstrated either negative or positive sportsmanship. Have each group present the story that they came up with to the rest of the team for discussion.
- o Additional questions for teams to consider:
  - What external forces influence poor sportspersonship? How do you, as a coach, counter that?

- Do your student-athletes think that as they get older it is more important to display good sportspersonship?
- How does sportspersonship affect all aspects of life, not only sports?

CHARACTER LOVES COMPANY

<u>Character Values (1-5)</u>:

1. *Respect for Parents*

2. *Sportspersonship*

3. **Respect for Coaches, Opponents, Officials, Rules**

4. *Gratitude (Love of Sport/Fitness and Opportunity)*

5. *Appreciation/Care for Others (Interdependence and Commitment)*

BUILDING BLOCK #3: Respect for Coaches, Opponents, Officials, Rules

One of my favorite movies growing up was *Chariots of Fire*,[67] and I still sing the theme song to myself whenever I go out for a run. This brilliant film portrays the 1924 Paris Olympic Games that pitted two rival Track & Field athletes who overcame the prejudice of the times between the Jewish and Christian faiths.

The film's star, gold medalist Eric Liddell, always displayed the utmost respect and admiration for his opponents, shaking their hands prior to each of his races for the opportunity to compete with them on such a grand stage. He also held strongly to his religious beliefs, and for this reason, he chose not to compete on Sundays. Holding firmly to his principles, he opted out of his best event, the 100 Meters, because the race was on a Sunday. Instead, he went on to win the gold medal in the 400M and the bronze medal in the 200M.

---

[67] *Chariots of Fire* was an Oscar winning film produced in 1981. This is definitely a terrific film to watch on a bus ride with the team.

Respect for coaches, opponents, officials, and **rules** is a foundational character value that is an absolute during the early years of youth sports participation. I once again turn to **BJ Bedford-Miller** *(Olympic gold medalist in 2000)*, in order to emphasize this value in character.

Continuing where I left off in my interview with BJ, she stated, *"At Texas, I learned how to win with grace and how to lose with class. But, I learned so much more from losing. I think it is important to have the ability to empathize…Go, be happy for that girl who won—be in the present and respect the game, the sport, your opponents."*

Her act of care and pure joy for her opponent from Romania in 2000 (whom she had never met), who had just earned a lifetime goal of winning a gold medal in the Olympic Games for her country, demonstrates true sportspersonship and **respect** for the hard work and sense of accomplishment. BJ wanted to make sure that her opponent did not miss out on this truly remarkable event.

-Lyman "Lee" Ellis III, EdD. *(40-year Youth Coach/Mentor; Athletic Director at Principia College; NCAA Head Women's Soccer Coach; Mentor of Mine):*

Here, a coaching-mentor and great friend of mine, Lee Ellis, shares a poignant message that unfolded over the course of his first 30 years of coaching. I hope that we all can draw from Lee's powerful message and philosophy about showing class and respect to our opponents:

A value essential to my coaching involves respecting opponents. Even at the earliest ages, children understand that it is not fun to just practice skills without getting the opportunity to try them out with an opponent in a game. This aspect of respect relates to the way one views the contest. Thinking of opponents as partners is a vital concept to understand if opponents are to be respected. If a given activity mutually promotes a quest for excellence, provides enjoyment, and creates an environment of anticipation and appreciation when players compete, then respect will result.

What happens, however, when these two values come into conflict? Playing hard within the context of a game can often result in an ethical dilemma for coaches and players, especially when the scoreboard disproportionally favors one side or one person over the other. At what point does the next goal, the next run, the next basket (aspects of playing hard) turn the contest into an activity that undermines and devalues the concept of respect for opponents?

A few years ago, I faced this right versus right dilemma. Coaching a collegiate soccer match, our side prepared for a good game, and I presume our opponent did as well. We were excited for the game and we greeted the other team graciously. We had a friendly rivalry with the team and the coach and I were good friends. Once the game began it became apparent that we were going to dominate. In fact, we scored nine goals; they didn't score any. We gave our best effort, kept a positive attitude and by the scoreboard account, had a great day. We showed little restraint in our play, but we didn't run up the score either. And, of course, we substituted liberally, but everyone wanted their chance to score. Our opponent didn't feel quite the same jubilation during or after the game. They actually refused to shake hands at the game's conclusion, were visibly upset and, as I found out later, felt humiliated by the lopsided score. What came to me later, after much self-reflection, was a different way of thinking in how to respect the game and, at the same time, how to respect the opponent.

What dawned on me was this concept: Our opponent had given their best effort. They couldn't have played any better, or they would have. We, on the other hand, had a choice. This is what we did going forward.

We started with team discussions about what it meant to play to the level the game demands, instead of up or down to the level of our opponent. We began introducing attitudes of play that would respect the game without disrespecting opponents who might not be performing up to our level on any particular day. We began working on numbers up and numbers down situations in practice, we talked about how we wanted to play, and we talked about how it felt from both ends of the perspective—winning and losing. We agreed that we would not score more than four goals in any half or more than six goals in a game. If another team came to play with less than a full squad, we would match the number of players they put on the field. To make the game interesting, we would sometimes leave the ball on the goal line instead of scoring or hit the ball wide of the goal or directly at the keeper. We would look to keep possession of the ball or look to score from a specific pattern of play. We did these things in lopsided games without fanfare, to respect the game without disrespecting our opponents. And, because we actually talked about and practiced our values regarding the game and our opponents, how we acted in those situation enabled our opponents to respect us.

Fast forward to last basketball season. My wife, Julie, and I decided to coach a sixth grade park and recreation team that included our son. Early on, there was a game that quickly became one-sided in our favor. We called a time-out and began discussing how it might feel being on the other team. We talked about how we might play differently so that both teams could enjoy the activity. We still wanted the boys to play hard, we just wanted them to work on other aspects of the game beyond purely scoring, because we could. So, we suggested left-handed layups from the left side, or shooting only three point shots (for sixth graders, making one of these is like winning the lottery), and five passes before attempting to score (an idea from the players). The game turned out to be very exciting and everyone had a good time. Our players learned something about respect and, at the same time, they had the opportunity to work on some of their skills in a game situation. Players on the other team were able to enjoy playing their best without losing sight of that effort because of a lopsided score…a win for both teams.

For some readers, I realize that this story and example laid forth by a 30+ year veteran coach is a tough concept to digest, as many of us have been taught that you play hard until the very last whistle or pitch. We have always been taught to never play down to our opponent, or in individual racing sports such as swimming and track and field, that you are always racing against your own personal best. These statements all have great validity. In this ego showcase-driven youth sports culture, I realize that it can be pride-swallowing and hard for young statistically-driven student-athletes to buy into, but humility and respect for others are much-needed life skills.

However, even in the MLB and other professional sports, there are unwritten rules of respect and not showing up the other team, as far as continuing to steal bases or advancing to the next base on a ball that gets by the catcher once the game is out of hand. No one likes to be on either side of a blowout.[68] Now, while there is not a magic formula that any of us can turn to in order to determine when mercy should be displayed on an opponent, as coaches and parents, we need to be guided by sound judgement. The scenario that Lee has presented above should be one that every coach takes some time to consider at the start of each and every season. It may even become one of the most meaningful life lessons that you are able to teach the young student-athletes on your team each year. It will undoubtedly provide a chance for your team to think, listen, reason, and communicate effectively about deeper issues than just the sport itself.

Great examples of leadership such as Lee's will be discussed in a later chapter where I will reemphasize the need to seek out these teachable coaching moments rather

---

[68] A "blowout" in sports is when one team dominates early and often and the victor of the game no longer becomes a question.

than blow right past them or miss out on a teachable moment like the coach of the 11-U team whom I depicted in my opening chapter. The important point is to recognize and own up to your main role as a coach, which is a mentor and teacher of life skills. This is how coaches can truly be leaders.

CV #3 Respect for Opponents, etc.: Activities and Drills to increase Retention/Assessment:

- When focusing on respecting those on the field with your team, such as opponents, officials, etc., it is very important for a coach to emphasize that young student-athletes can be respectful and still play with a passion, edge, and desire to compete to win. I think about college football, or even professional football, which can be a ferocious and aggressive sport. Despite the fact that these players are going back and forth all game long, I always appreciate how, after a hard-fought battle, you oftentimes see players stick around on the field afterward for a group prayer or to give their opponent a "man-hug" out of respect (win or lose). Another occasion where you see this extension of respect after a hard-fought competition is in the boxing ring. Those are my favorite moments to witness in the athletic arena.

- If you have a road trip with your team, rent the movie *Chariots of Fire* which I discussed in the early going of this section for **CV #3**. Pick out a couple of specific scenes that highlight respect for opponents, rules, etc. and have your student-athletes reflect in a journal about what they took from those scenes as it relates to them and their team. You could follow up on this during the team breakfast which would get the players up on their feet doing a bit of public speaking.

- Another good clip to show your teams occurs each year in the Army-Navy Football game. After each game, both teams meet up and go to the other team's sideline and lock arms respectfully saluting each other while listening to each band play that school's fight song.

- An excellent team activity is to have your players think about the scenario that Dr. Lee Ellis presented above regarding how to handle a "blow out." When your team is superior to the other team, you still want your student-athletes to compete with full focus and effort. Have them come up with a way to still do so as a team, but not to disrespectfully "run up the score" or demoralize their opponents. This can be hard for young, or even more mature student-athletes. They can be so focused on their own statistics, the opportunity to get selected for "All-Stars," or the looming college scholarship, that it can be difficult for them to buy in. More often than not, it is the parents who do not get the importance of building character through sports, who at times seem to care less about character and more about domination and accolades. If you have parents like that on your team, please give them a copy of my book.

CHARACTER
LOVES
COMPANY

Character Values (1-5):

1. *Respect for Parents*

2. *Sportspersonship*

3. *Respect for Coaches, Opponents, Officials, Rules*

4. **Gratitude (Love of Sport/Fitness and Opportunity)**

5. *Appreciation/Care for Others (Interdependence and Commitment)*

BUILDING BLOCK #4: Gratitude
(Love of Sport/Fitness and Opportunity)

"Gratitude is not only the greatest of virtues, but the parent of all others." –Cicero

-Addison Staples *(Youth Coach/Mentor; Founder and Director of Aces in Motion (AIM), non-profit organization serving underserved youth; Executive Director, Gainesville Area Community Tennis Association, Inc.):*

Addison Staples has been expressing his gratitude for the opportunities he has been given in his life through a commitment to giving back and providing life-long skills to underserved children, both domestically and internationally. Addison's non-profit organizations reach thousands of children each year through the major premise of making sports fun and relevant to life outside of sports.

If kids do not enjoy playing sports and do not realize that it is more than just about winning, they will walk away and never participate in sports again, and then that will lead to sedentary lifestyles and chronic disease. Then the inactive lifestyles lead to obesity and all sorts of other diseases...you can name your sickness. My thing is that there should be a better link between coaching education, values, character, and the cognitive and psychological developmental health of the child. It needs to be backed by science.

Addison went on to share with me during our interview that he was fortunate to have had two parents who spent a lot of time with him playing and learning sports, despite the fact that neither one of them happened to be a superstar athlete. They spent a great deal of time with him outdoors. His father taught him non-traditional sports such as water skiing and sailing, which eventually led him to become a competitive wakeboarder. While these sports taught him certain central skill sets and expertise, Addison pointed out how his parents allowed him to be his own person and chart his own course:

I think this is the important component that many parents are missing out on nowadays: It has to be the kid's thing that they love to do and not the parents living through them. Now, I realize that parents need to encourage and provide opportunities to try new sports and stick with them through a full season, but much of the time, I see parents who want it more than the kids.

Just like sailing and wakeboarding for me, why not encourage our youth to learn and love to play a sport for the sake of it? My thought with my youth outreach programs is to learn a craft, do it well, and truly enjoy it! Why do we always have to be competing? There is definitely a time and place for competition, but kids play more games year-round than ever before.

I love to play tennis and I have always loved trying to hit that ball as hard as I could, but to do it with precision. I took that passion and played tennis in college…and, now, I think it applies to running my business and learning how to do it well, and being a leader and how to do that well. I do think that the end result is about learning and loving what you do. That is how I approach my organizations.

As coaches, if we can help kids enjoy and have fun playing their sport and give all of their effort to playing the best that they can, then we have done our part. The only way that anyone loses (as coaches and young athletes) is if they are not having fun or not giving their all and making it their own—that is when they lose out!

I agree 100% with Addison. The reason why we do not see more gratitude and appreciation from our youth for the financial sacrifice or time commitment that parents invest in their child's athletic opportunities is due to the fact that many young boys and girls are playing the sport for dad or mom, rather than for the joy and thrill of the challenges inherent in sports. We need to work to tap into their learning styles and passions rather than our own.

I naturally think of Joe Maddon (the Chicago Cubs manager and previous Tampa Bay Rays skipper) who has developed a recipe that brings out the best in his players. He has a way of minimizing the stressors and distractions that can add to an already stressful game of baseball at any level while tapping into the childlike love for sports and competition. His teams have various competitions and team activities in the clubhouse and on the road to humanize the players and to help them let their guard down and have fun. Many successful coaches have tailored a similar approach that motivates youth to want to keep working hard through incentives, such as decals on helmets and the belt system in martial arts (which I will discuss in more detail with Master Boon Brown in an upcoming chapter).

In my interview with **Beth Work** (*Vice President of Operations, Boys & Girls Clubs of Manatee County*), I asked her about this topic of bringing out the gratitude and love for the opportunity to play sports:

> *Getting parents on the same page with the vision that matches or complements our programs is important. We hope that all of our coaches will use what they have learned through sports to teach the teams that they coach these vital life lessons…and it cannot just be about winning! We don't want the win-at-all-costs mentality. We are fortunate to have some wonderful coaches in our programs. We do, and will, continue to hold our coaches and players accountable to a high standard. If the coach isn't adhering to the right principles, then we will not have that coach come back because it doesn't seem like their priorities are right.*

In reference to her daughter who is now grown with a family of her own, Beth shared how her daughter's participation in sports (primarily swimming) is something that helped mold the strong, caring, and successful person that she is today.

> *It's not just about her accomplishments as far as winning and her personal best times, and actually, I don't reflect on that aspect much. Rather, I am grateful and feel that she learned a great deal from her coaches, teammates, and those whom she competed with. She learned so much from the variety of different teams that she was on growing up and it is apparent how it*

has carried over to other areas of her life. Looking back, it is not about the winning or the losing, but rather, it is about learning and the life lessons. I see how the life skills that my daughter learned through sports are positively affecting her as a young mom.

It is apparent that some coaches and parents really get this, and my hope is that all of our coaches will recognize the many values that they have the potential of teaching through a stronger emphasis on life lessons, aside from just winning. The things that our players learn through the example of their coaches (as well as their parents) will be what they most remember, and these will create similar habits.

Sometimes parents don't understand that it is not always about winning, or that their child will play every minute of every game. It is vitally important that parents are supportive of their child's coach and that they recognize that they are working together to teach these life lessons.

The philosophy of parents is going to be reflected in their kids…With today's society of winning-at-all-costs, I think that sometimes parents tend to forget what we are supposed to value about sports. Rather than helping to instill in their children a sense of gratitude and appreciation for their opposition, as well as for their coaches, parents too often get caught up in the wrong things.

In talking about bridging that gap or divide between parents and coaches that I emphasize in Chapter 3 (as well as in the Appendix), I asked Beth to expand upon this need. It takes a collaborative effort to teach the many lessons in sports ranging from winning on one end of the spectrum to having fun and enjoying the game on the other end. Beth stated:

Without a doubt, we need parents and coaches to realize that they are on the same team when it comes to teaching their kids. They play such an important role in teaching and modeling for their children a sense of gratitude towards their coaches and the officials who dedicate a great deal of time and effort to our children. Simple gestures of gratitude go a long way.

-Dr. Ken Wasserman *(MLB Team Physician for 20 years; Currently a Team Physician for the Baltimore Orioles since 2006; Helped establish the "Skin Cancer Screening Program" for MLB):*

I have become good friends with Dr. Wasserman and his family as I have coached his twin sons over the past few years. He has been around elite-level sports for two decades and I wanted to get his perspective on the commonalities that he has witnessed in the elite-level athletes whom he has come in contact with over the years. In our interview, Dr. Wasserman shared the following with me:

> *I have worked with MLB for 20 years now, and I have observed hundreds of elite-level athletes. Through my observations, I have come to believe that the players who have been close with their families and teammates have a higher sense of confidence which helps create a successful environment. Clearly, the respect that these players have for others leads to the development of a support system that promotes longevity and success over time.*

Aside from this trend that Dr. Wasserman has seen from professional athletes, he also candidly shared with me a similar sentiment of late from the NCAA National Champion Villanova Men's Basketball Team.

> *Over the past year and a half, our family has probably been to a dozen Villanova games at The Pavilion*[69] *on campus. At the end of the game, it is great to see many of the players interact and show appreciation for the families, friends, and fans. We have gotten to know Ryan Arcidiacono* [whose specific quote was presented in my CLD building block #1: Respect for Parents]. *He is great to our boys and someone who always expresses the utmost appreciation for his immediate and extended family who support him at the games.*

A big part of Ryan Arcidiacono's success, as well as the success of any athlete who has ever accomplished anything through sports, is attributed to the many mentors that steered them in the right direction and supported them along the way, such as parents, coaches, and close friends.

In talking about this need to unearth the passions of our youth through sports, **Rafael Perez** *(Major League Baseball, Director, Dominican Operations)* reflected back on how his father was able to emphasize that important message in him during his youth. Referring to his father, Rafael recalled, *"He taught me about passion for the game by leading by example. He had a passion for teaching kids and teenagers about life through sports, but most*

---

[69] "The Pavilion" is the arena where Villanova plays their home games.

importantly, he was passionate about the game. One day, he told me to always follow what I am passionate about and that true happiness will follow."

Similar to my own father, Oscar Perez allowed his son to make baseball his own. It does not mean that he did not play an active and integral role in guiding Rafael's life; he was with him the whole way but standing in the shadows. We need to do the same for our sons and daughters and let them run their own race with joy and passion. When we do so, we will begin to see our youth return the favor two-fold by virtue of their gratitude.

CV #4 Gratitude (Joy of Sport/Fitness & Opportunity): Activities and Drills to increase Retention/Assessment:

- ○ As a team homework assignment, ask your players to think about and write down on a notecard three things that they value about being able to participate in sports. This could be something that you collect at the next practice or game and keep in your coaching bag. When a player is struggling or facing adversity, you could remind them of what they value about the sport and their true purpose and intent for playing.

- ○ One of my favorite activities related to gratitude is to get young student-athletes to better appreciate their opponents. All too often it is about crushing one's opponent, and while I am all for striving with all one's effort to win within the rules, I want our young student-athlete to realize the value of their opponent. Ask your team to think about the following questions: What if the other team decided not to show up? What if the opponent decided not to try? Would that make for a fun experience? In the next section, I discuss in more detail the idea of interconnectedness, or interdependence, which ties in closely to this CV on **gratitude and appreciation for one's opportunities**.

- ○ An excellent team activity is to have your players get into pairs and have them think about and share how fortunate they are to be able to be a member of a team. Ask them to think about the sacrifices that their parents make to allow them to get to practice and games on time each week.

CHARACTER LOVES COMPANY

<u>Character Values (1-5):</u>

1. *Respect for Parents*
2. *Sportspersonship*
3. *Respect for Coaches, Opponents, Officials, Rules*
4. *Gratitude (Love of Sport/Fitness and Opportunity)*
5. ***Appreciation/Care for Others (Interdependence and Commitment)***

BUILDING BLOCK #5: Appreciation/Care for Others (Interdependence and Commitment)

"No man is an island; every man is a piece of the continent, a part of the main."

-John Donne, 16th Century English Poet

This building block is very similar to the previous building block on gratitude. Though they have some overlapping attributes, gratitude is primarily focused on appreciation for what you have received from others, while this current character value is most concerned with realizing the innate interconnectedness and interdependence with others. The cultivation of this quality of care and concern for our fellow mankind creates empathy, awareness, and an increased sense of the importance of community.

Within my UF research studies, I had over 20 coaches surveyed who have been involved in coaching/mentoring at the youth level of sports for over 40 years. That is a large well of knowledge from which to draw. These wonderful coaches and youth role models have done more than they will ever truly know for the youth and the overall well-being of their communities because of their care and commitment to others. You will be hard-pressed to find a father-son combination that expresses this ceaseless concern for the youth of their country more than Rafael and Oscar Perez. Here, I provide more on this important topic from the words of **Rafael Perez** *(MLB, Director of Dominican Operations; son of 50-year Youth Coach/Mentor in the D.R.)*:

> *My father taught me about* **caring for others**. *People approached my father and encouraged him to increase registration fees to participate in the league and to charge for uniforms, among other things, for profit. He was very emphatic about keeping things the way they were because he was not in it to take financial advantage of families for personal benefit. Leagues in the Dominican Republic are run as businesses and not as non-profit entities. I remember when I approached him about it; he made it very clear that he only cared about covering expenses and having some extra funds for any unforeseen expenses. The league was always about doing it for the love of the game and the enjoyment of impacting the lives of kids.*

The concept of **caring for others** is another critical value we all should focus on getting across to today's youth. This is the only real way to have influence in one's life. Rafael's dad could have exploited these families in the Dominican Republic by charging a high cost to partake in the league, but he wanted to make it affordable and not about maximizing profit for himself. Especially in today's booming youth sports economy, this is a powerful message about the importance of reaching out in underserved and low-income communities to include rather than exclude. My non-profit organization, **Character Loves Company**, does just that by providing an eight-week **CLD** curriculum for young aspiring student-athletes to learn about the many values that I discuss in this guidebook. In many instances, youth sports have become all about the money when they should be about the children. After all, as the quote at the beginning of this section from John Donne presents, we are all interconnected as human beings.

-Dan Duquette *(Long-time MLB executive; General Manager, Baltimore Orioles; Great contributor to youth development in sports)*:

I love the way that Dan framed the following contribution written specifically for my guidebook around this concept of instilling an appreciation for the upcoming generation, as well as for those who came before us in sports. Dan wrote:

At its core, coaching youth sports is about passing on a love for the game from one generation to the next and if kids will recognize the sacrifice youth coaches make to help them learn about the game and themselves, they can receive the gift. Just as you learn about being a ballplayer by watching other accomplished ballplayers work at their craft, you can learn about developing a love for your game by observing and listening to youth coaches. Coaches volunteer to help youth players get better access and opportunities to play and to help them develop their skills. Watch, listen, and learn from your coaches and maybe you can love your game, too!

Coaches, own this role of coach as a badge of honor as you teach and mentor our youth through the lessons that were instilled in you. And, youth participants, be open-minded to try new techniques and approaches to sports. Become students of the game and pay attention to the mentors that you have so that in 20 years you can have the knowledge and expertise to share with the newest generation.

As a youth mentor who makes a significant, positive impact on thousands of children each year, both domestically and internationally, **Addison Staples** (*previously mentioned Youth Mentor; Founder of multiple NPO's*) shares how important it is for all coaches and parents of young athletes to work to make the connection and relevance between sports and life-long successes. He remarked:

I wanted to get use of the skills that I had in sailing and incorporate that into what I do with my youth programs. I try to blend that same thought process to a passion and apply that to other important aspects of life such as friendships, parenting, and in a potential future job. That doesn't mean that you are going to love every minute of it, but I teach them to stick with it and learn how to do it, and do it well. I tell them to remember the struggle to get it right now. When they do end up getting it, they learn a lot from that stick-to-it approach. There are not nearly enough messages out there for youth in building character through adversity.

I am teaching a sport that much of the underserved community does not have access to in tennis. I just want to encourage them to learn something new and to stick with it, even if they don't find it easy. I think somebody is doing a disservice to many of these underserved kids by telling them that they are going to grow up to become a professional basketball player.

In the two hours that I had the privilege to spend with Addison in Gainesville, Florida, where his non-profit organizations are located, I was inspired by all that he is doing to help today's youth work together on the courts. In doing so, he is helping them to recognize that life is about learning new skills and challenging themselves to overcome previously conceived limitations. We all know that the chance of becoming a long-time professional athlete in any sport is like winning a lottery ticket, but the lessons learned are like riding a bike, or hitting a cross-court backhand with strength, accuracy, and **confidence**. These skills and others stay with you for a lifetime.

In order for any of us to make a difference in the lives of our youth, we have to truly care about them. That means that we need to sacrifice for them. We need to be disciplined and committed to living our own lives the right way to be that guiding light, beacon of hope, and rock for them to rely on. There is no more integral duty than being there for our youth, our children. However, as I previously pointed out, the current research shows that more than 24 million children in America grow up without their biological father,[70] many of whom also lack the presence of a consistent father figure. Being a father figure or role model in the true essence of the word and title is not easy. It takes all of the character values that I discuss in this book. I will return to this interconnected topic of care for others in Chapter 9 with my focus on the **CVs #17** and **#18** on **Sacrifice** and **Handling Adversity/Resilience, Toughness,** and **Grit.**

CV #5 Appreciation/Care for Others (Interdependence and Commitment):

Activities and Drills to increase Retention/Assessment:

- o Towards the mid-way point of the season, have your players take 10 minutes to jot down a positive quality that they admire or respect about each of their teammates. Be sure that they write the teammate's name next to each quality. Collect each of these sheets and take the weekend to type out the result for each player from their peers. This is a great drill to get your players to highlight and notice the positive qualities in one another. It is so easy nowadays to only see and dwell on the negatives, or what they do not like. The following practice, give each player a laminated notecard of the responses from each of their peers. You

---

[70] According to the "National Fatherhood Initiative" found at: www.fatherhood.org, we are facing a "Father Absence Crisis" in America, according to Ryan Sanders' (November 12, 2013) reference to the U.S. Census Bureau.

can decide whether to include the players' names who made the positive comment or not. You can also include a quality that you value about each one of them. This could be something that you hand out at the end of practice. I can guarantee that these positive comments from their peers will lift them up. Who knows, it may be something that they keep with them for the rest of their lives.

- o If you are working with slightly older student-athletes, perhaps in the 13+ age range, take a rain delay, traffic jam, or other period of lengthy time to burn and start a discussion on the transferable skills of sports to the business world, friendships, parenthood, or life in general.

- o The next team activity on interconnectedness and interdependence is one that I did with my first CLD curriculum in Southern California with a group of high school freshmen through seniors. This activity may take a bit more preparation, as I had them use the Internet and present their findings. I had them get into a few groups of four or five students. I then handed them each a topic and asked them to brainstorm, research, and analyze how their topic related to baseball. The topics each involved everyday processes that occur in nature that involve an interconnectedness of many moving parts to function. A few good topics were: the various roles and responsibilities of an ant colony, the inner workings of bees, and a more creative one, the process of photosynthesis. It was amazing to watch the creativity of these young student-athletes' minds at work in drawing the correlation between these topics and the importance of teamwork and interdependence in the sport(s) that they love.

CHAPTER 7—Level 2: CLD—Post-Foundational Level
(8-10-Year-Old Range)

<u>Character Values (6-10):</u>

6. *Coachability (Willingness to Learn)*

7. *Integrity & Honor*

8. *Concept of Working to a Common Goal (Teamwork)*

9. *Listening and Focus*

10. *Understanding how to Compete (Honestly & Ethically)*

BUILDING BLOCK #6: Coachability (Willingness to Learn)

Coachability is one of my favorite topics to discuss with athletes young and old. When I discuss this concept with coaches, parents, or children, I often refer to the works of world-renowned Stanford University psychologist Carol Dweck on the concept of human motivation and development. In her two major books (Dweck 2006[71] & 2012[72]), Dweck identifies and explains through her research two dichotomous human mindsets: the "growth mindset" and the "fixed mindset." An individual with a growth mindset is more willing to learn new things, whereas one with a fixed mindset is not, and thus the second individual becomes stagnant. This applies to athletics as much as it does to any other walk of life. There could not be a better walking or, in this case, sprinting billboard

---

[71] Dweck's 2006 book: Dweck, C. S. (2006). *Mindset: The New Psychology of Success.*
[72] Dweck, C. S. (2012). *Mindset: How You Can Fulfill Your Potential.*

to the power of a growth mindset than my first contributor to this topic: Paralympian and World Record Holder, David Prince.

-**David Prince** *(United States Paralympic World Record Holder in Track & Field in the 200M and 400M; Youth Mentor)*:

I could have introduced David in the last chapter, but I believe his most resounding character value to be his **coachability (willingness to learn and grow).** When David heard about my topic on character development in youth sports, he graciously agreed to sit down with me for a lunch interview after his rigorous morning training regimens in preparation for U.S. Team Trials leading into the 2016 Paralympic Games held in Rio de Janeiro, Brazil. Though our meeting was only supposed to be 30 minutes, we talked about character for over two hours and have since kept in touch sharing ideas with each other. Between the two of us, there was a great deal of passion about the topic of character and it spoke to the fact that "character really does love company!" The takeaways were both inspiring and motivational.

While the **CV** on **coachability** was my biggest takeaway from David, he quite possibly embodies all 25 character values, as do most of my contributors. Before digging into his growth mindset grounded approach to sports, and more importantly, life, allow me to return to the previous chapter and **CVs gratitude** and **appreciation** for opportunities and the interconnectedness with others as it relates to our interview. David had this to say:

> It is very rare to see someone thank their opponents, their coaches, their parents, their trainers, their doctors, their strength and conditioning staff, family, friends, sponsors, etc. After all, the athlete never could have accomplished anything alone. A lot of people support me in my life, and I am extremely grateful for them. My parents watched me struggle as a teenager but they stuck with me, and now they are more proud of how my character has formed. If I didn't grow in my faith and my life purpose, I don't think there would be as much pride in who I've become.

Oftentimes in the world of professional or Olympic caliber athletics, athletes who express their spirituality or faith can be ostracized and even lose out on endorsement deals. Along with his appreciation for his family, coaches, and friends, David expressed gratitude for his faith and spiritual unfoldment.

David's whole premise and perspective on life is based on the principles of a growth mindset that Carol Dweck presents. He stated it so simply, yet so eloquently, *"I am either going to win, or I am going to learn."* Wow, that is powerful. That profound approach to competition is David's *modus operandi* and sums up what sports are all about: a quest for excellence through growth and learning.

I hope that you do not misread, or misinterpret, what David means when he says, *"I am either going to win, or I am going to learn."* His statement is in no way cocky or arrogant, which are concepts that I discuss along with **CV #16** in the next chapter. Following David's powerful statement, he continued:

> *...and with this approach* [to competition], *I am unbeatable. I do not ever lose if my perspective is right! I either win or I learn. Nobody can beat me. I love the idea of constantly learning and bettering myself. I have won a lot of medals, and if it were only about the medal, it would be empty. It would not be worth it. It is silly that we go through so much effort for a piece of metal. Are the medals my identity? What is important to me is what I have learned through competition, whether I win a gold, a silver, a bronze, or even if I set a world record.*

Throughout the time that I spent with David, I was thoroughly impressed with his humility and perspective on the important things in life, such as care for his family, his spirituality, and a life of positive influence. However, like most of us, this was not always the case for David, as he recounted, *"I had plenty of role models growing up, but I didn't listen to my mentors back then. It can be really easy for young people to get stuck in the, 'I'm going to do what I want to do' mentality. Like many kids, I thought I knew all the answers."* Now, like I am, David is committed to helping our youth learn these valuable life lessons through his own personal story.

BJ Bedford-Miller *(Olympic Gold Medalist in Swimming; NCAA All-American)* has already shared some pearls of wisdom that she accrued through sports on the topics of sportspersonship and respect for others, and now she focuses in on **coachability** and how her growth mindset has allowed her to transfer her athletic success into corporate America:

> *Involvement in sports is the only place that I have found where you are allowed to fail. However, it teaches us to come back and bounce back and overcome...You have to be a kid*

and you have to have a dream worth chasing. When you give up on that dream, then what have you learned?

There is a cumulative effect from being in sports—it can help develop a growth mindset. For me, I have learned to love learning and having to keep learning and doing new things. For many athletes, there is always that steep hill or challenge to climb that motivates us. The feedback that sports gave me, either from coaches or sports themselves, always helped me strive to get better and improve.

This growth mindset has been forever engrained in the DNA of BJ Bedford-Miller, and she continues to rely on this learned value in the various professions and business ventures that she has taken on over the years. After her illustrious swimming career came to an end, she worked for Nike and other great companies before recently launching into a new career of Cyber security. It is a challenging and innovative field, but she relishes new opportunities as training grounds for exciting new growth.

-Jenna Marston *(Two-time Team USA Sportswoman of the Year; 2015 Pan-Am Champion Women's Baseball Player; NCAA DI Scholar-Athlete):*

Prior to Jenna accepting a college scholarship to play softball at the University of Missouri (Mizzou), I had the fortune of seeing her play high school baseball in 2008 for her father, who was a highly respected, long-time high school coach in St. Louis, Missouri. Jenna was not only on the team; she was the most talented player on the field. I left that game knowing that she was going to go on to be a superstar, due to the many characteristics that she displayed on the field, aside from merely her exceptional physical talent. When I caught up with Jenna earlier this year, this is what she shared with me pertaining to the topic of **coachability** and her growth mindset:

*I agree with you that **coachability** is one of the most important characteristics in an athlete. When you stop being willing to learn and grow, then you plateau. I believe experience is one of the most important teachers.*

The memory that always comes to mind is from the beginning of my freshman year of college. It was our very first intrasquad game in the fall and I was playing shortstop. The first batter was Rhea Taylor [a 4-time All-American]. She was a slapper[73] so I moved in knowing I'd have to get rid of it [the ball] quickly if she hit it to me. But, instead of tapping it, she absolutely smoked it right by me. It was a ball that I should have made a play on, but I probably didn't even move until it was past me and in the outfield. I remember instantly wondering what I had gotten myself into trying to play at that level. Luckily, I was able to make adjustments to the speed of the game and it all worked out over the following four years. But, that was a moment I'll never forget. I think it made me realize that it didn't matter what I'd done before, I still had a lot to learn.

Baseball and softball are sports that create the atmosphere of always learning. Watching games on TV, the announcers often talk about seeing something for the first time. When talking about coaches and players, they describe them as always learning something new. Even when discussing the greatest baseball minds, there's always that idea of wanting to know more. I think that is a big part of where I developed a drive to learn from everyone. If the most experienced and greatest coaches/players are still learning, then there is no way that I should ever believe that I have it all figured out.

You can always learn from someone who has more experience. I remember there was a time during an individual practice that a senior who hadn't had much playing time was giving me advice. I probably had more physical ability than she did, but she had more knowledge, and because I was open to it, I was able to learn from her and improve.

Last summer, I gave private hitting instruction lessons, and helped coach a 14-U team. The young athletes who were the best to work with were the ones who listened well, internalized the instruction, and made adjustments accordingly. The girls who thought that they already knew it all tended to make the same mistakes over and over.

I am not surprised by the extraordinary level of thinking that Jenna shared with me, as I have had the privilege of getting to know her parents, as well as her older brother, Chris (now the head baseball coach at Principia College), very well over the years. Jenna is very clear in stating that her family significantly influenced the person of character that she is today.

---

[73] In softball terms, a "slapper" is typically a left-handed batter who tries to slap the ball to the third baseman or shortstop while simultaneously sprinting out of the batter's box toward first base to beat the throw.

That story of Jenna's first college intrasquad game at Mizzou hits (no pun intended) on many concepts that I am working to instill in young student-athletes across the country. Many college-bound student-athletes think that when they get that DI scholarship or guaranteed spot on a roster, that they have accomplished something. As Jenna so clearly stated, that is only the beginning, and the learning curve starts all over again for those who want to continue to succeed at the highest levels.

Jenna is spot on with her depiction of a certain type of young athlete nowadays. She saw first-hand when she coached that 14-U team that some players think that they have it all figured out and, because of this attitude, they become stagnant in their growth and learning. These are the players who finish the coaches' sentences and give the "yeah, yeah" response, because they just do not want to listen to instruction. Sooner or later, no matter what the sport, this fixed mindset or poor attitude catches up to them, and they quickly plateau and fizzle out.

I have a lot of respect for Jenna's endless desire to learn and improve. She has accomplished so much athletically and academically, but despite all of this, she remains humble and is always striving to improve and get better. My next contributor was Jenna's high school softball coach, and he could not emphasize her growth mindset enough: *"She [Jenna] has always had a burning drive to improve and compete, and she is always looking for ways to get better in everything she does."* –Ken Leavoy (Jenna's high school softball coach)

-Ken Leavoy *(Assistant Coach and Gold Medalist with Team Canada's Women's Softball Team in 2015 Pan American Games; 3-Time Team Canada International Softball Federation Coach; 30+ year High School/College Head Coach/Mentor):*

Coach Leavoy sums up this **CV** on **coachability** very succinctly in sharing the recipe behind his success as a coach, which was modeled by his parents during his upbringing. The vital ingredients to harvesting an increased desire to grow, and a willingness to learn in our youth, come from that delicate balance between love and principle, similar to what **Betsy Mitchell** and others have discussed thus far. Ken had this to say on the topic of **coachability**:

> *I think that **coachability** is absolutely necessary for an athlete to truly grow. There has to be that humility in the athlete to be receptive, but there has to be a real hunger to want to be good.*

What helped me as a kid was the atmosphere I grew up in; my parents were a wonderful blend of love and principle. Very few limitations were put on me, in fact, when I talk to athletes today, they are shocked at times about what my parents, particularly my dad, expected of me. 'I can't' wasn't something that I was allowed to say. I was taught that there isn't anything you can't figure out and do. The expectation was always to 'figure it out.' My dad continually responded to my questions or doubts with, 'Well,...figure it out!' It taught me to think, to never doubt that there wasn't a way to succeed or find a solution to anything. I wasn't allowed to walk away. If I failed, I was expected to face the same challenge the next time with an expectation of 'figuring it out.' Excuses were unacceptable. Even today, I think of excuses as what those who lose use to soften the blow of their underachievement or uninspired effort. Winners get it done; losers make excuses!

Coach Leavoy is very well-respected in the communities where he coaches. I have no doubt that a big reason for this is that he empowers his student-athletes to accomplish more than they ever thought possible. He does not do it by holding their hands, but rather by holding them accountable and allowing them to figure things out, oftentimes on their own. As coaches, it can be easy to simply tell our players what to do and now that leaves them helpless when a coach (or parent or teacher, for that matter) is not around to help them through the difficult situation.

Now, every situation is going to be slightly different, and we have to adjust our *"figure it out"* approach according to the age of our players. If my young 6-year-old daughter asked me for help on her homework project, and I simply shout down the hallway, *"Figure it out,"* she would undoubtedly take that as, *"He doesn't have love or time for me."* However, if we have established a culture of learning how to work through things on our own first, I could then give her a subtle hint and allow her to ultimately figure the whole assignment out herself. In turn, she would gain a better understanding and be more willing to truly learn how to do something rather than be reliant on someone else to show her how to do it, or worse off, do it for her.

I close this **CV** on **coachability** and helping our youth to become more receptive to learning with one of my favorite quotes, *"Give a man a fish, and you feed him for a day. Teach a man to fish, and you feed him for a lifetime."* -19th century English proverb

CV #6 Coachability (Willingness to Learn): Activities and Drills to increase Retention/Assessment:

- According to Peterson & Seligman (2004, pg. 163) in their 800-page book entitled *Character Strengths and Virtues: A Handbook and Classification*, the authors state:

  It is likely that people with love of learning as a general strength would strongly endorse statements such as the following:

  - *I can't do this task now, but I think I will be able to do it in the future.*
  - *I like to learn new things.*
  - *I will do whatever it takes in order to do a task correctly.*
  - *Learning is a positive experience.*
  - *I care more about doing a thorough job than whether I receive a good grade.*

  The works of Peterson and Seligman (2004) provide a terrific resource from which to initiate a starting point for a team conversation on the topic of being **coachable** and having a **willingness to learn** through a growth mindset. For bullet point three above, I would potentially adjust the wording away from "whatever it takes" when discussing this idea with young children, as in their minds "whatever it takes" could become fuzzy and potentially encourage cheating within the realm of the statement. Perhaps "by all ethical means" would be a more appropriate statement as it relates to youth sports. The point here is that we, as coaches and parents of youth sports participants, need to be very *deliberate* and *intentional* about our messages. For the fifth and final bullet, the end statement of "receiving a good grade" could easily be replaced with "receiving a trophy or award or D1 scholarship."

- Reference the definition of a "fixed mindset" vs. a "growth mindset" that Carol Dweck discusses in her works. Have your players think about and actively choose to be an individual with a growth mindset.

- A fun activity is to take 36 cones and line them up in six rows of six. Chart out a path in your mind from the first cone to the 36th cone. Explain to the players that this is a game that takes the collective effort of all the players working together and learning from each other's mistakes. In the end, they will win if they stick together. The basic rules are that they cannot go backward. The first person steps up and tries to go from cone one to the next cone. If his or her step to cone two is correct, you say "yes." If their path is incorrect, you say "no" and then the next teammate steps up and tries a new path starting from the beginning. The next person always has to start from the beginning, but the emphasis is on paying attention to when their teammate went the correct way and followed their lead, while avoiding the wrong path (or cone) that they chose. What I especially love about this game is the **willingness to learn** from each other, but also the fact that no one can have an ego and simply do it all by themselves. When they figure it out in the end, the entire group should be excited about it. Sure, they all want to be that last person to complete the whole maze, but sports are about teamwork and continuing to grow and learn.

<u>Character Values (6-10):</u>

6. *Coachability (Willingness to Learn)*

7. Integrity & Honor

8. *Concept of Working to a Common Goal (Teamwork)*

9. *Listening and Focus*

10. *Understanding how to Compete (Honestly & Ethically)*

BUILDING BLOCK #7: Integrity & Honor

According to renowned psychologists Christopher Peterson, PhD. and Martin Seligman, PhD. (2004), **integrity** is defined as *"a regular pattern of behavior that is consistent with espoused values—practicing what one preaches."*

I begin this section of the **CVs** on **integrity** and **honor** with the most prized family story from my youth, as told by my father, **John Paciorek** *(50-year youth Coach/Mentor; MLB Record Holder)*. This recount is one that formed the image of a legend, my grandfather. I did not get to spend very much time with my grandparents, as they lived in Michigan and our family resided primarily in California. However, in my eyes, Grandpa was larger than life and greater than any professional athlete or American icon. As a young boy, I thought that he was at least 7' tall. For the purpose of this book, my father retold his memories of this powerful life lesson in **integrity** and **honor** that has framed his legacy:

> *One cold winter evening, Dad was putting on his boots which, five minutes earlier, he had taken off after shoveling the snow from the walkway in front of our house. I thought he had planned to spend the rest of his evening relaxing before going to bed, so I could not figure out*

where he was going. Plus, he had to get up earlier than usual the following morning to walk to work since the family car was at Uncle Zig's Garage being repaired. He had been out earlier that afternoon, walking half a mile through the snow to the store.

It was earlier that evening, while counting the money he had in his pants pocket, that he noticed a discrepancy in the amount that was there. The store attendant had given Dad $10.00 too much change in return for his purchase. To my way of thinking, being 10-years-old, Dad just made a $10.00 profit. So, I was more than a little annoyed when Mom told me he was on his way back to the store to return the extra money. I couldn't believe it! Who else would do that? I know I would not have, at that time. I remember thinking that if I had an extra 10 bucks, I'd have been in heaven. At least temporarily! Obviously, I did not yet understand the value of integrity and honor, but that memory of my dad has positively impacted the person that I am today.

I want to play out the parallels between the life lessons that my grandfather demonstrated through his actions for my father alongside the defining teaching moments that *MLB Director of Dominican Operations,* **Rafael Perez**, received from his father (who, like my father, has also been a coach/mentor of youth for 50 years). Rafael humbly shared the following narrative with me about **honesty** and **integrity**:

When I was in Little League, a scorer gave me an error on a ball that I believed should have been a hit. I tried to change the score myself at my house. My father always kept the stats' sheets at home and he caught me doing it. He sat me down and taught me about **honesty** *and* **integrity**. *He started by telling me that during the 12 years that he worked in the government in the Department of National Property, he had the opportunity to steal millions of pesos, but he never did. He looked me straight in the eyes and told me that he never wanted anyone to point their finger at us and say, 'Those are the kids of Oscar Perez, the corrupt government official in the National Property Department.' He continued telling me anyone can be* **honest**, *but* **integrity** *is being honest when no one is looking. It is between you and God.*

I hope that the character message on display from Oscar Perez resonates with you as well as it does for me. It is so important that we, as coaches, administrators, and parents, always lead by example in modeling the values of **honor, honesty**, and **integrity** for our youth to learn from. I remember being in a similar situation where I thought the scoring was wrong on a hit/error. Many dads, especially in today's times would go in as the head coach, after the fact, and change the error to a hit to benefit their own child. This is a disservice to the child, as Rafael so clearly points out.

Oscar capitalized on the "teachable moment" with his son Rafael by sharing a real-life choice that he had to make based on **integrity** and **honor**. He could have taken those pesos without anyone knowing, but his integrity and pride in who he was would not allow him to take the easy way to short-term reward. I cannot help but relate his decision of *"doing the right thing, even when no one is watching"* with the dishonest and corrupt decisions and actions of many corporate executives during the financial crisis and corporate scandals of the late 1990s and 2000s. In the latter case, many chose to "do the wrong thing" and it negatively affected our entire country. Similarly, the lack of integrity and honor during the "steroid era" almost brought down the game of baseball during this same time period. As coaches, parents, and administrators in youth sports, we need to capitalize on these defining teachable moments.

I am very grateful for the role models that I have had in my life while growing up, from my parents, grandparents, uncles and aunts, to older siblings, coaches, and teachers. My **integrity**, **honor**, and **honesty** were all tested during my career as a professional baseball player during the "steroid era." Despite numerous attempts by teammates and team personnel to negatively influence me to take shortcuts or cheat myself, my teammates, and opponents, I held to my morals and I refused the temptations to use PEDs. I am very proud of that, and I do not think that I could be the same coach and mentor that I am today had I cheated in baseball and in life.

CV #7 Integrity and Honor: Activities and Drills to increase Retention/Assessment:

o When discussing the **CV** of **integrity** and **honor** with your team or young student-athletes at this developmental stage of **CLD**, ask them if they would endorse the following statements on **integrity** as presented by Dr. Peterson and Dr. Seligman (2004):

- It is more important to be myself than to be popular.
- When people keep telling the truth, things work out.
- I would never lie just to get something I wanted from someone.
- My life is guided and given meaning by my code of values.

- It is important to me to be open and honest about my feelings.
- I always follow through on my commitments, even when it costs me.

o Relate these statements/questions now to sport-specific situations. This could be a way to create core team values about appropriate behavior. Examples of questions could be:

- When our team loses a game, we will still show respect to our opponent by shaking their hand and telling them "good game."
- When teammates make mistakes, we will not look down on them, but rather pick them up and support them.
- When the official/umpire/judge makes what seems to be a bad call or decision, I will respect his/her call and move on.
- If we have the opportunity to cheat in order to win, we will choose to do the right thing.

o Bring in a guest speaker, before or after practice, to talk with your team about a certain character value that you are working on to emphasize with your players. I did this when I was discussing the concept of leadership with my group of young student-athletes who were part of our BAT1000 youth development program in Pasadena, California. I invited out a friend and mentor of mine, **Fred Claire** (past GM of the Los Angeles Dodgers when they last won the World Series in 1988), and he spoke with the boys about what it takes to be a leader. The young student-athletes talked about their takeaways with Mr. Claire throughout the summer. Similarly, in the way that many young student-athletes want to do it all themselves and be the hero, oftentimes coaches do the same thing. There are many wonderfully successful individuals in our communities throughout the country who would jump at the idea to impart some of their knowledge for 15-20 minutes with the rising generation. You would be surprised by how many such individuals would be honored to jump at the opportunity.

o In discussing **integrity** and **honor** with student-athletes at this level of their development, ask your players to come up with a succinct and concise purpose statement that will help guide them when they are faced with adversity or a crossroads in life. I gave a group of high school student-athletes 30 seconds to think about it and write down their statement, and I was blown away by the clarity in many of their responses. Here are a few to note:

- "Integrity is doing the right thing when no one is looking."
- "Integrity is taking responsibility for one's actions, and acting with honor."
- "Integrity is being honest regardless of the personal consequences."

Character Values (6-10):

6. *Coachability (Willingness to Learn)*

7. *Integrity & Honor*

8. **Concept of Working to a Common Goal (Teamwork)**

9. *Listening and Focus*

10. *Understanding how to Compete (Honestly & Ethically)*

BUILDING BLOCK #8: Concept of Working to a Common Goal (Teamwork)

"Technology is just a tool. In terms of getting the kids working together and motivating them, the teacher is the most important." -Bill Gates

Teamwork is something that spills over into every facet of life, whether it be family life, the business sector, education, or athletics. With the increase in ego-driven showcases and weekend participation on teams for select tournaments for increased individual exposure, young student-athletes are not being granted access to the concept of teamwork which is developed through a common goal and common concern for one's teammates. No one who has ever accomplished anything great has done it alone.

My next contributor, **Coach Amanda Butler**, has a firm grasp on this **CV** of **working to a common goal**. I walked away from our interview inspired and encouraged about the future of youth and amateur sports. From one coach of character to another, I extend the highest degree of praise to Coach Butler by stating that I would be honored if one day my two daughters would be fortunate enough to play basketball for her, irrespective of whether that be at the University of Florida, where she is currently in her 10th year at the helm, or in a local recreational league.

-Amanda Butler *(Women's Basketball Head Coach, University of Florida; Mentor/Coach of the Year):*

This past fall, I traveled two and a half hours north of my home to Gainesville, Florida to take in a University of Florida Gators women's basketball home game with my two young daughters. Upon entering the grand arena, my children were enamored by the buzz of energy and excitement. From the crowd to the concessions, the poster schedules, the cheerleaders, the band, and the Gator team mascots "Albert" and "Alberta," my daughters were hooked. However, my ceaseless attention to sports and leadership immediately drew me to the court and to the game that had already begun. Though both head coaches that day from the SEC[74] talent-stacked rosters were impressive, I was drawn to the team dynamic that Coach Butler's basketball team portrayed. There seemed to be very little individual ego present in Coach Butler's team, despite the rough first half they had. It was ever-apparent, even from our mid-level seats, that her team displayed an unwavering amount of support and care for each other, a recognizable family-type pride.

The team went into halftime trailing by close to 20 points that night, but they stuck together and nearly pulled off an amazing upset victory at the buzzer. Not knowing anything about Coach Butler at that time, from what I witnessed from her demeanor and leadership on the sidelines, as well as her team's overall presence and commitment to each other, my inquisitive researcher's mind needed some answers. Upon the conclusion of her 2015/2016 season, I was able to gain access to this amazing coach. Unsure if Coach Butler would have the time and desire to impart some of her acquired pearls of wisdom with me and my readers, I revealed to her my focus on character development through sports and she immediately agreed to an interview.

Coach Butler has a keen and penetrating perspective on teamwork and working to a common goal. I asked her about **commitment to a common goal**, and if at her level it is hard to get some of her players to buy in to the team culture, as many elite-level athletes have become overly concerned with their own statistics and ego. Coach Butler

---

[74] SEC stands for the dominant Southeastern Conference, which is argued by many as the most dominant conference in all of college athletics.

responded to my inquiry about whether she has to deal with selfish egos with the following statement:

Occasionally, but I have to be honest—I don't see that as much and maybe that is attributed to the gender difference. However, when it comes to playing time, which is often regarded as an athlete's currency, that will always be highly sought after. It doesn't matter if you are a great kid or a great teammate, you are not just signing up to be on that team to get your name on the roster. Everybody wants to play. I don't think that we battle the 'I'm gonna get mine' mindset as far as the points and the stats go, as perhaps the men do. There are a ton of different lessons, and many angles to different books that one could write on the many lessons that sport teaches, but ultimately, the biggest lesson or value in team sports, in particular, is learning to be part of something that is bigger than just you. From a team standpoint, when I bring my best and you bring your best, we are striving for excellence together, whether as a teammate or an opponent. To quote a scripture from the Old Testament [The Bible], 'Iron sharpens iron'—and that is how we get better.

If you think about it, in just about every walk of life, you are talking about an individual with their family, or an individual in their church community, or an individual in a university, or an individual in their work environment; there are very few environments where you are just going to be totally 'riding solo.' You have to be able to fit into a picture, but not only fit into the picture, see the big picture and see how important your singular role is, while at the same time realizing that it is the big picture that matters most. There are positive and negative lessons to be learned from this, and if someone does not want to be part of it, they will be left behind. Hopefully, a message learned is that no one can win a championship by themselves—that it takes all of us.

It is my belief that we are wired, we are created, for community. And, sport is just a microcosm of that idea.

We actually have a name for our team culture and we refer to it as 'TLC' and it stands for Trust, Loyalty, and Commitment. Those are all things that are controllable, and whether it is pouting over a bad call, or projecting positive energy towards a teammate, those are two different things that are totally in your control. One is a misuse of energy, and the other is a fantastic use of your energy. The more that we stay focused on what we are actually in control of, the more we are going to succeed at a higher degree of channeling our energy in the direction that it needs to go. That is the strategic piece of our culture.

As coaches, it can be very easy in some regards to fall into that trap of 'do as I say and not as I do.' Now, if I am emphasizing to my team the 'power of touch' and we want to be cultivating positive energy, then I have to be very aware of the messages that I am sending as well. Sometimes as coaches, we can be the biggest babies on the floor, and we can be the biggest 'energy suckers' on the floor by the way we act and by our demeanor. It is as if somehow, as the coaches, it is okay for us to do that, but we don't want our players to do that. So, we really strive as a staff to assure that we are embodying that same standard that we are asking the team to perform to as well.

Coach Butler makes many integral points about the value of teamwork and how much greater the force of the whole is in comparison to the sum of the individual parts. As she imparted her knowledge and the secrets to her successful approach to the topic of teamwork with me, I was not at all surprised by her ever-growing accomplishments as a coach, and the immense amount of respect that she has inside and outside of the athletic arena.

Coach Butler humbly advises all coaches to be consistent in modeling the behavior that we wish to see in our players. She admits that, at times, coaches can say one thing and do another, and that approach creates an inconsistent message which, in turn, creates lack of continuity and poor leadership towards the desired cultural outcome. As coaches and mentors, if we want to help steer our teams and our players towards a common goal of good, then we need to borrow from the words of Gandhi who said *"Be the change that you wish to see in the world."* In our case, we need to be the role model that we want our players and children to follow.

Encompassed within this quote here from **Ryan Arcidiacono** *(4-year starter and captain of the 2016 National Champion Villanova basketball team),* he shares some valuable lessons that he learned on what it takes to be part of a team at a young age, which allowed him to be a leader and key contributor for Villanova. His Wildcats' team ultimately shocked the March Madness world during the 2016 NCAA Men's Basketball Tournament. Once again, Ryan stated, *"The family values that my parents instilled in me and my siblings not only helped me develop as a man but also improved my basketball game. The values they taught me growing up made me a better leader on the court; specifically, teaching me how to play together* *towards **one common goal** which helped our teams become successful and eventually win a national championship my senior year."*

I love this quote because in it Ryan expresses so much gratitude and appreciation, not only for his basketball **team** of brothers and coaches who make up his Villanova family, but more importantly, for his **team** at home comprised of his parents and siblings. From everything that I have read and heard about Ryan, he is the last person on his team who is looking for the glory and the press clippings, but rather, he is always about working towards the **team's common goal**. When that **common goal** of winning the NCAA Men's Basketball Championship became a reality, it was clearly evident when the team hoisted that trophy together demonstrating that it was a concerted team effort. At that moment, I was not surprised to see his family and the families of all of his teammates and coaches overcome with jubilation with the team.

CV #8 Concept of Working to a Common Goal (Teamwork): Activities and Drills to increase Retention/Assessment:

- o The team activity with the 36 cones and figuring out the path to victory as a team applies to this concept of teamwork and working to a common goal as well. Another version of this activity is to blindfold the person whose turn it is to go, and have the rest of the team guide them through the maze. Trusting in one another is an important component in working to a common goal.

- o Have your players come up with a team motto, similar to Coach Amanda Butler's team at the University of Florida with "TLC" (Trust, Loyalty, and Commitment). Ask them what three characteristics or qualities they want to embody each time they come together as a team, whether it be practice or games. When a teammate gets off track, it is very easy for you as the coach, or for a player, to simply remind each other of the team's motto or focus.

- o Coach Butler also talked about "energy givers" and "energy suckers." While this message could be a team message for everyone to hear, it could also be a great heart-to-heart with a player whose body language and demeanor needs an adjustment. This meaningful message will not only pay dividends for the team's culture, but more importantly, help that individual in all areas of life.

CHARACTER LOVES COMPANY

Character Values (6-10):

6. *Coachability (Willingness to Learn)*

7. *Integrity & Honor*

8. *Concept of Working to a Common Goal (Teamwork)*

9. **Listening and Focus**

10. *Understanding how to Compete (Honestly & Ethically)*

BUILDING BLOCK #9: **Listening and Focus**

"The secret of change is to focus all of your energy, not on fighting the old, but on building the new." -Socrates

I have believed for years that our school system across the country should add a **listening** and **focus** component to the academic curriculum beginning at the earliest of grades. There are many schools that have incorporated yoga and other classes designed to increase "mindfulness" and **focus** on the now. I hope that this is not just a trend, but rather a major approach to increase the willingness of our youth to learn and their ability to retain new information.

As I discussed in great detail earlier in this chapter under CV #6, one's **coachability/willingness to learn** is a key factor to lifelong success. However, that will only guide our youth to the watering hole. Once they get there, they need to be equipped with skills to watch and **listen** closely to understand when and where to drink. Just like learning anything new, this takes an ability to **listen** intently and **focus** actively on what is going on around them in order to thrive in any environment.

My next two contributors have mastered this willingness to learn simultaneously with a razor sharp **focus** and ability to **listen** in order to thrive in the competitive athletic arena at the highest levels. Both of these individuals have maintained the highest levels of humility during their athletic careers, and each would probably balk at any reference to them as gifted athletes, at least in relation to some of their teammates and opposition. However, they share a gift that, in my 20 years as a coach, I have rarely witnessed ranging from the highest level of professional sports to the lowest. This special knack is **focus** and the **ability to listen** to instruction, as well as give instruction. Their teammates would agree that these qualities make for great team leaders.

-David Ross *(2013 World Series Champion with the Boston Red Sox; 15-year MLB career; Team Leader):*

David was a teammate of mine for two seasons in the minor leagues with the Los Angeles Dodgers. He was one of the best teammates and leaders that I have ever had as a player, or witnessed as a coach. I recently caught up with David and we discussed a few different topics that are presented in this book. I specifically asked him about how he has been able to make the most of his abilities and talents and continue to successfully play this great game of baseball at the Major League level for 15 years. Here is what David had to say:

> *There are tough lessons in life, and if you are able to learn from those, you will be better next time. I try and pay attention to details, and how others make me feel and pull out the positives and learn from the negatives. I have had the chance to be around some of the great leaders like Bobby Cox, Joe Maddon, John Farrell, Dave Roberts, Robin Ventura, Brian McCann...I could go on! I have been around some wonderful people, and I have tried to learn from each of them and remember how they made me feel.*

I have no doubt that David's attention to detail and **desire to learn** from great baseball minds, who have managed him over the past 15 years, have paid great dividends in regards to the longevity and success of his career. From a teammate perspective, David is regarded as a leader and a phenomenal teammate, and this is something that he has earned because of his ability to **listen** and **focus** throughout his career.

Jenna Marston *(Two-time Team USA Sportswoman of the Year; World Champion Women's Baseball Player 2015)* has demonstrated these same vital factors to success.

I can vividly recall the first time I saw Jenna Marston compete. It was my second year as a college head coach in Southern Illinois and I had heard about this junior in high school on the other side of the Mississippi River who could flat out play, and by the way, she was a girl.[75] When I saw Jenna step into the on-deck circle, I saw something that I had yet to see while out on the recruiting trail. There was a look of intent in her eyes and a **focus** that was unparalleled. While most of the other players appeared from the shadows of the dugout searching the crowd for fans, friends, or even college coaches while they made their way to the on-deck circle, Jenna was different. She did not see me, she did not see the crowd, she was solely focused on one thing: the task in front of her.

One's preparation for an at-bat may not seem to be all that important for the casual fan, but from a coach's standpoint, it speaks volumes. I had never seen anything like it in high school. In fact, if Jenna was six inches taller, approximately double her weight, and from the land of the Dominican Republic, I would have thought I was staring at Albert Pujols preparing for his at-bat in the third inning of Game 1 of the 2005 World Series against the Detroit Tigers. Growing up a baseball fan in St. Louis, I am sure Jenna watched Pujols prepare on-deck for his upcoming at-bat many times. She may even recall the two-run homerun from Pujols off of Justin Verlander from that game.[76] In similar fashion, Jenna laced a double to the opposite field during her first at-bat.

Irrespective of what Jenna's end results or statistics were that day (three hits out of four plate appearances), I had dueling emotions as I headed back onto Interstate 270 North and over the bridge that led to Principia College. The first was a sense of "awe" for this young student-athlete destined for greatness on any field and in any classroom in America. The second realization was the fact that, within minutes of watching Jenna play with such attention to detail and **razor-sharp focus,** I had no shot of getting her to give up the countless number of scholarship offers that she would undoubtedly have to play

---

[75] Jenna Marston is one of two highly accomplished women included in my book who not only participated with boys on the same field at the Varsity level of high school competition in baseball, but they dominated. The other woman is Malaika Underwood, and her narrative is equally inspiring in CV # 18 Handling Adversity/Resilience.

[76] Justin Verlander was one of the top pitchers in the MLB during that time. I recall Verlander's fastball being clocked on the radar gun at upwards of 100mph.

DI[77] softball, in order to come play baseball at a DIII[78] college for me. Ultimately, she accepted a scholarship to play softball at the University of Missouri, where she was a stand-out scholar-athlete.

I was fortunate to have had the opportunity as a professional baseball player to have been around one of the greatest hitters in the history of Major League Baseball, Tony Gwynn.[79] During my five years as a ballplayer in the San Diego Padres organization, I had countless opportunities to learn from Tony Gwynn first-hand. As a young 20-year-old, I can recall racing to the ballpark during spring training, bypassing breakfast, and rushing out to try to beat Tony to the batting cages. Despite Tony Gwynn winning eight MLB Batting Titles, he loved to get out there and work on his swing. Oftentimes, while I was in my batting cage and he was in his, I would watch him go about his daily hitting routine. It was amazing to watch. Though I know that Jenna Marston would probably feel unworthy of being described in the same light as Tony Gwynn, her focus and approach to the game are much the same, as is the case with David Ross.

CV #9 Listening and Focus: Activities and Drills to increase Retention/Assessment: This CV on **listening** and **focus** is directly correlated to CV #6 being coachable. You simply cannot have one without the other. Listening and paying attention to directions are vitally important; coaches must find ways to engage our student-athletes and make learning relevant and fun.

- o While we, as coaches, understand the need for our student-athletes to listen well to instructions, we also have to realize that we need to be brief with our messages. There are coaches who will keep their teams after games for 30 minutes to an hour in an effort to really try to drive home a message. Some will even punish their teams with sprints until exhaustion. While there is

---

[77] DI college athletics, especially in the Southeastern Conference (SEC), is the highest level of amateur sports.
[78] DIII athletics are highly competitive, though they are typically a couple notches below DI athletics from a physical talent standpoint.
[79] Tony Gwynn, also known as "Mr. Padre," played for 20 years in the MLB. He was elected to 15 MLB All-Star Games, and he won an MLB National League record eight Batting Titles. Tony was inducted in the MLB Hall of Fame in 2007. He passed away in June of 2014, but his legacy as a baseball player, coach, family man, and individual of the highest character lives on.

some value from that, we have to realize that we may have their full focus for as long as 30 seconds. Yes, 30 seconds. Then, they will inevitably zone out. Obviously, with varying levels of SAs, we have increased concentration and focus and the message can be longer and more complex. However, at certain times, when explaining the directives for a certain drill, I have found that actually getting into the drill and having players try it and catch on to the flow of the drill is the best way for them to learn. It is more engaging and taps into the fact that we are all very visual as human beings in the way that we learn and retain information. Try a 30-second approach to messages of great importance. With longer explanations, try to limit it to three minutes. When this does happen, try to engage your team with questions and get them to speak and contribute.

o One of my favorite team activities of all time is "blind dodgeball." Be sure to locate soft snowball-type balls and enough blind-folds (bandanas) for half of the players on your team. Section off an 80 foot by 80-foot area of grass free of danger (i.e. sprinkler heads and holes.) Assign pairs to work together. One is to wear the blindfold and the other is to stand behind them and act as their eyes. A side note: I usually have the players throw the ball with their opposite hand to avoid injury, as well as make for more comedic relief. During this activity, the duos quickly realize how important focus, teamwork, listening, and clear directives are. Your teams will love the activity and want to play it far longer than time will permit. However, be sure to save 10 minutes at the end of the activity for player reflections on their takeaways from the activity.

o I have a simple **listening** and **focus** batting practice routine that can be adjusted and applied to any sport. I have the players say out loud after each pitch what the pitch was. If they cannot remember, they do not get that next swing. If they miss two, their round is over. Losing out on swings will get their attention. All of a sudden, the players who have focus problems in the athletic arena, or in the classroom, will suddenly find a way to lock it in. This is a concept that a few of my contributors discussed about youth and video games, and how kids can sit and play video games for hours on end with

razor sharp focus. Obviously, the more we can bring the "fun" back into sports the better. However, working on the process that it takes to improve one's craft is extremely fun and rewarding.

o   One thing that I have learned is that when it is a game, they lock it in. When it is a drill, they zone out. Simple phrases can draw them in, or freeze them out. It is true for all of us. Now, at the younger levels, the research discussed the importance of deliberate play (meaning more fun focus) as the primary mode of sport delivery. However, as children grow older, they do not shy away from drills as they begin to become a bit more **process oriented,** which is **CV #19** in Chapter 9.

o   In baseball, basketball, football, and many other sports, student-athletes loathe running or conditioning. As a baseball coach, it is very common to end practice by running the bases. Next time you have your players run from home plate to first base, take out your stop watch and record their times. When they cross first base, yell out their times. I can guarantee you that they will ask if they can do it again. Use that competitive edge that resides in all of us to make practice more fun and rewarding.

Character Values (6-10):

6. *Coachability (Willingness to Learn)*

7. *Integrity & Honor*

8. *Concept of Working to a Common Goal (Teamwork)*

9. *Listening and Focus*

10. ***Understanding how to Compete (Honestly & Ethically)***

BUILDING BLOCK #10: **Understanding how to Compete**

There are dozens of sports stories that come to mind on this **CV #10 Understanding how to Compete (Honestly & Ethically)**. For those of you who are avid tennis fans, Andy Roddick and the 2005 Rome Masters[80] may ring a bell. Roddick was the number one seed in the tournament and he had just defeated his opponent, Fernando Verdasco, to advance to the quarterfinals, or so it seemed. As the title of the 2005 *USA Today* article indicated: "Roddick's honesty turns out costly at the Rome Masters," Roddick wound up losing the point, and eventually, the match, due to his respect for the high ethical standards of tennis, as well as sports in general. During the news conference following the match, Roddick did not make a big deal about his honesty and nonchalantly remarked that his act was nothing special. It is apparent that Andy Roddick had been brought up **understanding how to compete both honestly and ethically**.

---

[80] According to the 2005 *USA Today* article, Andy Roddick was awarded a point that would have concluded the match in his favor. As he approached the net to shake hands with his opponent, Verdasco, he noticed the mark in the clay that indicated that Verdasco's ball was in. He alerted the judge, and the point was overturned in favor of Verdasco.

As this guidebook was on its way to print, many wonderful displays of this concept of true competition were on display during the 2016 Olympic Games in Rio de Janeiro, Brazil. The most memorable exhibition of this concept for me occurred during the 10,000-meter race. The reigning champion, Mohamed Farah of Great Britain, was inadvertently tripped up by Galen Rupp of the United States. There was no foul play involved as the two elite-level long-distance runners tangled up in the close quarters of the bunched up field of athletes. Farah fell down to the track hard and was nearly steamrolled by oncoming competitors like a pile up in NASCAR. However, after a few somersaults, Farah bounced right back up to his feet. He had now gone from the front of the pack to the back. Rupp slowed his paced drastically to assure that Farah was not injured and to signal his sincere apologies for the unfortunate accident.

When this event happened, I immediately sprung up to the edge of my seat to see how the champion, Farah, would respond. Had the fall taken the life out of his sail, or would he show the internal fortitude, toughness, and grit to fight his way back to the top? As a fellow American, I was flooded with pride to see my fellow countryman, Rupp, slow his pace dramatically to see that his competitor was alright. What amazed me even more was how the two "scratched and clawed" their way back to the front of the pack. Farah reclaimed the gold medal while Rupp finished fifth, just two spots from a medal that he had worked so diligently toward during the past four years. To see the two runners embrace after the race was a sight to behold and something that I hope receives the recognition that their noble acts of character deserve.

Far too often in sports (even at the youth level), the end result of such an accident involves bitter and disgruntled athletes, or more often, hyper-competitive parents (who think their child is going to miss out on his or her scholarship opportunity) getting into a scuffle in the stands or the parking lot. From a win-at-all-costs mentality, Rupp could have kept right on running without batting an eye. After all, with the reigning champion down, his chances of medaling were much higher. Instead, much should be garnered from the ethical manner with which two of the world's top competitors, Farah and Rupp, handled the situation with grace and mutual respect. As I will present in **CV #23**, an athletic endeavor is only worth winning if one wins the right way.

Continuing on this topic of how to compete the right way, I want to refer back to the narrative from Olympic gold medalist **BJ Bedford-Miller**. As you may recall, BJ and her University of Texas Longhorn teammates dominated the competition her freshman year, shattering the NCAA DI total points record en route to the National Championship Title. In contrast with her sophomore year, she and her teammates stood on the pool deck and showed class and dignity when Stanford defeated them in the National Championship. BJ capitalized on the lifelong lessons on display from her team captains that day regarding how to hold oneself in victory, as well as in defeat. This is evidenced in the following quote from BJ, *"At Texas, I learned how to win with grace and how to lose with class. But, I learned so much more from losing. I think it is important to have the ability to empathize…Go, be happy for that girl who won—be in the present and respect the game, the sport, and your opponents."*

Coach Amanda Butler (*UF Women's Head Basketball Coach*) also speaks to the importance of doing things the right way through the rigors of sports competition. There have been seemingly endless incidents in the media these days of coaches and players at all levels cutting corners and not adhering to high ethics in sports due to pressures to win and succeed. I asked Coach Butler to expand on her approach and commitment to competing the right way. Here is more from my interview with Coach Butler:

> *We have a couple of things that don't waiver in our program, whether it is the preseason, or a tough SEC game, or the middle of the summer. These are the things that we consider and refer to as 'the right things.' We want to do the right things and then we believe the right things will eventually happen. And, that is really an extension of our culture. It is reinforced and enhanced in the way we practice, the way we talk, and the way that we interact that is the strength of our culture. One of the beliefs that we hold is that culture beats strategy. We believe in continuing to do the right things no matter what the scoreboard says. Whether those right things mean effort, or to continue to support each other, or high fiving, or eye contact in a huddle, or the way we greet each other when we come on and off the floor, we are going to continue to do those things with the belief that eventually the right thing is going to happen. We spend a great deal of our time on our culture, really defining it in a specific way based on what we believe are the right things. Many of the concepts that you mention for your book are absolutely critical: the body language, the competitive spirit, the way we come out and compete, and fight the right way.*

I challenge each and every one of us as coaches or parents of children in sports to think about whether the cultures that our teams are forming are underscored by doing things the right way.

Coach Butler shared with me her affinity for the works of Dr. Jim Loehr, who has been a world-renowned leader in human performance and achievement, both in the world of sport and business.[81] She told me that she heard Dr. Loehr present and one of the key takeaways that she had from his presentation was in regards to the premium of "character health," which outshined physical, emotional, and mental health.

Coach Butler had more pearls on the topic of competing with character:

> *When you start talking about competing with character it draws you in to your absolute purpose for why you are doing something? I do think that you have to teach the value of sport beyond winning and losing without devaluing winning; and it is a very difficult thing to do.*

> *We have a generation of children who have been rewarded for just participating. So, we really want to teach them **how to compete**, and really **compete to win**, but understanding that the way you compete is more a reflection of who you are than what you do. That is an idea that we emphasize a lot. You see, basketball is what we do, but it is not who we are. Coaching is what I do, but it is not who I am. If it is also who I am, then I am going to be a 'nutjob' because I am going to be a bad person when we lose. There are far too many things out of my control that can dictate outcomes. That is not a healthy way to live. That is not going to enhance my character health.*

> *A challenge in sport today is that we have a generation of coaches who were raised by coaches and parents of the win-at-all-costs mentality, and many of them do not know how to teach character in a competitive setting. So, I love what you are after here. These concepts that we've talked about are huge here at University of Florida.*

What Coach Butler succinctly states above speaks directly to the fact that some coaches today are indeed "character illiterate." However, many of them were never taught values other than winning-at-all-costs. From that standpoint, they are teaching what they know, so perhaps we cannot blame them. But, what we absolutely can do is help educate them

---

[81] Dr. Jim Loehr is one of the leading experts in the field of human performance, and he has written many books on the topics: *The Only Way to Win* (2012); *The Power of Story* (2007); and *The Power of Full Engagement* (2003), as well as many more terrific reads.

on the foundations laid out within this guidebook. Let's not let another generation get skipped over when it comes to perhaps the most important of all types of health, the character health of our rising generations.

CV #10 Understanding How to Compete (Honestly & Ethically): Activities and Drills to increase Retention/Assessment:

- Share the example from above with Andy Roddick in the Rome Masters. He was honest to the line judge about a missed call. It ended up costing him the tennis match in the long run, as well as potentially $100,000 or more. However, in a day and age when greed for money and the win-at-all-costs mentality is raging, Roddick showed the world that you cannot put a price tag on one's integrity. Ask your players how they would have handled that situation if the Little League World Series, High School Championship, or College National Title was on the line. It is one thing to say that we would act a certain way, and quite another to actually follow through with it. By having this conversation, there is a much better chance that when a similar situation arises, your student-athletes will have at least broached the topic.

- Go ahead and play out some scenarios (there are scores of different temptations that can and do arise in each sport). Break your team up into smaller working groups, and give each group a different scenario to play out. After five minutes, have each group get up and present their case. Once again, this is a terrific way to work in a little public speaking and confidence building with their voices.

- Share the story that Olympic gold medalist **BJ Bedford-Miller** provided in this chapter regarding how to compete the correct way. This could be a great message leading up to the championship game, in order for your student-athletes to have a better perspective of what it takes to win with class and lose with dignity. As **David Prince** stated in CV #6 on coachability, there really is no such thing as losing because, when we lose on the scoreboard, we learn and grow more from it than when we win.

CHAPTER 8—Level 3: CLD—Mid-Level
(11-14-Year-Old-Range)

The mid-level of **CLD** is such an important stage in the world of youth sports. The bulk of the studies in the field show that this is the time when the majority of our country's youth are pushed out of sports for a variety of reasons. We, as coaches, administrators, and parents of youth sport participants, need to utilize **CLD** to help our children recognize and embrace the endless values of sports outside of just winning and playing solely for their own ego and the potential college scholarship. In doing so, we will keep our children in sports by increasing their stick-to-it-tiveness,[82] and promoting more awareness and appreciation for lifelong lessons through athletic enrichment.

---

[82] Stick-to-it-tiveness is a term similar to grit and perseverance, which I will discuss in great length in **CV #18 Handling Adversity.**

<u>Character Values (11-16):</u>

11. **_Discipline_**

12. _Timeliness (Time Management)_

13. _Humility_

14. _Work Ethic/ Sense of Accomplishment_

15. _Leadership_

16. _Confidence Without Being Cocky_

BUILDING BLOCK #11: Discipline

"Discipline is the soul of an Army." –George Washington

With the **CVs** of this chapter, we begin to shift our focus more into the development of characteristics derived from advancing levels of commitment to sport. This does not mean that the "play" or fun part of sports training and development should be lost and forgotten at the expense of incessant structured training sessions. One's appreciation for discipline should help develop an empowering sense of pride and commitment to something worth pursuing.

My good friend and past teammate, **David Ross** _(2013 World Series Champion with the Boston Red Sox; 15-year MLB Veteran, Key Player in Chicago Cubs Organization),_ learned this valuable lesson at a young age. Here is what he shared with me:

One story that comes to mind with regard to learning early lessons was tied to a bad report card that I came home with. I was around 10-years-old when I brought home a sub-par progress report in the middle of my Little League season. I was getting in a bit of trouble in school and my dad told me, if I was going to get grades like this, then I couldn't play baseball. I *had to get dressed in my uniform and go sit the bench and cheer on my team. 'What?' I declared. At the time, that had to have been the worst punishment possible! I loved playing baseball, and there was no way that I wanted to go watch and not play ever again.*

I think that was a great lesson in what my dad's priorities were and where mine needed to be. It was a lesson in what discipline, commitment, and loyalty are. As a teammate and leader, I have leaned on that. Hopefully, all kids are learning these tough lessons in life, and if they are able to learn from them, they will be better next time.

What a terrific recount from close to 30 years ago on the value of holding our children accountable by teaching discipline the hard way. The power of David's story really resonates on just how integral it is that we do not miss out on these life-changing "teachable moments" with our youth. I cannot help but think about Johnny Manziel and the direction his life has gone, despite all of his talent. In doing research on highly talented young athletes these days, many are given *carte blanche* during these formative years to do whatever they want because of their athletic prowess. For many such prodigies, the high standard of character excellence that David's father instilled in him may not have been emphasized to the degree necessary.

The message about the importance of being a student-athlete, or a student before an athlete, is something that all coaches, parents, and mentors involved in sports should be prioritizing on a regular basis. David learned that message at 10-years-old, and I am certain that his foundation in academics has paid exponential dividends for him, as he was an elite NCAA student-athlete prior to embarking on his 15-year MLB career. I love the fact that David's father made sure that he honored his commitment and loyalty to his teammates, as he still required him to attend the game and sit on the bench in his uniform to cheer on his teammates. At that young age, the two-hour game must have seemed like an eternity.

-Master Boon Brown *(35-year Instructor/Mentor; fifth degree black belt; Owner of Ancient Ways Martial Arts Academy in Bradenton, Florida; Educational background in Psychology and Counseling):*

Master Brown runs a transformative martial arts school in Southwest Florida, where he not only teaches young students and adults the requisite physical skills to protect themselves in any situation, but more importantly, he equips them with lifelong emotional and character growth skills. While Master Brown works daily with all of his students, teaching and training, he is equally masterful in assisting the parents of his students how to be *deliberate* and *intentional* in the manner at which they can help effectively transfer the skills that their children are learning from the martial arts studio to their home and school life. This bridge that he creates for parents through his well-crafted and timely weekly parent emails is invaluable. This is an excellent approach in order to maximize his students' experiences by getting parents on the same page. Our children need to be hearing a consistent message from both their coaches and their parents, otherwise, they end up being torn and confused. This topic of bridging the gap between coaches and parents is vital and the focus of my first essay on additional topics in youth sports in the Appendix.

During my interview with Master Brown, I asked him about the importance of discipline. Here is what he uncovered:

> *As a parent, sometimes you have to express your love by showing that you care by disciplining them. And that sort of goes against the overly-liberal side where some parents basically let their children get away with anything and everything; and most kids will exploit that. Meanwhile, the cat is dead, or the television has been pulled off the stand, or there goes another rock through the window.*
>
> *Some kids, nowadays, are screaming out to parents, and potentially even coaches, who are saying that they love or care about them, but yet when they do evil things or things that are wrong, nothing happens. We should be upset by the horrible things that they have done. They needed someone to be there for them. It could be as simple as a timeout. By being upset, it shows that you truly care about your child and want to take the time to express to them that you love them enough to not let this happen again.*

Master Brown's message here to parents and coaches fits in perfectly with the previous narrative from David Ross, whose father set the tone early in establishing a habit and expectation for excellence in his life. Even though young children may not be able to grasp the whole picture, or understand how habits are formed, they do realize when someone cares enough to respond to them.

Now, we do not want to throw the baby out with the bathwater, and each age progression demands a slightly different degree of discipline, and that does not necessarily have to be heavy-handed. As coaches, parents, and administrators of youth sports, we need to encourage the right way. If you just blast them all the time, especially at the early stages of development, they are going to continue to walk away discouraged without any lasting comprehension. We all need to build our youth up, establish care and trust, and then give them a pointer to work on. Master Brown provided more wisdom on such coaching efficacy strategies later in this chapter during **CV #15** on **Leadership**.

-David Santos *(Second Year Cadet at the United States Military Academy, West Point; Former student-athlete of mine):*

At the beginning of 2016, I had the opportunity to catch up with one of my past high school players whom I coached for two years, David Santos. Because of the skills that David acquired through his involvement in sports growing up, along with having wonderfully supportive parents who understood the balance between enjoyment and discipline, David is currently in his second year at the most prestigious educational institution in the world, the United States Military Academy, West Point. I asked David about the skills that are needed from his perspective in order to be successful as a cadet at West Point. Here is what David shared with me:

> *Being highly involved in sports all of my life has allowed me to enjoy working hard at something, while in the end seeing the rewards of my hard work. I am not sure if I would be where I am today had it not been for my participation in sports. Here at West Point, the people and the environment are amazing, but it is definitely not easy and you have to see the light at the end of the tunnel. I learned during my first year that **discipline** is vital to success. I am fortunate that the foundation of sports taught me **discipline** and how to be a person of high mental fortitude and integrity. Just as I could not cut corners in athletics growing up and expect success, it is the same way here. It is about doing the little things, whether that means Thursday morning uniform inspections, bed inspections, or keeping my shoes shined. It is all about the discipline of the little things that make a big difference.*

During my nearly two decades as a coach, I have witnessed strong character such as David's on display each and every day. However, David has always been one of the hardest working, respectful, and focused young men that I have had the fortune of coaching. The rigor of sports has been a great training ground and motivator for David, as it has taught him the discipline and mental fortitude that he needs to excel in the Army. I saw these attributes in him first-hand, on and off the field, as his coach.

Coach Ken Leavoy (*Champion Women's softball assistant coach for Team Canada in the 2015 Pan Am Games*) may have put into perspective the value of discipline for me as well as it can be said:

> *Discipline, as paradoxical as it sounds, leads to freedom. Genuine **discipline** or extended focus on improving a skill eventually allows that skill to be developed, and a new skill level is a form of freedom. What may have limited us in the past is no longer a limitation. That new sense of freedom usually gets us to 'buy in' even more to a strong sense of **discipline** and work ethic, which in turn gets us into an ongoing cycle of honest effort leading to improved skill and knowledge, which rewards us with freedom…and on and on it goes.*

What a wonderful recognition and acknowledgement of the awesome value of **discipline** and building for the future.

CV #11 Discipline: Activities and Drills to increase Retention/Assessment:

- o While we want children to keep fun first and foremost in sports, this mid-level developing stage is where we want to begin to emphasize the **discipline** that it takes to develop true skills. This is where the power of a short thematic story or parable can give the student-athletes something to relate to. Below I have provided a few great messages of success that came about through strong discipline and commitment toward a certain goal. The following list will give you as a coach some talking points that you can research further and make your own. The key to remember, especially at this age, is to keep it brief and to the point, and try to stimulate team involvement and players' perspectives and insights. This will increase their comprehension and retention. Potential topics:
    - Going back to the story of **Olympic gold medalist Betsy Mitchell** waking up at 4:30am on her own. If they found something that they were passionate about, do they think that they could do that? What would it take for them to rise up out of bed that early?

Would they have to sacrifice something on the other end (at night) in order to be more productive in the mornings?

- Ask them about the quote at the beginning of this section by one of our Founding Fathers and the first President of the United States of America, George Washington, *"Discipline is the soul of an Army."* Ask your players what that means to them and how it relates to sports and the concept of team.

- Favorite video game? What do they love about it? When they first played that game, were they good at it? How did they become good at it? Wasn't the challenge of learning how to play the game well a big part of the fun? Did it take discipline to sit there and be beat by their friends over and over until they figured it out?

- Ask them what they think about **Coach Ken Leavoy's** statement about how disciplined behavior leads to more disciplined behavior, which ultimately leads to building highly effective habits? Does this work both ways as it relates to establishing potentially bad habits?

- Come up with a team goal to increase their discipline. Tell them that you will do it as well. Perhaps it could be making their beds each morning when they rise. That simple act, first thing in the morning, will be their test that could trigger the tone for their willingness to be disciplined with their actions that day.

o Once you have covered this topic of the importance of discipline in their lives, make a call to action. Ask them about an area of their lives that they know would benefit greatly from becoming more disciplined. We all have areas to improve upon. After a few minutes of reflection, if you are willing, share an area of your life that you are working to become more disciplined in. Your leadership and humility will help break the ice for your team. When I did this exercise for the first time with a group of high school baseball players, I was amazed by the thoughtfulness in their responses, as well as their willingness to share.

CHARACTER
LOVES
COMPANY

Character Values (11-16):

11. *Discipline*

12. *Timeliness (Time Management/Preparation)*

13. *Humility*

14. *Work Ethic/Sense of Accomplishment*

15. *Leadership*

16. *Confidence Without Being Cocky*

BUILDING BLOCK #12: Timeliness
(Time Management/Preparation)

"Be quick, but don't hurry"[83] —Coach John Wooden

This **CV** of **Timeliness (Time Management/Preparation)** is one that many of the expert coaches that I have talked with over the years have found to be a critical characteristic of elite-level performance and productivity. Nothing productive has ever come when someone is scrambling to get somewhere, or trying to do something at the last second. Such counter-productive behavior results in chaos, tension, and ultimately, collapse. The quote, *"Be quick, but don't hurry"* by the great Coach Wooden, is one of my absolute favorites. At first glance, this quote seems contradictory, or paradoxical, but when you dig down and dissect what Coach Wooden is saying, his message of working with purpose and being prepared shine through.

---

[83] Coach Wooden's famous words, "Be quick, but don't hurry," are so poignant that he and author Andrew Hill produced a wonderful book (2001) entitled *Be Quick-But Don't Hurry: Finding Success in the Teachings of a Lifetime.*

Coach Amanda Butler *(Head Women's Basketball Coach, University of Florida)* discussed the above quote from Coach Wooden, for whom she holds the utmost respect. I specifically asked Coach Butler about this quote and how it relates to her coaching philosophies and the intent and purpose of her team's culture and goals. I saw this **CV** as clear as day in Coach Butler's team during that first game that I saw them play. They were down by a lot going into halftime, but they did not come out throwing wild haymakers. Rather, they stuck with the team game plan and they scratched and clawed their way back in and nearly won the game against a team that on paper (size and strength-wise) seemed superior.

Coach Butler, whose passion and enthusiasm for what she teaches about life exude out of her, seemed to appreciate this question and reference to Coach Wooden. She remarked, *"A confident and prepared team is a team that looks like they are trying to do things quickly, but under complete control. While the team that is unsure of its purpose, or at the core lacks confidence, that is a team that is going to appear hurried, rushed, and out of control, which infers a lack of preparation."*

I have found this to apply to every walk of my life, and I guess this is why Coach Wooden's and Coach Butler's words resonated with me so clearly. I teach public speaking classes at the college level, and this concept of "preparation builds confidence" rings true when preparing and delivering a speech. Yes, it is true that some speakers are more effective when they do not speak from a script, teleprompter, or notecards, however, do not confuse that with not being prepared. Typically, the above-mentioned speakers are more prepared than the rest because they have actually internalized their message over and over again in their heads so much that their message radiates out of their entire being.

In continuing the application of **timeliness** and **preparation**, there is validity in the old adage, *"If you are not 10 minutes early, you are late."* This is another terrific message that our youth needs to learn at a young age. If they are rushing into a tryout and pulling up their socks and tightening their belt as they walk into the athletic arena, then their first impression is not going to be a good one. The coach is going to notate the following on his or her clipboard: *"Late, probably not someone that I will want on my team."* Going into a job interview, the candidate who is rushed, out of breath, disheveled, and without preparation may, indeed, be the most intelligent and potentially most qualified for the job, however, they have already been crossed off the list because they were late and unprepared.

I think back to my first contributor to this book, **Betsy Mitchell**. Betsy took responsibility and ownership for her own swimming career by being on time and honoring a commitment to her team. As a teenager, Betsy wanted to start training early in the morning before school. Looking back on her desire to do so, her parents put much of the onus on her to make it her own. *"My dad immediately said that he would do anything to support me, including driving me at 4:30 in the morning before work, but I had to get him up. He would not get me up. So, that is what we did. I set my alarm, I woke him up and we went,"* remarked Betsy. What an awesome lesson for a teenager to have to set her own alarm and get up, get breakfast, and then wake her dad up to get to practice on time. If she did not have the discipline and commitment to get up on her own, she would have missed out on those early morning swim practices prior to school. It is hard to imagine Betsy being able to accomplish all that she did as an athlete, and what she is doing now, without that disciplined foundation that was established at a young age.

This mid-level age range of **CLD** is when children should be able to start making sports (and other experiences) their own; the period in their development when they start to develop ownership in their athletic endeavors. This does not mean that we, as coaches and parents, should not be there to encourage and support, but we cannot continue to force our past hopes and dreams on them. Imagine if Betsy's mother and father would have had to try and drag her out of bed every morning to get her to practice on time. How long would that have lasted? If we will allow our children to make the journey their own and begin to instill an understanding of work ethic and assertiveness in our children through the vehicle of sports, then the heights of what they can accomplish will become limitless.

CV #12 Timeliness (Time Management/Preparation): Activities and Drills to increase Retention/Assessment:

- o Present the following quote with your team: *"Tardiness often robs us opportunity, and the dispatch of our forces."* –Niccolo Machiavelli

  Have them discuss what they think it means. Begin to explain to them that this is the stage when they need to start taking a bit more ownership in their endeavors. Their parents should no longer have to lay out their uniform, carry their sport's bag, or backpack, nor remind them about what time practice starts. This is where timeliness and time management begin to develop in our youth.

- o Rainy Day Chalk Ideas:
  - Why do we ever cancel practice due to rain or weather? Unless it is unsafe to drive, if a coach can find a covered, sheltered and safe place indoors, there is much to be taught and learned regarding **CLD**. Practice is on!
- o Top 10 List:
  - Give each member of your team a notecard and a pencil (every coach should have a small box of golf pencils for team activities such as these). Have them take one minute only to quickly come up with the top 10 qualities of a good teammate, or captain. I can guarantee that the discipline needed to be consistent and show up on time will make many top 10 lists. After they spend one minute individually, have them partner up for two minutes and ask them to circle their overlapping responses. Then have the duo present in 30 seconds their findings to the entire team. This is a terrific way to get them up in front of the group sharing important ideas and leading the charge on character development. It is important that we empower them to use their voices and take an active role in their development and retention of **CLD.**
- o Similar to Coach Wooden's quote: *"Be quick, but don't hurry,"* have your team come up with a team slogan. Come up with a team slogan or philosophy regarding a team commitment to outwork the opponent while maintaining control and poise.

CHARACTER LOVES COMPANY

<u>Character Values (11-16):</u>

11. *Discipline*

12. *Timeliness (Time Management/Preparation)*

13. **Humility**

14. *Work Ethic/Sense of Accomplishment*

15. *Leadership*

16. *Confidence Without Being Cocky*

BUILDING BLOCK #13. Humility

"For those who exalt themselves will be humbled, and those who humble themselves will be exalted."
—Matthew 23: 12 (New International Version Bible)

The term **"humility"** and its importance have already been brought up multiple times thus far in this guidebook. The above quote from the Bible (NIV) is one of my favorite verses, as I believe it to be 100% accurate in all aspects of life, especially pertaining to sports. The need to express a sense of humility has been emphasized by visionary coaches through words and phrases such as: *"Stay humble, stay hungry"* or *"The game will humble you."* Despite the absolute truth behind such statements, we continue to witness an air of brash cockiness and hubris in many athletes (young and old) today, as if expressions of humility have become signs of weakness, or a character flaw. What I have observed over the years is the athletes who maintain their excellence over the long haul have a strong sense of acknowledgement and adherence to remaining humble and appreciative to a connection with others, or something greater than themselves.

Jenna Marston *(Two-time Team USA Sportswoman of the Year; Pan-American Champion Women's Baseball Player 2015; NCAA DI Scholar-Athlete).* I was moved and honored by the final statement that Jenna made in our dialogue together, *"...If we ever cross paths at a ballgame, I'd love to talk hitting and get to pick your brain."* Jenna has accomplished more than I ever had as a baseball player, and despite my longstanding background as a baseball coach and hitting expert, I was moved that someone with her resume[84] as a hitter could remain so **humble** and willing to learn from others. Jenna possesses that requisite **humility** that it takes to maintain lifelong growth. Her humility and willingness to learn should be an inspiration to us all.

Master Boon Brown *(35-year Instructor/Mentor; fifth degree black belt; Owner of Ancient Ways Martial Arts Academy in Bradenton, Florida; Educational background in Psychology and Counseling)* and I discussed **humility** and how much its emphasis is needed in our rising generations to combat the unrealistic expectations of the ever-prevalent win-at-all-costs mentality in sports. Here, Master Brown imparts his knowledge with us:

> *Everybody thinks that what it is all about is going pro or the scholarship, or always winning. But, sports allow kids to realize that they cannot always win, and that someone on a particular day might play better or perform better. The ones who are really going to succeed later in life are the ones who have had to face their failures head on. Just because you seemingly failed doesn't mean that you quit. In my mind, to fail means that this is the first effort and that I am going to try again.*
>
> *It is true in any sport, no matter how good you are at MMA,[85] anybody can beat you on any given day. If they land that front snap kick, that is all it takes. It is the same premise in MMA, or any other sport, such as football—if the quarterback has a bad day, or someone is sick, or the other team is having a good day, anything can happen. Not enough young athletes understand this concept, but they need to learn how to lose, because it is inevitable. If they believe they are that great and they have never learned the many lessons of losing, it becomes destructive.*

---

[84] Jenna Marston was a key contributor for Team USA in winning a gold medal in the Pan Am Games in the summer of 2015, as well as two silver medals and a bronze medal during the Women's Baseball World Cup in 2010, 2012, and 2014. In Venezuela, she batted .593 with eight extra base hits during the tournament, which led her team and was a close second to all participants in the tournament.
[85] MMA stands for Mixed Martial Arts, which has become one of the most popular sports in the world today.

A perfect example of this is Ronda Rousey. Master Brown and I turned our conversation to the fact that Rousey had been the most highly regarded MMA female fighter and UFC[86] Champion for quite some time. As a 2015 *Sports Illustrated* article attested to in its title: "The Unbreakable Ronda Rousey is the World's Most Dominant Athlete" (Wertheim), she seemed to be invincible before, as predicted, an opponent landed some unexpected blows that took her down for the first time. Rousey had not been accustomed to losing, and since this first loss, she has been struggling to find her footholds in order to get back on track.[87]

Master Brown continued on this topic:

Sports are so important for people to learn to win graciously and lose graciously and to recognize that just because you won, you are not better than someone else; and just because you lost that you are not worth anything. [Ray] *Rice,[88] the guy that you were talking about, a lot of athletes think it* [violence, and in this case domestic violence] *is a piece of the culture, the culture of sports, and it is not! It is a dysfunction, a disgrace, and it does not belong anywhere.*

The word 'gentleman' is not used well anymore, and we actually teach a course here [at the dojo] *in that. We teach a course in how to be a gentleman and how to be a lady. My wife comes in and teaches the one on how to be a lady. I am a firm believer that men and women in relationships should work side-by-side through life together with respect, and humility is a big part of that.*

I asked Master Brown to comment on how many traditional sports seem to be missing the boat on character, while martial artists seem to be more in tune with the chord of this book.

I appreciate how after a hard fought battle you should still bow to your opponent and show respect. Sometimes, you may not like the other person, or they may have thrown some

---

[86] UFC stands for the Ultimate Fighting Championship, which has been in existence in the U.S. since 1993. Though it has become an ever popular sport in the U.S., many question the ethical implications of airing the gruesome nature of the sport on national television.

[87] http://www.si.com/mma/2015/05/12/ronda-rousey-ufc-mma-fighter-armbar

[88] Previously in our conversation, I had brought up the brutal elevator incident with NFL football player Ray Rice and his then fiancée in an elevator. Rice violently abused his fiancée in the elevator knocking her unconscious, prior to dragging her out of the elevator. http://time.com/3329351/ray-rice-timeline/

cheap shots, but at the end of the day it is about respect. He or she still deserves my respect. Some schools actually teach unethical tactics and it is highly dishonorable.

As far as the dojo and the comparison to other sports, I like how at the end of a Little League game they all go down the line and shake hands with each other as a sign of respect. Now that is a start and the right message. I like what the Japanese do which is stand across from each other and bow to share the message that they appreciate the mere fact that they have an opponent to compete with or against. What martial arts has taught me is that we need each other in order to get to compete, and that mutual respect has got to be there. Unfortunately, in the world today, everything is about the 'selfie' and showing off what one has and what he or she can do. Where is the humility in that?

I love the many powerful messages that Master Brown shares with us on the values of respect and **humility**, and just how closely linked these two terms truly are. If people do not have **humility,** then they oftentimes cannot see the importance of respect for those who came before them, as well as those standing with them. These individuals miss out on learning opportunities because they become closed-minded (fixed mindset vs. growth mindset). There is a great deal of knowledge through lived experience, and Master Brown talks about methods that coaches and parents can use to better facilitate the learning process. In **CV #19** on being **process oriented**, I present some effective teaching tactics that Master Brown uses to facilitate increased student-athlete acceptance and retention in order to grow and become more coachable.

CV #13 Humility: Activities and Drills to increase Retention/Assessment:

- o There are many different ways to help young student-athletes, and children, in general, appreciate and learn to be humble. However, the most important approach is to model such behavior as a coach or parent. Are you demonstrating humility as a coach and mentor for your student-athletes?

- o A post-game tradition that my brother Mack (who has been a successful high school Head Baseball Coach for the past decade) does is to begin by pointing out what a great performance the obvious star of that game had. His point is that everyone was there, and they all witnessed the great accomplishments from that individual. It is traditionally not the extraordinary acts that make the difference in the end result, but rather the sum of all the smaller, less noticeable contributions all coming together towards a common goal. What Mack does, and what I have started to do, is to have the obvious star individual pick someone else to "brag on" for their contribution to the team's success. This is a way to not only get your team to comprehend the importance of the power of the entire unit, but it also minimizes some of the egocentrism that we see in youth, amateur, and professional sports. Try it out for yourself with your team.

o A team activity that I learned from one of my previous players is called the "Three Snaps Game." At the heart of this fun game is the necessity of members of a team working to get in unison with each other. The most effective teams and organizations have cohesion and continuity. Have your players get into pairs with a cone in between them. They are to snap three times and after the third snap say whatever word is in their head (be sure they are mindful and respectful with their words). Without giving each other any kind of secret signal, they are to work to eventually say the same word. After each turn, they should think for a second or two about what word they want to say next based on the feedback from their partner. Then they do their three snaps and say their next word. This is a good way to get players to adapt and adjust, as well as realize that if they want to succeed, they have to be on the same page as their teammates, and not living on an island all by themselves. (A hint as the coach is to come up with topics for them such as: sports, movies, music, etc.)

o Another terrific activity that I mentioned in a previous section is to work with your student-athletes on their interviews/meetings with potential future high school or college coaches. Sit down with each of them and ask them the tough questions that seek to gain information about their ability as athletes to adapt to difficult situations, how to be good team players, and whether they are concerned with the team's ultimate success rather than simply personal accolades. In the end, coaches want players with confidence in themselves, but more importantly, they want student-athletes who can be **humble** and who have an understanding of the power of a team all pulling in the same direction.

Character Values (11-16):

11. *Discipline*

12. *Timeliness (Time Management/Preparation)*

13. *Humility*

14. **Work Ethic/Sense of Accomplishment**

15. *Leadership*

16. *Confidence Without Being Cocky*

BUILDING BLOCK #14: **Work Ethic/**
Sense of Accomplishment

"Some people want it to happen, some wish it would happen,
others make it happen."[89] –Michael Jordan

-Fred Claire *(Los Angeles Dodgers General Manager 1987-1998; World Series Champion in 1988; 30-year Dodger Executive; Author of book:* Fred Claire: My 30 Years in Dodger Blue; *Leadership Expert; Professor at USC; Great Mentor of mine):*

In order to be a part of anything great, we have to work at it and commit our full efforts toward it. No one understands this concept better than my next contributor, Fred Claire. I have had the fortune of knowing Fred for the past 10 years, dating back to his mentoring and assistance for my master's degree thesis from California State University, Los Angeles in 2006. He has been a strong mentor of mine, and he is currently on the

---

[89] This quote found at Brainyquote.com defines the greatest basketball player of all time very well. For anyone who was fortunate to see "MJ" play, he was obviously one who made things happen on the court.

advisory board of directors for my non-profit organization, **Character Loves Company**. Fred has provided mentorship for me on the topic of emphasis in character for this book, and we have had many conversations about the importance of leaders making decisions based on integrity and sound principle. I had a chance to spend quite a bit of time one-on-one with Fred as it relates to the content and delivery of **CLD**. Here is some of what Fred shared with me pertaining to **work ethic/sense of accomplishment**:

> *The foundation of anything is the work ethic that we apply to whatever we choose to do with our lives. Certainly for me, what I was able to accomplish through the game of baseball was because of a tremendous work ethic. I, of course, had a passion for the game from a young age—I loved it.*

> *When the opportunities came my way, I was always prepared and ready. There was never a sense of entitlement for me. When the general manager position for the Dodgers* [one of the most cherished sports organizations in the world] *was offered to me by Peter* [O'Malley],[90] *I was prepared for it. Becoming the GM for the Dodgers was built on 20 years of experience with the organization. I had put in the time—I knew how it worked.*

Fred shared a keen analogy with me between his own work ethic and preparation for success with that of the Dodgers' young pitching phenom of the 80's, Fernando Valenzuela. In 1981, when Fred was the Dodgers' VP of Public Relations, he witnessed this mirrored expression in Fernando's desire to succeed, and what eventually led to Fernando-mania in Los Angeles. Here was an unheard of, young, left-handed pitcher from Mexico who spoke zero English. When the Dodgers' veteran ace pitcher, Jerry Reuss, pulled a hamstring prior to a game, Fernando was handed the ball and given the first start of his illustrious Major League career. No big deal for Fernando, who Fred vividly recalls mowing down the opposition that day as if he had been practicing and crafting for this his whole life, which he had. Fernando Valenzuela went on that year to become the only pitcher in MLB history to earn the "Rookie of the Year" and the "Cy

---

[90] The O'Malley family owned and operated the Dodgers' organization for more than 50 years from the team's days in Brooklyn through their move to Los Angeles prior to the start of the 1958 season. The O'Malley family was highly regarded as one of the most respected major sports ownership groups in the history of professional sports. In 1988, the O'Malley's sold the Dodgers to Fox News Corp.

Young" awards in the same season. Fred reminisced about Fernando breaking into the Major Leagues in the following way:

> *What impressed me the most about Fernando's brilliant performance that day was not how well he had pitched in earning the team the victory, but rather the calmness and confidence that he displayed. It was, and is still, almost eerie. Looking back on it now, and knowing Fernando the way I do, it makes perfect sense and it is very similar to when I was given the opportunity to lead the Dodgers as the General Manager. Fernando had worked so hard his entire life for that first start. He was raised in Mexico and he had a great deal of success in Mexico, as well as in the Minors.[91] Most importantly, he believed in himself and, boy, was that apparent when he stepped on that pitching mound.*
>
> *This is traditionally what happens when we have worked hard, and we are prepared to make the most of opportunities that are presented to us. It is about believing in oneself, which must be earned. It is impossible to get others to believe in us, if we do not first believe in ourselves. In the words of Coach Wooden, 'Hard work and preparation lead to confidence.'*

Staying on this same topic of working hard in order to accomplish anything worthwhile, I asked Fred about how his value for disciplined **work ethic** was formed back in his earlier years. After discussing how these habits were established through expectations and values taught to him by his parents, as well as through involvement in sports growing up, Fred took me back to the day he graduated from college in 1957:

> *So, now, let's reverse it and go back to '57 [1957]. In '57, I graduated from San Jose State and I needed to get a job immediately. I learned at a young age that you have to take initiative and make things happen. My folks lived in Pomona, so I wrote 30 letters to newspapers all across Southern California. The first newspaper that I contacted was the* Pomona Newspaper. *I still remember the lead editor, Mr. Johnson, telling me that they had nothing available now, but that they may have something open up in two weeks. I simply could not wait that long. I respectfully told Mr. Johnson that I would be back to check in and to keep me in mind if something opened up.*

---

91 "The Minors" refers to the minor leagues, which is comprised of typically six to eight different levels that "minor leaguers" work their way up through in order to advance to the highest stage, which is the Major Leagues.

Fred continued to tell how he spent the rest of the day traveling from newspaper to newspaper committed to having a job by the end of the day. *"We control our attitude and our work ethic, and I was going to make it happen that day! And I did. By the end of the day, I was given a job with the* Whittier Daily News," remarked Fred. *"It seems a little different nowadays for some young graduates."*

Fred is a visiting professor at the University of Southern California's Marshall School of Business,[92] and he shared with me a story that depicts how different the mindset is for some graduates these days. One of his graduate students had a great opportunity to take an internship with a wonderful company that could have been a springboard for a highly desirable job after graduation. The internship was the final summer prior to going into his senior year at USC. The student came to Fred for advice on whether he should take the internship, which would have been a lot of work, but a terrific training ground for his profession of choice after college. The other option was to stay home and relax during his final summer, after a tough and stressful year of hard work. Knowing Fred and his passion for principle, sound decision making, and work ethic, I was not at all surprised by his candid response to his student. I am fairly certain that his student took the internship, and that he thanked his lucky stars for Fred's principled mentoring after the fact. Here is Fred's response to his student:

> *'Should you take the position?'* [pause] *'Are you kidding me? You get up to Seattle and take that job!' You have to have a sense of urgency to make things happen, and I don't see that as much today nowadays.*
>
> *You see, for me, I never wanted anyone to give me handouts. I wanted to support myself and not have to rely on my parents financially after college. I joined the Army Reserves right after college, and every so often my parents would mail me a check for $25. While I greatly appreciated that gesture of love from my parents, I finally had to write back and say, 'Don't send me checks anymore. I don't need them because I want to support myself.' I took a great deal of pride in that, and I have always believed that there are no free rides (or handouts) in life.*

Fred has accomplished a great deal in his life. He is now 80-years-old (which is hard to believe as sharp and filled with passion as he is), and it could be understandable, or even

---

[92] USC's Marshall School of Business is one of the top business schools in the country.

expected, for him to put life on cruise control. You talk about a life well lived: He has been married to his wonderful wife, Cheryl, for over 30 years, he is a great family man, he won a MLB World Series, he served as a high ranking executive for the Dodgers for 30 years, he is a college professor, he runs his own leadership company, he has written a thought provoking book … just to name a few of his notable accomplishments. However, in my most recent talk with Fred, it is more apparent than ever that his drive for excellence and achievement are burning bright. The passion and enthusiasm in his voice for his latest endeavor, Scoutables,[93] a baseball analytics company, was reminiscent of the hunger for excellence that I am sure he exhibited that day in Whittier, all those years ago, that landed him his first job out of college. Much of what Fred speaks to clearly supports the **CV** of **Work Ethic/Sense of Accomplishment**, as well as CV #18 which focuses on working through adversity and showing true "grit."

CV #14 Work Ethic/Sense of Accomplishment: Activities and Drills to increase Retention/Assessment:

- o This is a perfect opportunity as a coach or a parent at home to encourage young student-athletes to put in some conscientious effort outside of practice time working to improve their abilities. No one ever became great at anything by accident. Over the years, I have seen some of the best athletes in the world train first-hand, and it was not an accident that they became great.

- o Give each of your players a note card and have them write their favorite athlete's name down on the card. Ask them to go on the Internet and do some research on this individual. Have them try to find out the secret to their favorite athlete's success. My guess is that hard work and passion will be at the root of what most of them find. Have them write their findings on the back of the card to share with their teammates. Unless you have a rain delay or long bus/van trip, you will most likely

---

[93] Scoutables (www.scoutables.com) was co-founded by Fred Claire and Ari Kaplan and the company provides data-rich, fact-based support for intelligent sports analysis and commentary by fans and professionals alike. Today, Scoutables produces daily machine-generated scouting reports on every Major League Baseball player as well as data visualization tools that allow users to explore Pitchf/x data.

not have time to get through all of them but you will be surprised by how many of them actually look forward to volunteering to educate their teammates on what they found out.

o Regarding Michael Jordan's quote at the beginning of this section on making things happen versus waiting or hoping for things to happen, ask your players whether they want, wish, or are willing to work to make their dreams become a reality. Talk and mentor them about what it takes to accomplish something great.

CHARACTER
LOVES
COMPANY

<u>Character Values (11-16):</u>

11. *Discipline*

12. *Timeliness (Time Management/Preparation)*

13. *Humility*

14. *Work Ethic/Sense of Accomplishment*

15. **Leadership**

16. *Confidence Without Being Cocky*

BUILDING BLOCK #15: **Leadership**

This topic of **leadership** is perhaps my personal favorite character value. I am a firm believer that one's positive influence towards others, and towards society as whole, is what life is all about. As I previously mentioned, I wrote my first master's thesis on **leadership** in the early 2000s. If I come across a book or an article with **leadership** in its title, I am immediately drawn in. I have been fortunate to have been around some exemplary leaders in my life. None more so than my mother, and despite her passing away when I was only 12-years-old, she continues to be my guiding light today. I now turn to four influential contributors in the world of sports who have all been remarkable leaders for quite some time.

-**Chivonne Kiser** *(Veteran High School Volleyball and Track & Field Coach/Mentor in the Houston area of Texas; Previous NCAA DI Volleyball player at Southern University; Mother and family person):*

Chivonne Kiser has proven herself to be an inspiring and motivating coach, role model, and mentor for all of her high school students over the past 15 years in Sugar

Land and Katy, Texas. Though Coach K's (as her student-athletes refer to her) teams have won their share of big games during her coaching career, she has always kept character and lifelong development at the forefront. Through my interactions with Coach Kiser over the past year and a half, I have always come away inspired. When I reached out to her for an interview for my book, she jumped at the idea. Her narrative here will provide you with the perfect set[94] from which to drive home a better understanding of the value of true **leadership**.

I began my interview with Coach Kiser by asking her about the influence that coaches, in general, can have on their players:

> *What I have learned over 15 years of coaching is that kids notice everything about you as a coach: from your mannerisms, to your sayings, to your demeanor. You cannot simply just talk the talk, but you have to walk the walk. Otherwise, they will see what you are doing and act on that rather than what you are saying. As coaches, we have such a powerful influence on our players.*

> *When we talk about the Johnny Manziels of the world, we need to look back over his path to where he is today. What happened along his path from his earliest years in youth athletics all the way up to his career in the NFL? Did his coaches miss out on the teachable moments in exchange for winning youth championships? Coaches need to hold all their players accountable, irrespective of how talented they are and how many championships they can help win.*

> *However, in our culture, winning is so important, even at the youngest of ages when it should be primarily about development. It is deplorable how caught up our culture is with winning-at-all-costs. We are failing kids as a whole when the coachable or teachable moments that are so vital to the development of young boys and girls are not being emphasized and taught. It is so critical that we, as coaches, are teaching our youth more than just the rules of the game and how to win. It sickens me to see the lack of sportsmanship [sportspersonship] or hear about it in the media pertaining to youth sports.*

> *I could sit here and talk about the championships and games I have won, but it is not about that at all for me. What means the most to me is the impact that I feel I have had on many young lives in a positive way.*

---

[94] A "set" in volleyball occurs when one player positions the ball for a teammate in a way that allows them to spike the ball for a point. The "setter" is the consummate team player, as she/he rarely gets a whole lot of acknowledgement, despite being vital to team success.

In 15 years of coaching at the high school level, a small number of my players have gone on to college to play NCAA sports. When they do earn the opportunity to continue as an athlete in college, it is a special thing for us as coaches to know that sports helped one of our players advance to college with a scholarship. However, most go on to college and they use what they learned in sports to be successful in college and in life afterwards.

For me, being invited to college graduations or weddings of my players, or their kids' first birthdays (which means that I am getting up there in age) shows the impact and influence that I have truly had in molding my players to be better people in life. The wins and losses are forgotten, but the life lessons of hard work and love stick with them. Many of them come back and help with tryouts voluntarily. Some even tell me that they want me to coach their kids someday and that is, to me, the ultimate compliment.

I could not agree with Coach Kiser more with regard to everything that she stated during our interview, however, her last statement is what coaching is all about. There is no bigger tribute that any previous player could give to you (as their coach) than their desire for you to coach and positively impact their own children in the same way that you affected them. You obviously have to withstand the test of time and longevity as a coach, but that is a legacy. She continues:

I think about the great coaches—The Coach K's[95] of the world. How they stay relevant is by building lasting relationships with their players. As a coach, I am marketing a brand of trust, and giving my kids [my players] my absolute best brand, whether times are good, or when faced with adversity. They are going to see how I respond as an example, and I am not going to lose my composure, or use foul language, because there is too much on the line as a coach and mentor.

I have an army of successful individuals that I have coached in high school athletics who have gone on and made me proud. Whether they won or lost [on the court or track], they have learned valuable life lessons. I want to help others to want to reach out and help the next generation through coaching. Nothing made me more proud than to have been able to hire one of my past players to run the freshman program at our high school. I see a little bit of me in her, and that is rewarding as a coach.

---

[95] "Coach K" is Mike Krzyzewski, the legendary Duke University men's basketball coach. He is a terrific role model and, similarly to Coach Kiser, a mentor who has always placed character development front and center.

I have figured out that coaching is, first and foremost, about teaching! It's about teaching how to be productive citizens and leaders. Character lasts. Look at Coach [Tony] Dungy. Look back into his years of coaching and see the lives that he has influenced in a positive way. When I think of Peyton Manning and all that he has accomplished in his career, he has done it with lasting character. Who were his coaches growing up? I want to look back at the line of coaches that played a part in his development, starting with his parents. No doubt they deserve some of the credit, and I have no doubt Peyton would be the first to tell you that.

Coach Kiser's remarks above are mirrored by **Coach Ken Leavoy** *(Champion Women's Softball Assistant Coach for Team Canada in 2015 Pan American Games; 30+ year High School/College Head Coach/Mentor).* I asked Coach Leavoy how important trust in **leadership** is in sports in order to truly make an impact as a coach and mentor. Here is what he told me regarding coaching **leadership**:

Some coaches are way too concerned about their win/loss record and thus the genuine development of their athletes is secondary to their ego. Instead of putting the development of the athlete first, and by that I mean, development as a person first and then as an athlete. Oftentimes, they just want wins. All athletes need to know that they, as people, really matter to their coach, and when they feel that, they will become more coachable.

Coaches have an extraordinary influence on kids and that is a double-edged sword. They can be a very positive influence or they can be the opposite. I absolutely believe that sports are a wonderful avenue of development and growth for kids in preparing them for life. So many of the necessary life skills can be enhanced through sports. That, to me, is more important than any win/loss record for a coach. The coaches that get it right have former athletes staying in contact with them for life and the relationship after is very special. Coaches who don't get it, who don't put the personal development of a child ahead of wins, are hated and despised and have no long lasting friendships with their athletes.

This is synonymous to what Coach Kiser emphasized as well, as the coach who only cares about winning is going to let the end result on the scoreboard supersede everything else. The student-athletes will realize quickly that such a coach does not truly care about them, but rather sees them as interchangeable figures, similar to pieces on a chess board, in the winning machine. When the Coach/Player relationship is based entirely on wins and losses, there is no cultivation of that mentor relationship of trust and influence that a coach can have. When student-athletes know that their coach has their backs, they become much more receptive to learning, and that is where real growth can occur. A coach who truly cares will seek out the coachable life-learning moments, and not shy away from them in order to be liked by the superstar player. If that means benching the star player in a big game for not adhering to expected team principles, then so be it. That is how you truly win, both as a coach and as a student-athlete. Coach Leavoy picked up on this point about principled leadership:

> *The thing that I remember most about the Pan Am gold medal was the collective effort of the athletes and coaches. Open-minded and humble coaches listened to their athletes and were willing to do what was necessary to meet the athletes where they were. The athletes responded with respect and appreciation and a total buy in to the guidance and direction of coaches. The gold medal was the result of a team that came together, coaches and athletes, with a trust in each other and a faith that we could win, that we knew we were really good and wanted to prove it. The final out was such an extraordinary moment.*

Coach Leavoy and I talked at great length about the trust and humility of coaches and players working together, and just how important **leadership** is in creating the team over the individual concept. Even at the highest levels of competitive sports, there needs to be a sense of commitment to others through a common goal, which can only be identified through strong **leadership**.

Another great leader who understands the importance of leading by example and creating an environment that values doing things "the right way," or in this case, "The Dodger Way," is **Fred Claire** *(Los Angeles Dodgers General Manager 1987-1998; World Series Champion in 1988; 30-year Dodger Executive; Leadership Expert; Professor at USC)*. As I mentioned previously, Fred is one of the most respected leaders in the world of sports. Here, he shares an inside look into the role that leadership and strong culture played in the Los Angeles Dodgers' World Series Championship in 1988:

> *You have to have the right people on the bus with you who are willing to stay committed to a common goal as well. It didn't happen for us* [the Dodgers' organization]

in a day, but rather, it took a couple of years. It was playing in the dirt, and figuring things out in order to get the most out of our potential. Author Jim Collins hits on this idea in his book, Good to Great,[96] when he talks about the fly wheel and how you have to stay at it day after day after day.

When Fred took over as the Dodgers GM in 1987 in the midst of some organizational turmoil, many felt that he was not the right choice, despite his 20+ years as a high executive within the organization. As I will demonstrate in the next section on **confidence,** Fred knew he was the right person to lead the organization back to greatness. Fred told me how he immediately began to make some changes within the organization in 1987 (i.e. key player acquisitions) that were setting the stage for what turned out to be the pinnacle of success just one season later. Some of the early trades that Fred made may not have seemed to be pivotal moves on paper, but what he was doing was getting the right people on the bus, who were willing to do things "the right way," and he knew and understood the principle of operating the "fly wheel" each and every day.

At a young age, Fred spent time in the Army Reserves, and that is where he began to learn and value the role of **leadership.** Not knowing about Fred's service in the Army, he shared an important acknowledgement that his military training gave him. He told me, *"While I was in the Army Reserves, it became very clear that a military unit had to believe in the person leading the way. If that person shows any sign of weakness, doubt, or shying away—that is not the good type of leader."* Fred went on to express to me how this applies to all areas of **leadership,** whether it be the military, the business world, or the sports world.

I have always had such a deep appreciation and respect for those who have served and protected our great country in the United States Military. I have gained an even deeper level of respect for this great mentor of mine, Fred Claire. He stated, *"I trained in advanced military, but what I did in the Army Reserves, and what I was able to accomplish with the Dodgers, is nothing compared to what people who went to war and fought for our country did and continue to do!"*

---

[96] *Good to Great,* written by Jim Collins in 2001, is an excellent book that Fred Claire often cites as a guide to leadership. It is a prerequisite for leaders in any walk of life.

I want to conclude this section on **leadership** with a brief statement by another World Series Champion, and one of the best leaders and teammates that I ever had the fortune of competing with, **David Ross**. David is one of the most respected players in the game of MLB. He is currently in his final year of a 15-year career in the Major Leagues, and despite having no coaching experience, he is already being considered by numerous baseball experts to be one of the leading managerial candidates at the Major League level upon his retirement at the end of the 2016 season. While that is not the traditional path of most managers in MLB, managing others is ultimately about caring for them, and leading them toward a common goal. David Ross has been doing that since 1999, when we were teammates and California League Champions in San Bernardino, California (as well as Southern League Champions in Jacksonville, Florida) in the Minor Leagues, and most likely long before that.

Here, again, is what David told me about what he has learned about **leadership** during his remarkable MLB career, *"I try and pay attention to how others make me feel and pull out the positives and learn from the negatives. I have been around great leaders like Bobby Cox, Joe Maddon, John Farrell, Dave Roberts, Robin Ventura, Brian McCann...I could go on! I have just been around some wonderful people and I always try to remember how they made me feel."*

David Ross' **leadership** and willingness to make others around him better are characteristics shared by my uncle Tom Paciorek (18-year MLB player) and many other long-time great athletes. One of my contributors to this book, Jenna Marston, shared with me a *Baseball Tonight on ESPN*[97] podcast interview by Buster Olney[98] with 7-time All-Star, and 2-Time MVP, Dale Murphy (who is known as one of the best teammates of all time). During the interview,[99] Olney asked Murphy about the veteran players who greatly impacted his growth as a young, up-and-coming athlete. It brought great pride to hear Murphy talk about my Uncle Tom's character and willingness to help mentor him and the younger ballplayers develop, despite knowing that these up-and-comers would most likely take his position someday. That is what excellent teammates and leaders do.

---

[97] ESPN is the world-wide leader in sports news and entertainment.
[98] Buster Olney is a long-time and highly respected American columnist for ESPN.
[99] The Buster Olney podcast can be found at: http://podtail.com/podcast/baseball-tonight-with-buster-olney/red-hot-sox-5-26-16/. The interview with Dale Murphy begins at the 21 minute and 30 second point.

I have no doubt that David Ross' keen attention to detail and his desire to learn from the great minds around him have molded his leadership and positive influence on others. David is a field general, and people listen to him when he has something to say. They know that he is not in it for himself, but that he is in it for the betterment of the team. He has earned respect and that is what real leaders do. I want to repeat his final statement because I believe it is a powerful message for all of us who interact with student-athletes of all ages: *"I have been around some wonderful people and I always try to remember how they made me feel."* My challenge to you as leaders of your teams is to follow David's lead and always think about how your words and actions are making your players feel. Are you building them up or breaking them down?

CV #15 Leadership (Mentoring): Activities and Drills to increase Retention/Assessment:

- o Building Team Culture: Ask your student-athletes what it takes to be a great leader. Have them think of situations when it would be tough to be a leader. For instance, can a leader just simply coast and go along with the crowd?

- o Homework exercise for your players prior to the next practice or game: Ask them to come up with a good captain/leader in professional sports, and why he or she is an effective leader.

- o As a coach, come up with your own Top 10 Qualities of a good Team Captain. Share your list with your players. Ask them if they possess what it takes to be a true captain of the team? Are they willing to make the sacrifice and stand up for the high standards and principles that you demand? There are many wonderful captain and leadership training books for young student-athletes at the high school and college levels. As a coach over the past two decades, I have been guided and inspired by many such books. I have come up with and used what I call my "Top 10" essentials of an effective captain. I am not one who takes "captainship" lightly, nor one who automatically rewards an upper-classman with the title and honor. The right to be a captain has to be earned at all times. During my coaching career, I have gone a year without a player-captain. I have also relinquished two players of their title of captain, one of whom earned it back. I have also been fortunate to coach some of the most gifted and natural leaders and captains in youth and amateur sports. In my mind, the team captain (or captains) is someone who will always lead by example, despite the consequences or backlash that he or she may receive from their teammates, or the media. A captain is no higher than his or her teammates, and a true captain would never want to be regarded as so. A player-captain is someone who acts as a liaison, or link, between the players and the coaches. Two absolute characteristics that such a captain must possess are trustworthiness and respect.

CHARACTER LOVES COMPANY

Character Values (11-16):

11. *Discipline*

12. *Timeliness (Time Management/Preparation)*

13. *Humility*

14. *Work Ethic/Sense of Accomplishment*

15. *Leadership*

16. ***Confidence Without Being Cocky***

BUILDING BLOCK #16: **Confidence Without Being Cocky**

In working closely with a great deal of high school and college student-athletes over the past nearly two decades, I have paid close attention to the differences between **confidence** and cockiness. There is a very fine line that many young and developing student-athletes seem to have a difficult time with. I have witnessed this phenomenon first-hand in professional athletics as well, which speaks to the fact that this takes a constant self-regulating system of checks and balances. For this reason, this final **CV** in the mid-level developing stage spills over into the advancing stage of **CLD.** In our society as a whole, **confidence** displayed through high self-esteem and self-worth are qualities that we look for in others, especially our own children, or those whom we coach and mentor. However, what we loathe is the individual who thinks the world revolves around him or her.

Having spent a great deal of conscientious thought and analysis on these two dichotomous terms, I have formulated definitions to differentiate between contributing characteristics of **confidence**, and contributing characteristics of cockiness. **Confidence** is derived from years of preparation and practice, which lead to a certain degree of expertise. Vitally important to the concept of **confidence** are three established **CVs** that were previously learned: respect for others, appreciation and interconnectedness with others, and a demonstration of humility. Cockiness, on the other hand, is a puffed up image based on an over-inflated ego and a focus solely on one's self. It is vitally important that we, as coaches and parents of developing student-athletes, work to delineate between these closely identified yet completely divergent terms.

Whether it be in the world of sports, the field of business, or the medical field, we all want highly competent and confident individuals on our team or in our company, as well as in the operating room. The quality of confidence makes the "Top five" list in every field, as it is absolutely imperative in order to be a successful leader and person of influence. I love the story of self-**confidence** without being cocky that my mentor, Fred Claire, shared with me dating back to his early days with the Los Angeles Dodgers.

For those of you who may not be avid baseball fans, **Fred Claire** and Tommy Lasorda were paired together as the Dodgers' general manager (Fred) and field manager (Tommy) when the Dodgers reached the ultimate triumph of winning the World Series Championship in 1988. However, their relationship began close to 20 years prior to that, when they both were at the lowest levels of the organization working hard to make an impact and move their way up to the top of the organizational ladder. I love these two interconnected stories about **confidence** underpinned by respect and humility that occurred during Fred's journey to his pinnacle of influence within the organization. Fred stated:

> *Now Tommy* [Lasorda] *and I were always great friends and we had a great relationship. It dates back to one of our early interactions back in 1969 when I was working for a small, local newspaper covering the Dodgers in spring training in Vero Beach, Florida. Tommy was a young, up-and-coming manager for the Dodgers' minor league team in Spokane. I told Tommy that I used to play ball and that I'd like to take batting practice with the team someday. As I was boarding a traveling team bus to Orlando, Tommy spotted me and shouted out that he needed an extra player at second base for his Spokane team's home game that day. Most likely thinking that I would back down from his challenge, considering I was in street clothes on the first step of the departing bus, he must have figured that his invitation would put an end to my quest to join the team for batting practice. However, people that know me know that I am not one to back down to challenges.*

After tracking down the clubhouse attendant in order to be fitted with a Spokane uniform, Fred quickly hustled out to one of the back fields at Dodgertown,[100] which are designated for the minor league teams within the organization.

> *Tommy was now probably a little worried that within a matter of a few minutes, I was in full uniform ready to go play second base. Tommy shouted 'Claire, go coach first base.' I approached the ever-charismatic future Dodgers manager [19 years later, both Fred and Tommy would win a World Series Championship with the same Los Angeles Dodgers as General Manager and Field Manager, respectively], and I told him that I came here to play and not simply waste my time coaching first base, no disrespect. I am sure that was Tommy's voice of reason saying that he had better not get a news-reporter hurt in a game that he put him in. However, I was going to hold him to his promise and get in that ballgame to show what I could do. In the next inning, Tommy told me to 'go replace Valentine[101] at second base.'*

> *I played second base for the remainder of the game and made a few routine plays. I will never forget my first at-bat that day. As I entered the batter's box, the young catcher remarked, 'Hey, you were with the big club last year weren't you?'*

As Fred shared this story with me, he had the same passion and excitement reflecting back on that day (some 45 years ago) as a young kid at Disneyland for the first time. He was 31-years-old entering the batter's box against a hard-throwing left-handed pitching prospect for the Giants' organization. Fred remembered the adrenaline that was pumping through his veins that day, and the nerves that came from staring down the barrel of a 96mph fastball. Despite this fact, Fred's body language must have exuded the confidence with which he always embodies, warranting the catcher's question about him playing in the "Big Leagues" the previous year. One's body language (which I will discuss further in CV # 20) and the way we carry ourselves are vital. It is not about being cocky, but rather, it is about believing in yourself and knowing that you are capable of success.

---

[100] Dodgertown, located in Vero Beach, Florida, was the premier spring training facility in MLB. The Dodgers' organization has since moved its spring training operation to Arizona, undoubtedly to be closer to Los Angeles.
[101] Bobby Valentine was the Dodgers prized first-round draft choice from the 1968 legendary MLB Draft.

It was remarkable to hear Fred recall his fond memories of that day in the sun in 1969. What seemed like a meaningless spring training game for a low-level minor league Dodgers farm team was a proving ground to demonstrate his character and **confidence**. *"That was just how I was raised. I have never been fearful to take on a challenge,"* stated Fred. That was something that he developed as a youngster playing sports and competing with others. We all should work to instill **confidence** through hard work and preparation in our teams and players. It would be a shame for our youth to miss out on opportunities awaiting them simply because they did not learn the **confidence** needed to take on challenges, advances, and promotions that lay at their feet.

To prove this point, let me fast-forward Fred's narrative from the hidden back fields of Dodgertown in 1969 to one of the grandest stages in all of professional sports, Dodger Stadium,[102] where Fred led the Dodgers to the pinnacle of success in 1988. Fred became the Dodgers' new general manager just prior to the 1987 season.

The Dodgers finished the 1986 season with more losses than wins, and despite making some key trades in his first year at the GM controls in 1987, the team finished with another sub-500 season. This was not acceptable for Dodger fans who had become used to winning West Division Titles and making playoff runs in the 1970s and 80s. Naturally, the Dodgers' owners and management looked to appease their fans and demonstrate that they would, indeed, return the organization to its past glory. One of the big rumors throughout the city of Los Angeles was that the Dodgers were shopping around for a big name general manager candidate to replace Fred going into the 1988 season, after only one year at the helm.

Despite the fact that the 1987 team record on paper seemed to parallel the lack of success from the previous year, Fred knew that the dynamic of the team was starting to gel. He told me that he truly felt that they were a few key player acquisitions away from making a real run at a championship. He believed in himself and the management team that he had around him, including his field general, Tommy Lasorda. Despite the rumor-mill about the potential of Fred being replaced, he believed in himself and was not going to allow the media or anyone else to take away what was rightfully his. His self-confidence, despite the whirlwind going on around him, is inspiring:

---

[102] Dodger Stadium is one of the finest venues in all of sports, and the Dodgers are one of the most storied sports franchises in all of sports.

I loved that job. I wanted to remain as GM of the Dodgers, and I knew that I was the right man for the job and up for the challenge. I loved the competitive side and I knew that I could have a significant impact. I had set the stage for the 1988 team with key trades prior to acquiring Kirk Gibson (who everyone remembers as the team MVP and catalyst), and I knew the 1988 team was going to have a shot to do something special.

Fred essentially told the Dodgers' President, Peter O'Malley, that if he went with someone else and thought that Fred would accept a lesser executive role in the organization, there was a strong chance that the Dodgers would lose him:

My motive to Peter [O'Malley] was never threatening as we had the utmost respect for each other, and we had worked together for 20 years up to this point. I had built confidence through the rigors of the 1987 season, and I knew what I had to do to build a champion. Peter knew that nobody was going to outwork me. It was about confidence rather than fear.

Needless to say, the O'Malley family ownership stayed with Fred at the helm, and the rest was history that will forever engrave Fred Claire in the hearts of Dodger fans around the world. Most MLB executives and players work their whole lives dreaming of winning a World Series, and yet only a very small percentage actually accomplish this feat. An overwhelming sense of inspiration and admiration came over me as Fred shared just how close he was to being on the outside looking in. There is no doubt that it was his **confidence**, built on years of preparation for the job, that eventually earned him the vote of confidence when it mattered most. The chips were on the table, and Fred was all in. Fortunately for the Dodgers' organization and its fans, they retained Fred Claire. Otherwise, who knows if they would have been denied this miracle season without Fred orchestrating the symphony.

We will all be faced with times when our knowledge and abilities will be challenged, or when roadblocks and obstacles will try to hinder our paths. The chance to win a World Series Championship may not necessarily be on the line, but we have to be confident in our own abilities and training during these times of adversity. As Fred stated earlier in my interview with him, *"It is about believing in oneself. It is impossible to get others to believe in us, if we do not first believe in ourselves."*

CV #16 Confidence without being Cocky: Activities and Drills to increase Retention/Assessment:

- This is the perfect age in which to take the time to emphasize the difference between confidence and cockiness. Come up with your own definitions, or borrow from my ideas as laid out in this chapter. The key is to help your young student-athletes discern between the two dichotomous terms.

- Have your players practice walking from the on-deck circle to the batter's box, or likewise stepping up to the free throw line, starting blocks, etc., with the entire team watching. Every elite-level performer has a routine that allows them to embrace the situation with confidence. Have them work on their own routines of confidence in preparation for competition.

- Ask your student-athletes to go home and think about their fears. Do any of those fears get in the way of their short-term or ultimate goals? If they do, ask them to challenge themselves to be confident in addressing challenges head on. After all, they don't want to miss out on something due to fear or lack of confidence.

- When your student-athletes break through a limitation, or address a challenge head on, be sure to highlight that. A simple, *"I see you working"* goes a long way.

- In CV #20 on **Body Language Awareness**, I will share some activities or exercises to improve your student-athletes' non-verbal communication which, in turn, affects their outward and inward appearance.

CHARACTER
LOVES
COMPANY

CHAPTER 9—Level 4: CLD—Advancing Level
(14-16-Year-Old-Range)

By reaching the "Advancing Level," or fourth stage, of **CLD** indicates that the student-athletes should now have a well-established character foundation on which to build. As **CLD** takes root in the world of youth and amateur sports, more and more of our youth will see the great value in continuing to participate in sports, aside from merely winning and the zero-sum game that I have discussed. At this advancing stage, you can expect to find more committed and passionate student-athletes, which makes for an exciting period of development. It is also at this advancing level that we will see the *potential* for increased coachability and a conscious effort and receptivity to a lifelong love of sports. Let's embrace this exciting period in their development.

<u>Character Values (17-22):</u>

17. *Sacrifice*

18. *Handling Adversity/Resilience*

19. *Process Oriented*

20. *Body Language Awareness*

21. *Community Service/Outreach*

22. *Honest Evaluation (Self & Peers)*

BUILDING BLOCK #17: **Sacrifice**

Sacrifice is closely linked to many other **CVs** that I have discussed thus far within **CLD**, such as appreciation, interdependence, integrity, teamwork, discipline, humility, and leadership, to name a few. This can be a concept that is difficult for developing student-athletes to comprehend and apply, and for that reason, I have placed it in the advancing level of **CLD**.

In my mind, the ultimate example of **sacrifice** throughout the history of our great country is from those who have served the United States in any of its five branches of **The Armed Forces**: Airforce, Army, Coast Guard, Marine Corps, and Navy. Though I have not served our country in that capacity, I have the utmost respect for any and all of our country men and women who have. I want to give tribute to these brave and courageous citizens, as well as their families. Leading into the final CV #25 Legacy, which is the highest and most advanced level of **CLD**, I provide a tribute to a true American hero, **Scott Studenmund**, who gave the ultimate sacrifice of his life for the safety and protection of our country.

Continuing with the value and emphasis on sacrifice, I return to my father's narrative on his youth, and his recollection of the example of sacrifice of self for the betterment of others set forth by his father. My father, **John Paciorek** *(50-year youth coach/mentor; MLB record holder)*, reflected back on the many **sacrifices** that his dad made for his family of 10 growing up in Hamtramck, Michigan. At the time of his youth, he did not fully appreciate the extent of his dad's **sacrifice**, but it still left a lasting imprint in developing similar characteristics in him. Here is more of my father's narrative:

> Dad [Grandpa] *always made sure that there was enough good food available for Mom to prepare at meal-times, even in those harder times when we were on welfare. None of us kids (eight in total: five boys and three girls) wanted to go with him to pick up the groceries with 'food-stamps' (for fear of being seen by someone we knew). I also remember seeing him waiting until the entire family finished a tasty, nutritious dinner before he sat down and finished what was left, even if they were merely the scraps off the plates that we had left behind.*
>
> He could hardly afford it, but he made sure that his children had a good Catholic School education. For some reason, he did not want to send us to public school, even though it was free! Transfiguration was a flourishing Polish-Catholic elementary school six blocks east of Moenart on Syracuse Street where we lived. I have no doubt that the Church gave us a significant discount, since I recall Dad doing things for them in his 'spare-time.'

I have always pondered how my father's family, growing up in a blue-collar town on welfare with parents with little to no athletic history, produced eight high school sports stars, five professional baseball players, three of whom were Major Leaguers. The answer I now know is grounded in this life learned value of **sacrifice**. My grandparents may have had the genetic makeup hidden inside of them to be sports stars, but they were not able to develop such skills growing up in poverty during the Great Depression. My dad shares how my grandfather left school and went to work for Chrysler when he was only 15-years-old to help his parents provide for the family. He continued as a dedicated employee for Chrysler until his retirement more than 50 years later.

It is my belief that the longer one is involved in sports, the easier it becomes to fully grasp the concept and tremendous value of **sacrifice**. **Sacrifice** is a **CV** that I feel is truly embraced within my family, and sports and the commitment to family have played equal roles in developing this appreciation, while passing it down through the generations.

This concept of the great **sacrifice** that it takes to accomplish anything worthwhile brings me back to my very first contributor, Olympic gold medalist **Betsy Mitchell.** As you recall from CV #1, Betsy had an agreement with her father based on **sacrifice** and many other values in character. For a teenager to wake up at 4:30am on her own for swimming practice takes great **sacrifice**, as well as grit and resilience that I will discuss in the upcoming CV.

Another Olympic gold medalist in swimming, **BJ Bedford-Miller**, demonstrated her understanding of the value of **sacrifice** for team throughout her illustrious athletic career and into her life after sports. She remarked, *"I learned about the importance of sacrifice while I was at UT.*[103] *As a freshman, I swam the 100M butterfly. I didn't get to swim my best event because I did what the team needed. You see this a lot in football, as well as other sports, where these elite athletes at the college level are able to adapt and adjust in changing positions in order to play in the NFL. Versatility and sacrifice are so important in life."*

This is an excellent message from gold medalist BJ Bedford-Miller about sacrifice that has gone awry in today's ego-driven showcase culture. As young and promising student-athletes get older and move up the ranks, there has become a trend of parents voicing the prerogative for their son or daughter to solely play one select position (i.e. Shortstop, Middle linebacker). I have seen it first-hand where such parents will make a big stink, or even threaten to remove their son or daughter from the team, if they do not play their position of choice 100% of the time. As the coach, administrator, and parent of student-athletes, this is the wrong message to children on so many different fronts.

In talking to hundreds of college coaches, as well as professional sports organizations nationwide in an array of different sports, these qualities of adaptability and versatility are what they look for, along with coachability, teamwork, and willingness to sacrifice their own self-interests for the betterment of the team. As coaches, we should

---

[103] The University of Texas was, and continues to be, a powerhouse in NCAA Swimming. Two contributors to this book, Betsy Mitchell and BJ Bedford-Miller, hold many distinguished records and noteworthy accomplishments at UT.

work to prepare all of our players, especially the more advanced athletes, to excel in other positions for future growth and opportunities. Keeping players at one sole position is a disservice to all team members, especially the elite athletes who have a chance to advance to the next level(s).

Take the following scenario: Your most skilled shortstop in softball is a high school All-American. She is far superior on the field in comparison to any of her teammates and opponents. With all of her success as a student-athlete, she is highly sought after and is being recruited by colleges and universities from the SEC, ACC, Big 10, Big 12, or PAC-12.[104] She elects to attend the top-rated university in the country with a full scholarship. All of a sudden, she is a freshman in a new program, and that college's current shortstop is an NCAA All-American. Who is going to play shortstop: the high school All-American with no experience at the collegiate level, or the college All-American who led the team to the College World Series the year before, and who has proven herself at that advanced level? We all know the answer to that question. In situations such as these, which occur more frequently than you may think, if this young freshman wants to get on the field, her experience playing other positions in the past will pay big dividends. The ability to sacrifice one's desires now for future gains needs to be embraced and developed now before it is too late.

This **CV** on **sacrifice** segues right into the next topic of adversity. In both cases, as well as with all of the CV's that I present in this guidebook, they are foundationally progressive from one to the next, and they can only be fully grasped with an identification, demonstration, and retention of the preceding building blocks of **CLD**.

CV #17 Sacrifice: Activities and Drills to increase Retention/Assessment:

- o Have the players think about sports other than the one that you are coaching them in currently, and try and think of where sacrifice for the team goal is necessary (i.e. bunting in baseball, the extra pass in basketball, participating in a certain event in swimming or track and field). Perhaps the sacrifice itself is not the player's best event or skill, but that person is simply the best woman or man

---

[104] The SEC (Southeastern Conference), ACC (Atlantic Coast Conference), Big 12 (Big 12 Conference) and PAC-12 (Pacific Athletic Conference) are viewed as the five most dominant and talent-rich college sports conferences in the country.

for the job. When sacrificing for the betterment of the team, there exists a willingness to put the interest of others above one's self.

o   On a similar note above, instead of applying the importance of sacrifice to sports, have your team think about how **sacrifice** relates to success in business, or family life.

o   Share the exact scenario that I presented above about the high school All-American and the NCAA All-American. Ask your players to think about who the coach is going to play at shortstop, or whatever the preferred position is in your sport. At this point in their **CLD**, they should all have the requisite character values to answer and acknowledge the validity of this analogy as it pertains to their need to learn to play multiple positions, or run or swim a variety of events.

o   Another great team activity for a rain delay is to have the players on your team think about sacrifices that they are going to have to make in life, and perhaps even sacrifices that they have already begun to make in order to be a dedicated and successful student-athlete.

o   If you have access to a projector screen and Internet access at a hotel on the road, get your team together and have them view what I feel is one of the most inspiring commencement addresses of all-time. Naval Admiral William H. McRaven, 9th Commander of U.S. Special Operations Command, gave the 2014 commencement speech at the University of Texas. He covers many of the CVs that I discuss in this guidebook, and one that really stood out to me was the **CV** on **sacrifice**. You can find a transcription of the speech at: www.news.utexas.edu as well as find the 20-minute video on YouTube.

Character Values (17-22):

17. *Sacrifice*

18. *Handling Adversity/Resilience (Grit & Toughness)*

19. *Process Oriented*

20. *Body Language Awareness*

21. *Community Service/Outreach*

22. *Honest Evaluation (Self & Peers)*

BUILDING BLOCK #18: Handling Adversity/Resilience (Grit & Toughness)

Peterson and Seligman (2004, pg. 229) provided the following reference to one of America's most successful individuals in relation to this **CV Handling Adversity/Resilience (Grit & Toughness):**

> *In the summer of 1855, 16-year-old John D. Rockefeller needed a job. He had just completed a three-month course in bookkeeping, and he made a list of the companies in his hometown of Cleveland that might need a bookkeeping assistant. Cleveland was booming with business, but none was willing to take a chance on someone so young and inexperienced. For weeks, Rockefeller spent six days per week walking hot streets in his suit and tie, trying to find work. He was rejected from every business on his list. Rockefeller responded to this potentially crushing setback by simply starting over, requesting interviews from the same firms that had denied him days earlier. Eventually, a produce shipping company executive rewarded Rockefeller's persistence and hired the boy who would become the richest and most powerful*

businessman in the world (see Chernow, 1998, for an account of Rockefeller's job hunting travails).

My contributors to this section are living and breathing testaments to Rockefeller's example of never giving up and facing adversity head on. I want to prepare you now that this section on **CV #18 Handling Adversity/Resilience (Grit & Toughness)** is filled with pearls of wisdom.

David Prince *(Paralympian and World Record Holder in the 400M and 200M)* will enter the blocks first for **CV #18,** and for good reason. His words and his story are remarkably inspiring and motivating testaments to the power of **adversity** and **grit.** I do not say that because of the fact that what he has accomplished in the athletic arena has been done with an amputated right leg below the knee. What impressed me the most about David during our two-hour interview was the simplicity with which he embraces adversity. David led the way under CV #6 on Coachability and growth mindset, and now you will see how **resilience** and **dealing with adversity** go hand-in-hand with one's willingness to grow and learn.

When I asked David about the concept of **overcoming adversity**, I thought for certain that he would point to his right leg. However, in the first two hours of our meeting, David did not even mention his leg, as he does not want anyone to feel sorry for him or think that he is limited in any way. The obvious reason for this is because he is most certainly not.

After spending time with David, the brilliance of his message began to crystalize and come together for me. As I mentioned in the section on coachability, David's *modus operandi* is, *"I am either going to win, or I am going to learn. I can never lose."* While I was sitting there with David waiting for him to talk about how tough it is to be a world-class athlete (let alone track star) with an amputated leg, David was on a different level with respect to **adversity.** In David's mind, true growth can only be accomplished through the trials and tribulations of adversity. Whereas most of us do anything in our power to steer clear of adversity, David looks it straight in the eye each and every day and he not only accepts it, but rather, he embraces it.

David used the analogy of the traveling salesperson who goes door to door selling his product in order to make a living. The law of averages tells us that for every door that closes in the salesperson's face with a "no," that salesperson is one step closer to the next "yes." When David decided that he was going to commit to training himself to become a competitive world-class track and field athlete, after the motorcycle accident that left him with an amputated leg, he did not see the fruits of his labor for many years. He stated, *"It took over five years of losing in order to make my first team* (Team USA). *Nothing was easy and there was a lot of pain throughout the process. That is where I developed my attitude toward failure. Actually, I feel that there is no such thing as failure; it is simply one more step toward success!"*

David is approached on a regular basis by fans of the sport of track and field, as well as those whom he comes in contact with just walking down the street. They tell him how inspiring he is to them for persevering through what many may see as a limitation. To this, David explains:

> *I am definitely not trying to be inspiring. I am just working with what I have. There is nothing easy about having one leg. I would give anything to have my leg back. It is hard. When I wake up in the morning, I have to put on a cold leg. But, I definitely don't want anyone to feel sorry for me. When someone tells me at the store that I am an inspiration to them simply because I am walking around with a prosthetic leg, I tell them, 'you should see me run.'*

That is an understatement if I have ever heard one. Watching David come out of the blocks and take off running is not only inspiring, but remarkably motivating.

-Malaika Underwood *(Current Captain & 10-year Member of Team USA Women's Baseball Team; Medalist in five World Cups; Full Scholarship Volleyball Player at the University of North Carolina, Chapel Hill; High School 3-Sport athlete, including baseball):*

Malaika has had the opportunity to demonstrate **resilience** and **grit** throughout her athletic career. First off, Malaika made it very clear to me that she never would have had the strength and courage to persevere the way she did without the support of terrific parents, for whom she has the utmost respect and appreciation. You see, Malaika was born and raised in the sports crazy county of San Diego, California, where legendary baseball players such as Ted Williams and Tony Gwynn have streets, restaurants, and sports arenas named in their honor. Malaika took to baseball at the youngest of ages, despite it being a sport played primarily by boys. She had a knack and passion for the game that continues to fuel her competitive spirit today into her mid-30s. I could immediately relate to Malaika's story and struggles to continue to play the sport that she loved so dearly due to being a girl, or young woman. My sister Christy had a similar talent and affinity for the game of baseball. However, she was marginalized and steered away from her passion by the general public while still in the developing stages of Little League. I was filled with hope after hearing Malaika's travails, and I had a feeling it would conjure up tears of inspiration for not only my own sister, but also a great number of young boys and girls across the country. Here is part of Malaika Underwood's story of **perseverance**, **toughness**, and **grit**:

> *Despite my parents' support, by the time I was 13-years-old, the pressure to play softball grew as other people, mostly coaches and friends' parents, said I should switch for the chance to earn a college scholarship. It felt like the whole world had their own plans for my future. So, I took the matter into my own hands and wrote a letter to the baseball coach at every high school I could possibly attend – public, private, charter – because it didn't matter to me where I went as long as I got a fair chance to play baseball.*

Here is a replica of the letter that Malaika took the initiative to send out to a number of head baseball coaches in San Diego County leading into her freshman year of high school, in hopes of finding just one who would give her a fair chance to earn her way into the baseball program. Keep in mind, she wrote this letter as an eighth grader:

Dear Coach,

My name is Malaika Underwood. I am interested in attending your school. I am in the eighth grade and am presently attending O'Farrell Community School: Center for Advanced Academic Studies. I am in the process of choosing what high school I would like to attend.

I am a young lady 14 years of age. I am interested in playing baseball, not softball! Last year, I played on the Chollas Lake Senior Minor Team for 13- and 14-year-olds. I am a pitcher and second basewoman. Last year, I batted third in the order, hitting .557. We played a total of 25 games, I had 61 at bats and 34 hits. I made no errors at second and had an ERA of 1.85 as a pitcher. I presently play for the Chollas Lake Senior Major team for 14- and 15-year-olds. We are currently playing games. We will start the Tournament of Champions in about a week. After the Tournament, I will begin games for All-Stars.

Now that you know a little about me, I would like to let you know that I don't expect some special placement or treatment, but I do expect a fair chance.

I would like to know if you have anything against women playing on your high school team? Has any girl tried out for your high school football and/or baseball team? Has any girl ever made the team?

I would appreciate if you would write me with the answers to these questions and anything you would like to tell me about the school, yourself, the athletic program at your school, or your team.

Thanks for taking the time to read and reply to my letter.

—Malaika Underwood (1994)

After a variety of responses to my letter that included indirect no's, contact information for the softball coach, a few maybes, and even fewer yeses, I landed at La Jolla High School. In my estimation, La Jolla High Coach Bob Allen had been the most open to the idea and the most honest when he said, 'If you're good enough to play, you'll make the team.' That was all I asked. I would go on to play two years of junior varsity and two years of varsity baseball for the La Jolla High Vikings.

The process of writing the letter and trying to convince baseball coaches to give me a fair shot taught me a lot about myself and about the positive things that can come of unwavering determination. Maybe 13 or 14 seems like a young age to face these types of challenges, doubt, and adversity head on, but this early lesson has served me time and time again – in other sports endeavors, in academics, and in my professional career.

I was lucky enough to excel in other sports in high school and, by my junior year, I had received a number of college scholarship offers for volleyball and basketball. Ultimately, I would accept a volleyball scholarship to UNC Chapel Hill (1999-2003). But, as luck would have it, I would stumble on the opportunity to play baseball again. In 2006, after I finished graduate school at UNC and while working for the UNC Development Office, I found out that USA Baseball was based in Cary, North Carolina and they were hosting open tryouts for their Women's National Team. The team would compete in the second International Baseball Federation Women's World Cup in Taiwan later that year.

I jumped at the opportunity to get back into baseball, and there is no doubt in my mind that the lesson I learned about determination helped me focus in on what had to be done to make the team. That summer, we beat Japan in the gold medal game. I've been fortunate to play on the USA Baseball Women's National Team every year since. It has been an honor representing my country on the baseball field over the past 10 years.

Malaika's story speaks to the soul of sports, and I love the fact that she is a true ambassador for the value of embracing being a student-athlete. Malaika made the most of her educational experience at the University of North Carolina, Chapel Hill, where she earned an undergraduate degree in International Studies and a Master's degree in Sports Administration. Along with being the team captain of the USA Baseball Women's National Team, which is currently ranked number two in the world, she also works as Vice President, Licensing for The Brandr Group, LLC.

One of Malaika's Team USA teammates, and another contributor to my guidebook, **Jenna Marston** *(2-time Team USA Sportswoman of the Year, among many other notable accomplishments)*, first informed me about Malaika's inspiring story. It has been said that if you really want to know about a person's character, the truest witness is from a teammate who has worked side-by-side with him or her on the field of battle. Here is what Jenna had to say about Malaika:

She is an extremely talented athlete, but more importantly, she is an all-around great person and leader. She is basically the face of the women's baseball team, and I honestly cannot say enough about her. She burns with a competitive fire, but she still maintains that character that you are talking about in your guidebook. Long story short, I have an incredible amount of respect for Malaika Underwood, and I am certain that you will not find anyone with a better combination of character and competitiveness.

Jenna's statement regarding the high quality and consummate example of her teammate's character is summed up in Malaika's final remarks to me regarding her contribution to my book:

I hope your guidebook inspires all types of people and, to whatever degree my story touches people, I am thankful. I've never regarded myself as an activist or role model. As a matter of fact, for a long time, I just put my head down and focused on playing, because that's what I love to do. But, at this point in my life, I realize that if I don't tell my story, nobody will hear it. And, maybe, just maybe, somebody needs to hear it.

-Mr. Jeremy Peterson *(Served as a Ranger in the United States Army for six years; Fought in the Second Gulf War in Iraq; Third Degree Black Belt; Current Youth Coach/Mentor):*

Mr. Jeremy, as his karate students refer to him, had a "rough upbringing" to say the least. Because of this, he is the only sibling in his family who still communicates with his parents. His brother ended up walking away from a bright future in professional baseball as a pitcher when he ripped his potential contract to shreds in front of a professional baseball scout in order to prove a message to his parents that he was done with the pressures that his father had put on him in sports. His brother has never returned home, nor has he communicated with his father ever since (over 25 years ago). Despite his rough upbringing, Mr. Jeremy found a way to find a silver lining in it all, which has allowed him to embrace adversity and form his unshakeable resolve, **grit**, and **toughness**. Here is what Mr. Jeremy told me during our one-on-one interview:

*I am who I am today because of my father. I know it wasn't the best way for youth to learn because he was especially harsh and critical, but the qualities of knowing how to **persevere through adversity** and the discipline that I have had in my life make me who I am.*

I have learned that life is more about losing than winning. I don't mean that in a depressing way. What I mean is that who we are is often molded by losing and our struggles and failures. Go ahead and find a book on success written by someone who did nothing but succeed. You won't find one.

Through a great deal of hard work, I earned my Eagle Scout with all three palms.[105] The discipline and resilience that I learned from my father is why I earned that. My father made me stay with it. If he had left that completely up to me, I would have quit many times over. It is because of him that I stuck with it. When I was 19-years-old entering Ranger school in the Army, which is an intense leadership program, I was immediately promoted to the rank

---

[105] Eagle Scout with all three palms is the highest level of a scout. The rank of Eagle Scout and palm requirements must be earned prior to one's 18th birthday.
http://usscouts.org/advance/boyscout/bsrank8.asp

of PFC because of my Eagle Scout status. It meant that I knew something about perseverance and sticking with things.

I asked Mr. Jeremy about his decision to enter the Army at the age of 18, as well as the many life lessons that he learned during his six years of service to his country.

I went to the Army angry and anxious to get away from my family turmoil. Once I was there, I realized that I could not leave because I needed it as much as the Army needed me. I made up my mind from the outset to enter a special Army Ranger training program. I started my Ranger program in basic training, and then entered advanced infantry training, followed by RIP (Ranger Indoctrination Program). From there, I joined the 82nd Airborne Division.

Ranger school was intense like nothing I had ever done before. I will never forget during one of my first days in training the commanding officer approached a young baby-faced kid in my platoon and asked the kid's age. The commander was shocked to find out that he was 19 years old. He then asked me how old I was. I responded that I was 19-years-old as well, followed by 'Sir.' After giving me a double take in disbelief that I was also only 19-years-old, he responded, 'Boy, you have had a hard life.' Yes, I had, and being in the Army for six years was a very challenging but rewarding time in my life.

I watched grown men cry at night because they wanted out; they no longer wanted to be part of the awful realities of war. They did not want to be that person anymore. It was indeed rough.

It was not more than a few weeks after I was sent home in 1992 for a health issue that a platoon that I would have certainly been a part of was sent in to Somalia for 'Operation Black Serpent.' The entire platoon was wiped out. Three soldiers who I went through basic training with had been killed in that mission.

Because of a health issue, after six years of serving our country, Mr. Jeremy was served his separation papers from the Army. He had returned to civilian life a new man with many life lessons and newly acquired skills. As he told his story, it was obvious that he continues to be driven to make a positive impact with the second chance that he has been given. To this day, Mr. Jeremy has been mentoring and guiding the lives of youth in his hometown, where he has undoubtedly influenced more lives than his strong, caring, and humble self would ever boast or brag about.

As you can see from all three of the moving narratives shared in this section, **adversity** can either break us or make us stronger. Let's work together as coaches and parents of student-athletes to build a sense of **toughness**, **grit**, and **resilience** in our children through the vehicle of sports. In order for this to happen, we have to be willing to allow them to fail and even, fall at times. This does not mean caring less; it actually takes more love and compassion to allow them to fall, and then allow them to pick themselves up. This also does not mean that we are not going to be close by to give them the affection and support they need. However, our hope should be that as student-athletes reach this advancing level of **CLD** that they will know how to get back up, dust themselves off, and get back in the race. Grit and toughness are formed by facing challenges head on, and not shying away from **adversity**. All three of my contributors in this section have learned to embrace **adversity** as a chance to grow stronger, rather than running away from their problems or responsibilities.

Unfortunately, for many men in America today, the **toughness**, **grit**, **integrity**, and **discipline** that it takes to face **adversity** head on are clearly lacking when it comes to their greatest responsibility: being a dad. The lack of a father figure in the lives of our youth has become an unfortunate epidemic throughout our country that has pervaded our homes. In Chapter 6, during CV #5 Appreciation/Care for Others, I broached the topic of the shrinking visibility of father figures in American homes. As previously mentioned, more than 24 million children grow up without an active presence from their biological father, many of whom have no father figure whatsoever. Men who add to this alarming statistic represent the "character illiterate" individuals who were either never taught, or were unable to grasp, these character values of caring for others and the importance of **dealing with adversity**, which stimulate positive character growth. Facing adversity head on and overcoming challenges and difficulties create better men, better women, and a better society. However, if the sole value that our youth is learning through sports is the benefit of winning, then we, as coaches, parents, and administrators of sports, are missing out on the "teachable moments" that create lifelong lessons.

Life is not always easy, and rarely ever does it go according to our own game plan. We have a duty to teach and emulate the requisite skills needed to persevere, such as **toughness**, **grit**, **care**, and **concern for others** through athletics. There is no better vehicle, in my mind, than the venue of sports from which to do so, but we have to be *deliberate* and *intentional* with our emphasis on **CLD**.

CV #18 Handling Adversity/Resilience (Toughness): Activities and Drills to increase Retention/Assessment:

- ○ Here, again, is another terrific opportunity to open up a dialogue with your players or children about the overlapping values between sports and life. The message could be as simple and powerful as never "quit" something in the middle of a season. When things get tough, or they don't get along with all of the teammates, they need to learn to persevere and battle through them. (Now, there are extenuating circumstances when safety or physical/emotional harm trumps the loyalty and stick-to-it-tiveness). In a job, they may not like their boss or a co-worker, but they need to find a way to work together despite differences in opinion or taste.

- ○ I recently heard about and watched the **Invictus Games** that took place in May of 2016 in Orlando, Florida. The Invictus Games were created by Great Britain's Prince Henry as an international event to honor, celebrate, and support the athletic pursuits of excellence by injured war veterans. I recommend that any coach and his or her team stayed tuned in for the next Invictus Games in order to witness the honor, bravery, **perseverance**, and **grit** on display by true heroes.

- ○ Share the example that I provided to start this CV on Rockefeller's **grit**.

- ○ Share an example of the way life works in nature. For example, a tree curves, contours, and adapts in order to stretch toward the light. It is constantly bending and reaching outward. That is what we as human beings need to do.

- ○ Talk about the **resilience** that it took for President Lincoln to become the President of the United States, and all that he was able to accomplish in his tenure.

- ○ When your players think that they have had to endure some tough times to get to where they are in sports, share the story of **grit** and determination from Malaika Underwood to follow her dreams.

- ○ Life will oftentimes throw us curveballs. The more that your teams and student-athletes learn to adjust and adapt, while continuing to move forward, the better. A fun and carefree activity to play with your team is the "Adjustment Game."

This is a game that I learned from my brother Mack, who I mentioned earlier is also a youth coach. I actually play this in my public speaking classes to help get my students out of their shells a bit, and to tap into their creative minds. The way it works is that you have a player/student come to the front of the group. You then ask them a question, such as: "Tell us all about your favorite vacation." As the individual is telling his or her story, you are confirming with a "yes" throughout. However, as he/she gets rolling, you interject a "no." For every "no," the individual now has to adjust his/her story without getting flustered, and simply go with the flow. It is fun to hear how creative they become, and how they are able to react on the fly. Try it, as it is always entertaining.

CHARACTER
LOVES
COMPANY

<u>Character Values (17-22):</u>

17. *Sacrifice*

18. *Handling Adversity/Resilience*

19. **Process Oriented**

20. *Body Language Awareness*

21. *Community Service/Outreach*

22. *Honest Evaluation (Self & Peers)*

BUILDING BLOCK #19: **Process Oriented**

"Excellence is not an act, but a habit." –Aristotle

Being **process oriented** involves both sacrifice (putting off immediate satisfaction for long-term results), as well as learning how to fight through the adversity of tough times (mental fortitude), toughness, and grit. As the revered philosopher Aristotle points out, excellence is not a one-time event, but rather a habit or process. As it relates to sports, many great coaches will work to instill a message of "trusting the process" rather than focusing exclusively on the end result.

Mental toughness is an imperative prerequisite to becoming and maintaining a **process driven approach** to all aspects of life. The three courageous contributors to the previous section (**David Prince, Malaika Underwood,** and **Jeremy Peterson**) all have had to fight through difficulties and extremely challenging road blocks along their paths to excellence. However, they trusted the process, despite not seeing the immediate desired results. As parents and coaches, we have to be role models in this regard, which can take a great deal of patience, discipline, and grit on our part to hold on to and follow a **process oriented** approach to coaching and mentoring.

As a coach/mentor himself, as well as a devoted father, I asked **David Prince** *(Paralympian and World Record Holder in 400M & 200M)* if there was a specific message that we had not discussed that he wanted to share with young student-athletes, and/or the parents and coaches of such athletes. Here is an interesting perspective from David:

To children: Playing sports is a lot like playing video games. You have to keep trying until you figure out how to do it right, how to do it better. That is how you advance from one stage to the next. It is about learning from previous mistakes and staying with it until you conquer it. We all have the ability to work to figure things out.

To parents and coaches: Kids know how to persevere through difficult stages and challenges. They do not mind having to fight through adversity. To pass a certain stage or win a game, they will stay at it for 20 or 40 or even 200 times. If it is something that they enjoy doing, they will stick with it.

I love this message from David because it is a wake-up call to all coaches and parents that we need to remember that we are working with children, and we have to adapt and find ways to make it fun. If that means tapping into the video game culture through the use of video analysis or references to popular teen culture, then so be it. However, we cannot make them love what we loved and we cannot do it for them. It dawned on me as David was discussing the topic of the video game culture that perhaps that is why young people enjoy them so much—because it is their thing! That took me all the way back to what **Betsy Mitchell** *(Olympic champion)* praised her parents for in CV #1, which was allowing swimming to be her thing, and not their thing.

As coaches, we need to do a better job of helping our student-athletes see the relevance of sports to other areas of life and to their future growth. As was discussed in CV #18 on adversity, children (actually, all of us) learn so much from their mistakes. David's point here is a salient one that sheds light on why today's youth enjoys video games. They have to progress through the process themselves, and they love it. Now, I am not endorsing the gamers (as everything should be done in moderation). Kids, do not tell your parents that Coach P. said it was okay for me to stay up all night in order to conquer the game. However, we do need to translate that "never give up mentality" to all walks of life.

The million-dollar question that you are most likely asking yourself or tearing your hair out over is, "*How do we do this?*" My next contributor is an expert and, literal, master at this who has 35-years of experience from which to draw. **Master Boon Brown** *(Master Instructor; 5th Degree Black Belt; Long-time youth coach/mentor)* has been **process minded** in his philosophy and approach to teaching his students life lessons that will remain with them long after they earn their black belts. Here, Master Brown shares some of his proven techniques to help young student-athletes become more **process oriented** and accepting to instruction:

> *Most parents have the desire to do what is best for their kids but they do not have the tools, or the understanding of how to do what is best for their kids in the long run.*
>
> *What we do to deal with this, or to empower more coachable kids here* [at Ancient Ways Martial Arts Academy] *is 'Praise, Correct, Praise.' Say I have a kid with his hands down too low, and I come up as the instructor and say, 'Put your hands up.' So, what he is going to do is put his hands up, and then when I walk by, he is going to stick his tongue out at me or worse. He is not going to respect me and he is going to think that he is a poor student. Often, this could not be further from the truth. Simply, what he is doing needs correction, but in his mind, what he is doing is bad and I am mean. So, what I instinctively do now is say, 'Wow, Joe, I really like your stance; it's really strong. You've got your black belt focus straight ahead! Now, let's bring those hands up just a little bit.' [Student brings up hands.] 'Now, that looks better. Give me a high five. Now you look like a warrior!' I have made it a habit of doing this so instinctively that I do it now without having to really think about it.*

As Master Brown went through his process of student correction, or constructive criticism, I could vividly see a young 13-14-year-old's demeanor completely changing for the better simply through what he masterfully refers to as the praise, correct, praise technique.

> *We also do what is referred to as 'proximity praise.' So, say we have a kid over here who is just totally out of it and I cannot find anything to praise because he is so out of control and unfocused. I will look at the kid next to him and say, 'Wow! Everyone, check out Jimmy's warrior stance.' All of a sudden, Joey next to him has refocused and fixed his own positioning, and he is back on track. Proximity praise really works, even with a group. Simply say, 'I love*

the focus or energy from this side of the room,' and all of a sudden, the other side steps it up and now you have an entire room locked in.

We also have what we call 'spotlighting,' which is when we have the whole group stop what they are doing and take a knee. Then, I will point out what Kayla is doing well. It is a little breather for the group, and it makes Kayla feel great. Most importantly, it allows everyone to see exactly what I am talking about with the technique, and hopefully next time they want the example to be from them. These are practices that we use in the martial arts field, and they work.

So, now, with someone a bit older in age, or an adult, in general, we have another approach that is highly effective, that I call 'PPCP,' which is 'Praise, Permission, Correct, Praise.' Let's say that I have an elite student on the floor, and they are doing some great front kicks. However, they are not recoiling it very well. So, I might say, 'Hey, really great front snap kicks, and I like how your hands are working, but can I give you one tip to make it even better?' If you have established that agreement of respect, they are not going to say 'no.' They always say 'yes.' Then I follow up with, 'Well, try to get a bit more recoil on that kickback.' Now, what have I done? I have treated them with respect, and I am much more likely to continue to get such positive behaviors and improvements because of that. Afterwards, give them the final praise and maybe a high five and you are moving on. That is PPCP—praise, permission, correct, praise.

Master Brown and I then began to discuss transferrable skills learned in martial arts that could easily be incorporated into more traditional sports. He told me about a parent of one of his karate students who ran a tennis academy in Florida. This individual was enamored by how engaged and excited his own son was to go to karate practice three days per week, yet many of his students seemed to lack that same enthusiasm for tennis. This tennis instructor began to take note of the various forms and combinations that Master Brown and his instructors were teaching his son and the rest of the students. There was no ball to hit, kick, or throw, yet these martial arts students were locked in and focused on the key movement patterns that they worked at tirelessly and without complaint.

This tennis coach approached Master Brown and asked him if he thought it would be possible to apply such a routine to other sports, such as tennis. Here was Master Brown's response:

I said that he could absolutely apply this to tennis. I explained to him how a fighting combination (or Kata) is just like the sequences that occur in many other sports. Start with the serve and then what comes next? The man said, 'Well, it depends... you could do one of two things: You could rush the net to take away the angle on the return, or you could stay back looking for a return.' Okay, I told him that he could simulate a serve and return kata, a rush the net kata, a doubles kata, and now the kids are going to learn and they don't even need an opponent. They are going to move and they are going to work on their tennis kata. And, you know what, he did just that.

He also loved the idea of the belt system that martial arts utilizes as one progresses and develops through levels. The reward system keeps people motivated and moving forward. So, he thought about putting hand grips with different colors on the tennis rackets, so you start off with white and then go on to yellow, etc. I think a lot could be gained from the reward system of martial arts and applying it to other sports. I suggested to a local aerobics instructor to try that same reward system out with his classes. He started giving out different color wrist bands and suddenly his retention went up. The reward system has to be built in there for motivational purposes. It makes a big difference for people.

Our approach is to empower the kids through the reward system. Kids don't have to be perfect at the early stages to advance to the next level, but if he or she is not trying, then that is not okay with me and there are many times when students will not pass the belt test. Once you get closer to earning that black belt, now you have to be close to perfect, but they have been trained to understand that and they know how to achieve it. The higher expectations are there.

Try out these pearls of wisdom from a Master Instructor, as coaches and parents across the country can use these to make sports more fun and rewarding. These are proven methods to give constructive criticism, but in ways that empower kids rather than techniques of breaking them down. Our ultimate goal should be to help each and every young student-athlete whom we are fortunate to coach and mentor. If we can get through to them and relate to them using any and all of these techniques that Master Brown suggests, then we have a good chance of helping them improve and grow. You even see this concept in play at the highest levels of NCAA DI college football through the helmet decal system. For instance, if an Ohio State football player makes a noteworthy play, he is rewarded with a Buckeye decal to put on his helmet. Players take a great deal of pride in that type of reward system knowing that their play contributed to the team's ultimate success.

At the end of the day, if student-athletes feel as if their participation in sports is worthwhile, and that it helps them develop as an athlete and person, then there is a strong likelihood that they will stick with it and continue to value their sports involvement. If you choose the option of unnecessary roughness and you are overly critical, then your student-athletes will shut down and shut you out. If this is constantly the case, then sooner or later, they will say enough is enough and leave sports altogether.

To become adept at anything, we have to struggle to figure it out for a while. As **David Prince** described, the video game expert does not acquire mastery in one or two tries. They struggle at it and they make adjustments based on past miscues. And, guess what, they love it! If you think that children cannot be **process oriented** enough to stick with something and figure it out on their own, then you have obviously never sat and watched them play video games for hours on end. They will get defeated over and over, yet they keep at it. Why? The answer is because it is fun and for the thrill of a tough challenge. As coaches or parents working with our youth in sports, let's work to encourage the **process minded** approach that is needed to succeed in any endeavor. The key is to give guidance, but to still allow them to make it their own when helping them connect the dots between the **process** and the desired results.

CV #19 Process Oriented: Activities and Drills to increase Retention/Assessment:

- o Ask your players to think about the quote by Aristotle at the outset of this chapter: *"Excellence is not an act, but a habit."* Have them write in their journals for a few minutes on what that statement means to them and how it relates to their **process** of improvement in their sport. A good follow-up question is to ask them to think about the progress that they have seen during this season, as well as what areas they will improve most if they keep "**trusting the process**."

- o A good take-home activity in terms of **trusting the process** is to have your student-athletes do some research on "watering the bamboo." In order for bamboo to show signs of life and growth, one has to water it every day for two years. There is typically no growth for a full two years. This is a great analogy and lesson for growth in sports, as well as in life. This will teach our rising generation about the importance of reaping what you sow.

o   As Paralympian and World Record Holder in the 200M and 400M, David Prince, points out, children do know how to **work the process**. They do it every day, sometimes for hours, as they play video games. Though I am not a big proponent of video games, I have observed in amazement as some of my players sat locked in like a fighter pilot, conquering stage-by-stage, paying attention to the fine details that it takes to learn and adapt in order to conquer the game. Because many young people love playing video games, we need to tap into that passion and find ways to use a **process oriented** approach in the athletic arena or classroom.

o   A valuable activity at this level is to practice the "college coach: player interview" with each player individually at this 14-16-year-old range and above. Help them gain a better understanding of what college coaches are looking for in recruits. This is a great activity as student-athletes will get better and better at this with practice and from your coaching tips. The biggest mistake that I have seen parents make is that they try to do all of the talking for their son or daughter with the college coaches. This stunts the process of growth for student-athletes who are aspiring to play in college. College coaches are turned off by the recruits who cannot speak for themselves. However, this takes repetitive practice. I have heard parents tell me that they feel that they cannot resist the urge to speak for their son or daughter because they are much better at saying all the right things. Well, actually, that could not be further from the truth. Such parents could also do their son or daughter's science project for them, but in the end, how does that prepare their child for success in life?

o   If you are a junior high or high school coach, you could devise a decal reward system based on whichever measurements you find to be important. As Coach Wooden says, what we emphasize gets improved upon. You could do what I did when I was a DIII head baseball coach trying to motivate my players to "buy in" to the team concept. I created an 11x17 laminated card stock board for each player. My assistant coaches and I then put them up on the outside of their lockers (obviously, they each did not have their own helmet as football players do). I then came up with ten different decals for big plays such as: "SAC" for a sacrifice bunt or sacrifice fly, a lightning bolt for sparking a rally, or a "GC" for a game-changing play. As a coach, you can have fun with it, but from a **CLD** standpoint, there has to be a character/teamwork component to the decals. For instance, in football, to emphasize **integrity** or **compassion,** a player could be rewarded a decal for a big-time crushing tackle followed by the same player helping his opponent back up off the turf after the end of the play. Such a sign of **sportspersonship** could be rewarded with a decal. There is nothing "soft" or "weak" about a linebacker lighting up an opposing ball carrier and then showing respect for his opponent by helping him back up in order to line up and have the challenge of doing it again on the next play.

o   To add more buy in from your student-athletes on the **process** of doing things the correct way, or team way, have them work in pairs to each come up with a specific decal and then have the duo present their idea to the team. You could take it a step further and have them go home and design the artwork for the decals. The cost is very minimal for the internal rewards of seeing your players begin to see how paying attention to the minor details of the game leads to better overall performance over the long haul.

o   Emphasize to your student-athletes that at this age-range the current "best" players can have a tendency to become content with their abilities and, thus, they stop working the **process** of getting better. The player who is driven by a purpose of improving a little bit each day oftentimes surpasses those early bloomers. Take Michael Jordan who, in my mind, is the greatest basketball player of all time. We all know the story—he was cut from his team in high school as a freshman. Imagine if he would have stopped working the process?

Character Values (17-22):

17. *Sacrifice*

18. *Handling Adversity/Resilience*

19. *Process Oriented*

20. *Body Language Awareness*

21. *Community Service/Outreach*

22. *Honest Evaluation (Self & Peers)*

BUILDING BLOCK #20: **Body Language Awareness**

Over the past 15 years as a coach, **body language awareness** has become one of my biggest emphases. I wish that I would have had a coach work with me on this when I was young because I know that it could have benefitted my outward and inward perception, and, inevitably, my performance. As the head baseball instructor and camp coordinator for many years at IMG, the world's most prestigious youth sports training grounds, I would always take the opportunity to impress upon the thousands of baseball campers who arrived on campus each summer the importance of their **non-verbal communication**. I wanted them to become more aware of the message that their **body language** was giving to the outside world. I have found that the mid-teenage range is the most appropriate age to receive, comprehend, and retain this important message. These formative years are also where the worst displays of **body language**, in regards to respect, humility, and dealing with adversity, are outwardly manifested.

Body language awareness has a close correlation with CV #16 on confidence, as you will see from the expertise shared from my first contributor.

-Dr. Angus Mugford *(Director of High Performance, Toronto Blue Jays & Special Assistant to the General Manager; Former Performance Institute Director at IMG Academy for 13+ years):*

Prior to Angus joining the Toronto Blue Jays' organization as the Director of High Performance in 2015, he worked closely on the performance and mental side of sports development training with elite-level tennis players at IMG Academy. I had the opportunity to spend a couple of hours with Angus at the Toronto Blue Jays spring training complex in Dunedin, Florida in March of 2016. I asked Angus to share his expertise on non-verbal communication and **body language awareness.** Here is what **Dr. Angus Mugford** revealed about the power of body language:

> *One's body language was always important to me while I was at IMG. You definitely see it in the world of tennis. Tennis is a brutal sport when it comes to this concept, especially at the junior level. If you want to see examples of good body language and bad body language, look no further than tennis. It is a grind from point to point. Then you look at the greats over the past few decades—from Pete Sampras, to Nadal, to Federer—they are all examples of **positive body language.** It was tough to tell whether they won or lost the point. Body language can drive the positivity of your own thinking, as well as communicate exactly how you feel to your opponent. Awareness of this and emphasizing the importance of it is necessary for the players in the Blue Jays organization, too.*

> *It is either a threat or a challenge, and it is simply the way that you look at something. If you see adversity as a threat, then the most common result is going to be a negative response leading to increased tension. If you see each at-bat, or point, as a challenge, then your body is going to respond differently. You have got to be loose and relaxed in order to increase physical performance—it is an opportunity to be excited about.*

Wow, where was Angus when I was playing? His comments on how to maximize performance by taking control of one's response to the inevitability of adversity brought me back to David Prince's philosophy: *"I either win, or I learn. I can never lose."*

Angus referred to an excellent book co-authored by a friend of his, Ashley Merryman, called *Top Dog: The Science of Winning and Losing.*[106] This book discusses the concept of how the way one views something can have a lasting effect (either positive or

---

[106] *Top Dog: The Science of Winning and Losing* was written by Bronson and Merryman (2013).

negative) along with many other relevant topics on motivation and competition in the world of sports, academia, and business.

During our dialogue, Angus also referenced the works of Dr. Amy Cuddy, a Harvard Business School professor, who discusses the psychological and physiological reaction from your body language, and how science shows that there is nothing fake about one's body language when it comes to performance. Cuddy has written multiple articles, as well as a 2015 bestseller on this topic entitled: *Presence: Bringing Your Boldest Self to Your Biggest Challenges*. Cuddy is probably best known for her 2012 Ted Talk:[107] "Your Body Language Shapes Who You Are." During her talk, she discussed the power of body language control and awareness. She states, *"We are influenced by our own non-verbals. It is about opening up…Our bodies change our minds. Our minds change our behaviors. And our behavior changes our outcomes."*

Cuddy goes on to talk about how power poses such as the "Wonder Woman" or "Superman" pose can significantly increase testosterone which raises one's confidence levels. At the same time, and equally beneficial, these poses lower cortisol levels, which affect stress levels when faced with adverse situations. There is an inverse relationship between testosterone and cortisol, as they work in opposite directions. Dr. Cuddy says that all someone needs to increase positive testosterone and decrease negative cortisol is their body, some privacy, and a few moments prior to a big job interview, in the on-deck circle, awaiting a free throw, or in the waiting area before a race. We all need to find our best power pose.

Here, Angus shares his agreement on the concept of the power pose, as well as a first-hand recount of the role that **body language** plays in performance and success:

> These power poses are about awareness of the message your body is sending. The classic thing about confidence is that most people base confidence on results, whereas your most effective confidence needs to be in the absence of results. It takes courage and confidence to have a game plan. Everyone is going to have negative thoughts, but how you have prepared your game plan is what is important. An example would be going into an exam—you have studied and you are prepared for it. Now, you combine that preparation with effective body language [i.e. a

---

107 Cuddy's 2012 Presentation entitled: "Your Body Language Shapes Who You Are," is the second most watched Ted Talk. You can find her talk at the following link: https://www.ted.com/talks/amy_cuddy_your_body_language_shapes_who_you_are?language=en

power pose] and you are setting the chemical conditions to be at your best. After all, sport is not about who is the best player, but performing the best when it counts.

I have a great example for you about body language. Picture the 16-year-old tennis prodigy, who is the best in the world for his or her age. When that individual enters the professional side, they are now a boy in a man's world or girl in a woman's world.

Angus saw this situation play out right in front of his eyes. More often than not, the end result of the first few years of the scenario of boy or girl meets world is one of great trials and tribulations. However, tennis star Kei Nishikori had been trained at IMG Academy where Angus had worked closely with him and seen him grow since he was a 13-year-old boy. Kei Nishikori is now one of the top tennis players in the world (bringing home the bronze medal in the 2016 Olympic Games in Rio de Janeiro).

The year was 2008 and it was Kei's first U.S. Open (at only 18- or 19-years-old). He had advanced to the third round now and he was competing against the number four player in the world, David Ferrer. It was a classic New York late night match at Louis Armstrong Stadium[108] that went all the way to the fifth set. Many had ruled him out, as they felt that the kid had no business being on the court, but Kei didn't buy into it.

Angus shared how the commentators continuously stated how impressive it was to see Kei appear to be unfazed by his more experienced and much higher ranked opponent. In essence, he looked like he belonged. Whether he was faking it until he made it on that night or not, he made it loud and clear for the tennis world through his actions and presence that he had arrived.

Despite playing a veteran who had proven himself many times over, Kei demonstrated the value of practicing for these moments, and all he had to do was fall back on his level of training and that was reflected in his body language and performance. [Nishikori ended up winning the match.]

What I am excited about here with the Blue Jays is translating what I have seen in tennis over the past 15 years with baseball.

The excitement and passion in Angus's voice as he thought back to that night at the U.S. Open more than eight years ago reverberated through the phone. It was obviously a

---

[108] Louis Armstrong Stadium was the third largest U.S. Open Stadium at that time with a capacity of 6,000 fans.

resounding testament and validation to the power of preparation and **body language awareness** for Angus to see this event unfold first-hand.

Coach Amanda Butler *(UF Head Women's Basketball Coach)* is also a strong proponent of the importance of **body language awareness**. As a matter of fact, she actually charts it on a daily basis, as the "power of touch" is extremely important in forming her team's culture. Coach Butler spoke with me about how important non-verbal communication is in her program at the University of Florida:

> *One strategy we use is to find ways to measure the things we value. In many cases, this is very challenging because you are talking about intangibles. One of the things that we started to do that has been very successful for our team is measuring the power of touch. Now, we didn't come up with this. It is something that has been studied in other places, and it is prevalent in a few programs in the NBA. We basically had an individual on our staff at every practice and during every game who charted how many times we supported the team concept through the power of touch; whether it was a high five, or a chest bump, or putting your arm around someone, or patting someone on the leg. Every day, we charted the power of touch and, at the end of practice, we read off those numbers so that everyone knew how well they did at communicating something, and hopefully, in a positive way to their teammates. We also did that in games. It is difficult to find ways to measure everything that we value, but when you do value something, you have to find ways to make it important and to measure if you are improving in that area day to day, game to game, year to year.*

I love Coach Butler's specific focus because it brings so much awareness to her players' body language. Are they sulking at the end of the bench because they blew a layup or because they were benched, or are they creating positive energy through their body language? Nowadays, more so than ever with the egocentric showcase approach to sports, young student-athletes can be easily caught up in their own performance and miss out on the bigger picture of the team. The fact that **body language awareness** is a team emphasis helps student-athletes quickly transition away from their own ego for the sake of something bigger. This awareness will undoubtedly stick with Coach Butler's players and overflow into family life and relationships after sports.

To sum up this **CV** on the influence of **body language awareness**, I return to **Ryan Arcidiacono** *(4-year captain and leader of the 2016 NCAA Men's Basketball National Champion Villanova Wildcats)*. I have to admit that I did not have a chance to watch much of the March Madness NCAA Tournament this year. However, I made an agreement with two young 13-year-old brothers whom I work with in baseball that I would watch some of the finals because Villanova was their team and Ryan Arcidiacono was their favorite player. Now, these two young boys had been well-versed in my interest and passion in character. When I asked them what they liked about Arcidiacono aside from his physical abilities, they had much to say that demanded my interest. They told me that he is a great and true leader, a hard worker, that he is tough, and that he was nice to them and talked with them after games. I liked what I heard, so I agreed to tune in to the finals.

When I turned the game on, it was midway through the second half and the commentators just happened to be talking about Arcidiacono. I can recall them raving about his ability, poise, awareness, floor presence, and leadership, similar to the scene from *Braveheart*[109] when William Wallace's countrymen talk about how they imagined him to be over 7' tall. I was expecting to see a 6'10" point guard like Magic Johnson running the show for Villanova. Now, do not get me wrong, Ryan is put together at 6'4" and 200 pounds, but he plays much bigger than that. In my mind, that is one of the ultimate compliments because it means that one is tapping into his or her full potential and utilizing the intangible characteristics that define greatness. I was impressed with what I saw from Arcidiacono, and I would not be surprised to see him lead his future teams as a professional[110] to many more championships.

CV #20 Body Language Awareness: Activities and Drills to increase Retention/Assessment:

   o   Start with an effective activity in "Power Stance & Statement" building. Lead a team activity where each member of the team has to come up with a 30-second confidence building game plan filled with reminders for strong body language and positive self-talk.

---

[109] Mel Gibson's 1995 blockbuster hit movie, *Braveheart*, depicted a 13th century war hero who defied all odds in fighting for Scotland's independence against King Edward I of England.
[110] Ryan Arcidiacono signed with the San Antonio Spurs of the NBA in 2016.

- The best activity for emphasis and retention of the message of effective body language and awareness is by recording your student-athletes live during pivotal moments in games. Film them just before an event, race, at-bat, free throw, penalty kick, etc. Ask them to critique themselves. Do not allow them to beat themselves up too much, as we can easily become our own worst critics. As Dr. Angus Mugford and the research by Dr. Amy Cuddy emphasized, one's body language (good or bad) will impact not only how others view that person, but how that person views themselves.

  *In order to do this activity, first gain permission from the parents of your student-athletes. It is always critical for parents and coaches to be on the same team, and this would be an excellent way to join forces in emphasizing this important life skill development.

- Another activity that will help young student-athletes to become more conscious of their body language is to have an assistant coach tell a story and pick a few players to watch your mannerisms while sitting on the bench or huddle amongst the other players. The coach will tell the same story three times. The first time you will show mannerisms of the disengaged SA (or player who is too cool to listen). The second time you will portray the rude and bored SA (yawning and checking phone). The third time you will impersonate the SA who is coachable, attentive and fully engaged. Ask the three players standing to notate to the rest of the team who they would want as a player. This drill is both educational, and eye opening for many young SAs.

CHARACTER
LOVES
COMPANY

Character Values (17-22):

17. *Sacrifice*

18. *Handling Adversity/Resilience*

19. *Process Oriented*

20. *Body Language Awareness*

21. *Community Service/Outreach*

22. *Honest Evaluation (Self & Peers)*

BUILDING BLOCK #21: **Community Service/Outreach**

"It is more blessed to give than to receive."–Acts 20: 35 *(New International Bible)*

There are so many uplifting daily examples of giving and **community service** throughout our society, yet many of them go unrecognized simply because the giver is not doing so for outward recognition and glory. Rather, it is the intrinsically inherent reward of helping another in need. However, this innate sense of looking out for one's brother, sister, neighbor, teammate, etc. that we all have buried within us is often suppressed by overwhelming self-pride, egotism, and self-absorption.

When discussing the concept of teaching our children how to get outside themselves, and instead, look to assist another in need, I have actually had parents of overserved[111] student-athletes remark (on multiple occasions) that lifting another up

---

[111] The term "overserved" in this instance is juxtaposed with the term "underserved" defined below. Overserved children in sports are those who have been exposed to any and every avenue from which to increase one's sports development and performance. Overserved student-athletes often have been over-worked, over-exposed, and become disenfranchised with their sport and become burned out.

could have an adverse effect in the long-run for their own child. When I pressed further on each of these occasions, the parents rationalized without hesitation that if another child is given the same access to elite-level training then that individual could potentially take their child's rightly deserved college scholarship. This "character illiteracy" that I speak of can inevitably infiltrate the minds of our youth in sports with selfish, ego-centric, and other counter-intuitive and counter-productive character traits contrary to the true intent of youth and amateur athletics.

As I mentioned from the outset of this guidebook on **CLD**, the many values of sports participation are neither good nor bad in and of themselves, but rather they are the byproduct of the content and delivery system. Currently, many sports theorists have concluded that the derivatives of youth and amateur are not promoting a concern for others in need, but rather a *"get mine at the sake of others mentality."* As coaches, administrators, and parents of youth sports participants, an emphasis on concern and service to others demands our high priority. Here are a couple of great examples on how to get our student-athletes to focus less on self and more on team, community, and their connection with others.

-Dr. Michael Sagas *(Founder of Twinnor; Professor and Chair of the Department of Tourism, Recreation and Sport Management at the University of Florida; Former NCAA DI Student-Athlete):*

In 2015, Dr. Sagas founded Twinnor, a non-profit organization focused on providing for underserved[112] individuals seeking opportunities to grow and advance through their love of sports. The premise behind Twinnor connects back to **CV #5** which is awareness and care for others, as well as many other **CV**s that I have discussed. During our interview, Dr. Sagas explained where his idea originated and how such an approach of assisting others, not just in our own neighborhoods, but around the world, can help return some of the intrinsic values of youth sports:

> *Twinnor is an interesting story. The idea is based on paying it forward[113] and that it is a duty as an athlete (one who gets to play, develop, and benefit from sports) to aid others. It*

---

[112] The use of the term "underserved" has more appropriately replaced the use of the word "underprivileged" over the past decade relating to individuals receiving less than adequate service because of financial circumstances.

[113] To "Pay it Forward" is to give or provide for another without seeking anything extrinsically in return. Rather, the individual who receives the benefit (benefactor) simply seeks out another to return the favor to. So, in essence, they are doing precisely what the phrase implies "paying it forward," rather

should be viewed as a privilege and not an obligation. Twinning is an idea that teaches a character value that is two-fold: pay it forward by reaching out to someone else in need, as well as respecting and appreciating the opportunities that one has.

Twinnor is built on the idea that the legacy created is indeed a one-for-one exchange. The concept is that every kid can adopt (so to speak) and fund or support one other kid, whether it be through equipment needs, league participation fees, or mentoring. It is a way to setup a mentoring system between two individuals to provide positive reinforcement on both sides.

Dr. Sagas and I discussed how the concept of Twinnor is different from Crowdfunding,[114] which is primarily based on financial support.

Twinnor and the concept of Twinning goes beyond the concept of raising money for someone else. Twinning is the pairing of two people for the benefit of both people through social, emotional, and psychological support, while teaching basic life skills. It doesn't have to necessarily be about the money, but about the time and the care towards others.

The concept of Twinning is such a simple yet profound concept. It is truly a two-way street or interaction that Dr. Sagas talks about; it mutually benefits both parties. If the concept of **community service/outreach** is delivered appropriately, it can also help our youth become more cognizant of the blessings in their own lives. As one who has worked with youth and amateur student-athletes closely for nearly two decades, I love the potential of grasping important life lessons through Twinning, especially an understanding that value is not only measured monetarily or extrinsically. I have been part of teams that have worked to build houses for Habitat for Humanity here in the United States, as well as teams that have helped paint houses and a school in the Dominican Republic. Activities such as these enable students to experience the power of giving first-hand.

---

than seeking immediate return on investment. A 2000 hit movie entitled, *Pay it Forward* starring Kevin Spacey was based on this concept. The concept is both inspirational and motivating.
[114] The concept of Crowdfunding has been around for quite some time, however, modern crowdfunding has become popular since the turn of the 21st century as a millennial approach to the means to a financial end. It is similar to Crowdsourcing as a way to generate funds.

An important point to emphasize from Dr. Sagas is that our young student-athletes need to have some "skin in the game"[115] or "sweat equity"[116] in their service to others. We cannot do **community service** for our children. Though it is impactful to donate significant sums of financial support to worthy causes, **outreach**, in this case, needs to come from our children in order for the resonating impact of giving to take root and make a lasting impression. I can visualize a young boy or girl mowing neighborhood lawns all summer long, or working as an umpire or official at the local recreation center, in an effort to earn $200 from which to provide for a "Twin" match in need in his or her own hometown or abroad. What a powerful legacy of paying it forward that such one-on-one exchanges can build in our rising generations.

I think back to a previous contributor, **Addison Staples** *(Founder of multiple non-profit organizations, such as Aces in Action),* who has made it his passion and profession to provide elite sports and life skills training to underserved children throughout the broader Gainesville, Florida area, as well as in many third world countries abroad. Similar to Dr. Sagas's Twinning concept, Addison provides leadership and direction toward the interconnectedness of serving others. Through his non-profits and interaction with youth, he is passing on what he learned from coaches and mentors whose support he needed and valued as a young man.

Perhaps one of the student-athletes under your guidance and mentorship will go on to start a multimillion-dollar company that provides world-wide philanthropy, like Blake Mycoskie, the founder of TOMS.[117] I love what TOMS is doing, as it has that similar one-for-one exchange of Twinnor. In the January-February, 2016 issue of the *Harvard Business Review,* Mycoskie remarked on the competitive advantage that TOMS has in the industry due to its overarching concern for the well-being of others in need. He stated, *"That is our greatest competitive advantage: It allows us to build an emotional bond with*

---

[115] Having "skin in the game" is a reference to the conscientious effort that must be invested into anything for it to feel worthwhile.

[116] "Sweat equity" is another way to look at having "skin in the game." One has created "sweat equity" when they have put forth a great deal of effort and labor to accomplish something. It is an investment in their sweat, hard work, and maybe even blood and tears.

[117] TOMS is a shoe company that started out of an apartment in Southern California built on a vision and purpose to provide for others in need. TOMS has grown into a company with profits upwards of $300 million. The basic premise is that for every pair of TOMS shoes purchased, the company donates a second pair to a child in need, often in third world countries.

customers and motivate employees, because they know they are shopping and working for a movement bigger than themselves."

In the proceeding section, as always, I provide a variety of activities and drills for the reader to utilize to increase retention and provide for measurable assessment of their teams and individual student-athletes. I have listed some of the invaluable organizations that your teams can get involved with for a weekend team building, or season-long, activity. As Dr. Sagas identifies, **community service/outreach** is a blessing to both parties and a true win-win. The overserved population gains perspective and shows care and concern for those who are less fortunate, while the underserved gain access to life-changing opportunities for growth and development.

CV #21 Community Service/Outreach: Activities and Drills to increase Retention/Assessment:

- o The most important approach with **Community Service** and **Outreach** is to get your teams out in the community serving others
- o Charitable Events for student-athletes of all ages:
  - Local Challenger Leagues
  - Miracle League
  - Make a Wish Foundation
  - Canned food drive for Homeless
- o As Student-Athletes get older and more mature"
  - Homeless Shelters
  - Children's hospitals
  - Big Brothers & Big Sisters
  - Animal Shelters
  - Offer sports/tutoring lessons for younger kids
  - Volunteer to umpire (if you want to give your players some perspective)
  - Volunteer to help at B&G Club or YMCA as a coach/mentor

- Team Outreach Concepts that take more Planning on Coach or Parents
  - Take a team trip in HS or College to the Dominican Republic (play three or four games with the local talent, but, more importantly, help build a house through Habitat for Humanity, help with youth camps like I did. It was one of the top five life-changing events in my life, after getting married and having children—it truly was an inspiration.)
  - Something that my brothers and I do with our BAT1000 youth sports development programs is to fundraise to provide for three homeless children from the Union Rescue Mission to take part in our weekend activities in Southern California.
  - Twinning (The student-athletes need to raise the money themselves—maybe through a team car wash to raise $200 for equipment and fees to sponsor a team in Guatemala, for example). Parents cannot simply buy it for them—the message needs to be taught on the intrinsic rewards of sacrificing something (as a team, or individual) and accruing "sweat equity" to provide for others in need. Go to www.twinnor.org to find out more.

CHARACTER
LOVES
COMPANY

Character Values (17-22):

17. *Sacrifice*

18. *Handling Adversity/Resilience*

19. *Process Oriented*

20. *Body Language Awareness*

21. *Community Service/Outreach*

22. Honest Evaluation (Self & Peers)

BUILDING BLOCK #22: Honest Evaluation (Self & Peers)

"You're never as good as everyone tells you when you win, and you're never as bad as they say when you lose."—Lou Holtz, Long-Time Coach at Notre Dame

I love this quote from Lou Holtz, the legendary University of Notre Dame head football coach and life mentor of thousands of student-athletes during his illustrious 40+ years in collegiate athletics. Athletes are often elevated to superhuman status when they perform well, or kicked to the curb when they do not. As coaches and parents mentoring in sports, we need to work to instill an honest and healthy sense of value and self-worth in all of our student-athletes. The major emphasis here holds true to the impetus of this guidebook, which is to help all who are involved in youth and amateur athletics to identify with and appreciate the countless character values that are developed through sports participation (aside from just winning).

This **CV** on **Honest Evaluation (Self & Peers)** has not been given much emphasis in today's generation where individual egos and perceptions of abilities have been highly inflated by the trophy and showcase generation. I have found that young student-athletes have a difficult time with their own self-evaluation when it comes to their current athletic abilities. Now, I am all for young student-athletes setting big goals in life to strive toward and having the confidence to believe in themselves. However, if they have been brought up through sports participation the correct way, with **CLD** at the core, once they reach the end of this "advancing" level of athletics, they should have a more balanced perspective and appreciation for the value of sports outside of merely the college scholarship or professional contract.

In order for this balanced perspective to be instilled in our rising generations through sports, we (as coaches and parents) need to emphasize that all the hard work, energy, and commitment to becoming the best athlete and teammate they can be will have a remarkable return on investment in terms of transferrable life skills that will enhance their success in life after sports. Not every young athlete is going to be able to play in the NBA, WNBA, NFL, MLS, etc., and, actually, the odds are less than winning the lottery. As **Addison Staples** *(founder of non-profit Aces in Action)* stated so clearly, *"Kids need to stop being told that they are going to be NBA players, because it is leading to them putting their eggs in the wrong basket that, ultimately, creates a pathway to disappointment and, more alarming, failure to develop and value life skills."*

Honest evaluation in any endeavor in life is vital to growth and the maximization of one's talents. **Honest evaluation** helps to identify flaws or weaknesses and areas of needed improvement. However, it is a tight rope for coaches to walk, and it takes a savvy approach to give constructive criticism that will be well-received, as Master Boon Brown attested to in the section on CV #19 focused on teaching student-athletes to be process oriented. At this advancing stage of **CLD**, we need to be honest in our evaluations. In doing so, it is integral that a foundation of trust and respect is underpinning the coach/mentor: student-athlete relationship. Our goal should always be to build our young people up but not to give them false hope.

I discussed this concept of **honest evaluation** with long-time and highly successful high school coach, **Chivonne Kiser**, to share how she has been able to assist her student-athletes, as well as their parents, about this important focus on the development of honest evaluation. Here is what Coach Kiser shared with me:

I have conversations with the student-athletes and their parents at the beginning of each season regarding the importance of competitive sport, and what the ultimate aims of sport participation should be. The main thing that I let my student-athletes and parents know is that the ultimate goal is an education, and that needs to be priority one with or without an athletic scholarship. I emphasize that athletic participation is something to be a proud part of - something that helps form one's identity while empowering them with key building blocks for a successful future.

Coach Kiser made it very clear to me that she is highly competitive and one who wants the young women who she coaches and mentors to learn how to win on the court. However, in more than 15 years of coaching, she has never evaluated herself, or her players, by the win-loss record or whether they hoisted a state championship over their heads. For Coach Kiser, her definition of success is determined by what her student-athletes absorb and take away from her program about how to succeed in life after they graduate. When the overwhelming majority of her student-athletes move on to college, whether or not they continue to participate in intercollegiate sports, most of them understand how to honestly evaluate who they are and what they want to become.

However, Coach Kiser admits that this can be an ongoing struggle each year, as some student-athletes and their families want to measure self-evaluation and self-worth in terms of the quest for an athletic scholarship. Over the years, I have fought this battle that Coach Kiser speaks of with many of my own student-athletes. They become so infatuated with the DI college scholarship, or the link to a big name university, that their quest to reach that level becomes a debilitating obsession. When the college scholarship or professional contract becomes their means of evaluating their self-worth, they often miss out on many of the character values that I discuss in this guidebook.

Coach Kiser shares her approach, and in doing so, she gives some excellent advice for coaches and parents of student-athletes looking to help build a better sense of self-worth and self-evaluation in those who they coach and mentor:

The best thing I can say is that I'm completely forthright with parents and athletes about my expectations and I share my experiences with them about my interscholastic and intercollegiate careers. I share the benefits, pitfalls, mistakes, triumphs, insecurities, humbling experiences, and other life lessons learned that may guide them along. So far, parents and students have valued and respected my opinions and assistance, and they seem to appreciate what I honor about sports. They may not always have agreed with my tactical decisions, but they appreciate the positive experiences their daughters have encountered during their four years in the program, and really that's been the most important thing to everyone involved. When they ask themselves, 'Was all of the sacrifice worth it in the end?' Inevitably, their answer is, 'Yes, it was!'

What Coach Kiser and I discussed is that, ultimately, what we are teaching and learning through sports is never truly over. Rather, it is always a springboard to developing a consistent approach for how to persevere through life's challenges and succeed.

As you recall from Olympic gold medalist **BJ Bedford-Miller**, she learned a valuable lesson her sophomore year in college at the University of Texas during the NCAA Finals about honest self-evaluation, true competition, and humility. During my interview with BJ, she shared that during her freshman year she and her team at UT were on top of world. However, a short year later they had to take a long look in the mirror of honest self-evaluation in order to find a way to get back to where they knew they belonged.

As they sat there and watched Stanford celebrate the coveted championship during her sophomore year, it undoubtedly helped BJ and her teammates fully grasp the joys of triumph and the sorrows of defeat. It helped them realize that they had to get back to work; they needed to out-train and out-prepare their opponents at Stanford if they wanted to taste the ultimate triumph once again. Sure enough, a year later, they were back as National Champions.

What I love about the concept of true self-evaluation is that it highlights what can be controlled: approach and effort. At the end of a competition, student-athletes should be learning to measure themselves based on effort, attitude, preparation, focus, commitment, and character. Rather than teaching our rising generations that self-worth is tied to winning every game, earning a scholarship, or turning pro, we need to be more focused on things that they have control over. As coaches and parents of student-athletes do a better job of this, they will see their teams and players become much more coachable and receptive to constructive criticism.

My mentor, **Fred Claire** *(GM and World Series Champion for the Los Angeles Dodgers)*, summed up the importance of focusing only on that which one has full control over, such as effort. Fred shared with me a powerful story of honest self-evaluation from former Dodger outfielder and leader, John Shelby:

> *What stays in my mind about John Shelby to this day is his last at-bat at Dodger Stadium in 1990* [Shelby was at the tail end of his career and close to retirement after more than ten years in the MLB]. *John hit a routine ground ball to second base. It was an easy out, but what struck me was how hard he ran down the line to first base, as if he was a 20-year old rookie trying to make the ball club. He ran that ball out as hard as he possibly could, and that meant a lot to me as the general manager. For young kids out there, I would tell them that someone is always watching. How you work on a daily basis at the routine things is an indication of the type of person you are. That is a résumé!*

CV #22 Honest Evaluation (Self & Peer): Activities and Drills to increase Retention/Assessment:

- o Honest evaluation can be a difficult thing for any dedicated student-athlete. However, at this advanced stage of sport development honest and fair assessment is vital.

  What I have found at this level is that a written assessment to accompany a post-season face-to-face evaluation is the most effective approach to allow for growth in each student-athlete. It is typically a good idea to have your assistant coach in the room with you to give additional insights, but also to combat any potential disagreements.

- o Give your players 10-15 minutes after a practice towards the end of the season write a self-evaluation in their player journals. Be sure that they are not simply evaluating the physical performance on the field but all areas of their lives: athletically, socially, family, relationship with peers, character, and leadership.

- o It can be very easy for young student-athletes to fall into the trap of only caring and focusing on their own improvements and development.

When you are having your post-game meeting, ask each of the players to think about something about a teammate that has impressed you. Give them a few minutes to think about the person to their left or right. It is a rewarding activity to hear and see each of these young SA's complimenting one another.

o   At the mid-way point of the season, have your student-athletes identify their three biggest strengths related to the sport of focus, as well as their three biggest areas for improvement. Perhaps you can give them a print out for them to fill out prior to the next practice or game.

o   For my end-of-the-season player evaluation, I usually give the players a blank copy of my evaluation form and ask that they fill it out to the best of their ability prior to our meeting. Prior to disclosing my assessment, I ask the student-athletes to rate themselves followed by my assessment, line by line. This is an excellent way to highlight any incongruities and help them to be more realistic in areas of needed improvement, or for some, unrecognized strengths. The players typically appreciate this approach, though they may not like the honest feedback. An important note: At this point, you have hopefully been able to get to know your players well enough and together you have earned a mutual respect that would invite honest and constructive feedback. There is a fine line between constructive criticism and demoralizing a player, but at this stage, student-athletes need to be given honest feedback in order to move forward.

CHAPTER 10—Level 5: CLD—Advanced Mastery Level
(16-19 & 19-23+ Year-Old-Range)

Character Values (23-25):

23. **Winning (How to Win the Right Way)**

24. *Servant Leadership*

25. *Legacy (Impact on Others Now and in the Future)*

BUILDING BLOCK #23: Winning
(How to Win the Right Way)

"At every step, individuals and organizations in sports and in business may choose to bend the rules and spirit of the 'game' or to play, and perhaps win, with integrity. Building commitment to ethical conduct in sports and business requires building a culture that aligns individuals and organizations around core values. Doing so demands leaders who are attuned to broader societal issues and values that influence their organizations and teams."—Center for Ethical Business Cultures website, 2016[118]

The above statement from the Center of Ethical Business Cultures underscores the importance of character development programs such as my **CLD** curriculum. While I hope the entire quote speaks to you, the part that jumped off the page for me as it relates to my mission is: *"Building commitment to ethical conduct in sports and business requires building a culture that aligns individuals and organizations around core values."* As I have highlighted

---

[118] http://www.cebcglobal.org/winning-with-integrity-a-conversation-on-sports-ethics-and-leadership/

throughout this book, there have been countless businesses, corporations, sports teams, and individual athletes over the past few decades who have completely sacrificed integrity and morals in pursuit of winning or maximizing profits. This win-at-all-costs mentality needs to be replaced with the focused approach of this **CV** on **winning the right way**.

I have spoken directly to this need to win the right way throughout this book. The many narratives from highly successful athletes during and after life in sports are proof that one does not have to sacrifice high ethical values to win in any endeavor of life. **Winning the right way** is the only way to build lifelong habits of success.

An overwhelming majority of my contributors emphasized just how vital it is to **win the right way**. **BJ Bedford-Miller's** testimony *(Olympic Gold Medalist and NCAA All-American)* and the juxtaposition of emotions from winning the NCAA National Title her freshman year to the sheer disappointment the next shows how sports have a way of teaching life lessons in a manner that nothing else can. When you make up your mind to **win the right way**, and compete the right way, it is not always the scoreboard that will dictate whether you truly won or not. **Fred Claire** was also very clear about just what made that 1988 World Series Champion team with the Los Angeles Dodgers so special, *"That 1988 Dodgers' team was one of the highest character!"*

My first contributor to this section is **Jeremy Peterson** *(Former Army Ranger who served America in the Gulf War; Youth Mentor/Coach; 3rd Degree Black Belt)*. Mr. Jeremy, as his young karate students respectfully call him, shared a vivid memory about a recent illustration of **winning the right way**, or what he refers to as "triumphing" the right way.

The following incident took place more than 20 years after Mr. Jeremy last served our country as an Army Ranger. A young, brash 20-year-old, who may have reminded Mr. Jeremy of a shell of his old self, decided to pick a fight with the wrong guy. Mr. Jeremy retold this story in the same manner that I had heard him share many similar parables to his karate students in the Dojo in an effort to help them better understand a key character learning moment. Though he did not give this story a title, it could have been called, *"What It Takes to Be a True Man (or Woman)."*

A macho, testosterone-filled young man in his early 20s jumped out of his car in an effort to instigate a scuffle with Mr. Jeremy having thought that he had purposely almost backed his vehicle into him. The young man was screaming every profanity in the book and basically challenging him to a fight right there in the parking lot. This young man had no idea who he was messing with, as Mr. Jeremy is not only an extremely strong human being but also a third degree black belt, and a trained American soldier. If this arrogant soul had any clue who he was messing with, he would have apologized immediately and simply walked away in one piece. However, it was Mr. Jeremy who maintained his poise while peacefully and humbly admitting his honest mistake. Unfortunately, that was not enough for this individual who leaned in asking for trouble. Here is how Mr. Jeremy turned this potentially ugly scenario into a triumph:

> I told him, 'I am going to give you what you want, and then I am going to give you what you need. You want an apology, so I will apologize again for almost backing up into you.' The young man responded, 'Yeah, and what do I need?' [Mr. Jeremy responded,] 'You need to learn to let it go. I was once much like you, but life has taught me forgiveness, tolerance, and the importance of accepting faults, as well as the importance of being humble. So, my question for you is, how long are you going to hold on to this? It is not worth it. Move on. I've been there, I've done the thing that you think makes you a man…It is not beating someone else up, or winning that is going to make you a man.'

I could not help but ask Mr. Jeremy what a younger and less experienced version of him would have done to that young man right there in the parking lot. Rather than answering my inquiry, he stated proudly, "I triumphed as a person in that incident by simply shedding some ego. I've learned that if I try to show that I am stronger than someone else, that gets me nowhere in the long run. Be the strongest version of you rather than trying to beat someone else!"

I love that story because I know what Mr. Jeremy could have done to that young man, and some may say rightfully so. However, Mr. Jeremy is a husband and father, and a role model to hundreds, if not thousands, of young children. What he did instead was take the high road. In doing so, he *deliberately* and *intentionally* chose to **win the right way**. Relating back to the previous **CV** on community service/outreach, perhaps Mr. Jeremy set an example by paying it forward for someone else in a similar situation down the road? What a terrific life lesson that was capitalized on by a true leader and hero in his community.

Similar to Mr. Jeremy, my next contributor has also chosen to serve our country in the United States Army. **David Santos** *(Second year Cadet at West Point; past student-athlete of the highest character)* is all about **winning the right way**, which is something that he learned through the vehicle of sports at an early age. David had just finished his first year at one of the most prestigious institutions of higher learning in our country, The United States Military Academy, when I interviewed him for this book. Knowing David's background in sports, I asked him to share a defining memory from his youth in the athletic arena that molded the person who he is today and prepared him for the discipline and consistency that it takes to succeed at West Point.

He recalled his seventh grade baseball season in junior high school growing up in Georgia. He earned the starting position at second base on a solid team comprised of mainly eighth graders despite being one of the smallest players on the team. His team was playing in the semi-final game of their league playoffs and the game was on the line in the final inning. David was at-bat with a chance to tie or even win the game for his team:

I had a full count [three balls and two strikes], *and the pitcher delivered the pitch that came in high and outside off the plate. However, the umpire called it strike three. I was out and the game was over. I immediately removed my helmet and threw it onto the ground as my coaches and our team's fans were going crazy over the notably poor call. My coach came running out and was livid towards the umpire.*

Though the reaction from coaches and fans demonstrated that the umpire had indeed made a bad call on the pitch for strike three to end the game, I realize that I missed out on an opportunity to lead and demonstrate discipline and integrity. Now that I think back on that defining moment in my growth, I am sure that I embarrassed my parents and myself by responding the way that I did. What stands out is not that I struck out, but how I responded to that adversity and that I did not seize that opportunity, though I did learn a great deal from it.

Now, many years later, that event has helped mold who I am today. There are so many values and tests of character that come through sports and though I may have failed to show my true character that day, I have used that moment to better prepare for the many adversities that I have faced since. I am learning to seize those moments and hold true to integrity and honor for who I am and what I stand for.

The 1st Superintendent of West Point Academy, General Douglas MacArthur, stated the following about his viewpoint of athletic competition: 'Upon the fields of friendly strife are sown the seeds that upon other fields, on other days, will bear the fruits of victory.'

It was highly evident from David's perspective and appreciation that the mission and vision of West Point was the perfect fit for him to continue to learn, and grow, and serve. He not only knew that quote from General MacArthur by heart, but he is living it.

As David's coach in high school for two years and someone who has coached youth sports for more than 15 years, I was most impressed with David's work ethic, discipline, and integrity on and off the field of play. When David shared this defining moment from that seventh grade baseball game with me, it was ever-apparent that the event had truly been a life-learning moment in how to **do things the right way**. David is a testament to what General MacArthur stated many years ago about the great value of sports in the development of a stronger American society.

I asked Coach **Amanda Butler** *(University of Florida Head Women's Basketball Coach)* about the importance of her players graduating from her program knowing how to compete and **win the right way**. Here is what Coach Butler had to say:

> *I think that **winning the right way** is vital. Ultimately, if you are trying to figure out how to be successful in sports, and not just wins and losses, you have to focus on the **right things** and helping to develop effective habits. These are the ways that we, as coaches, can make a positive and lasting impact. The other part of it is that, quite simply, this approach to **winning the right way** is a much more fulfilling way to compete. If you are just going to measure success by whether you won or lost, then that can be somewhat out of your control. You are not going to win every game. Eventually you are going to lose, or miss a big shot, and if those are the factors or triggers for fulfilment, then you are going to be up and down all the time. When players prioritize the process of **doing things the right way**, it is a much more fulfilling way to put on your uniform, lace up your shoes, and go to a game or a practice each day.*

Coach Butler hits on a central theme here regarding the intrinsic values of athletic participation that go far beyond the wins and losses. However, if student-athletes are being trained from a young age to buy into the zero-sum game, which posits that the only value is winning and doing so at all costs, then their journey through sports is going to lack true fulfillment. Eventually, student-athletes will choose to opt out of the volatility and lack of a clear purpose for participating in sports.

Nowadays, parents and coaches are seeking entry into competitive environments where they are "playing down"[119] against lesser competition to boost their own stats and ego. This is greatly limiting the development of our student-athletes, both physically and mentally, because they miss out on needed growth opportunities that come about through adversity and struggle. This goes back to **David Prince** *(Paralympic World Record Holder; Youth Mentor)*, whose motto is: *"I am either going to win, or I am going to learn."*

Today's young student-athletes are missing out on this vital ingredient of competing and winning with the right perspective. This is rooted largely in overprotective parents or coaches who do not ever want to see their children or teams fall, or seemingly fail. As David Prince and the other contributors to my guidebook have emphasized so clearly, falling is not failing unless you do not get back up and try again. However, many young student-athletes are prolonging such life-learning opportunities until much too late into their athletic careers. At that point, if they do not have a strong foundation deeply rooted in the 25 values of sports participation, then they will not know how to embrace and grow from adversity. I think of athletes such as Tiger Woods, Johnny Manziel, Ronda Rousey, and Josh Hamilton—all of whom were the best of the best in their sport, but when they fell (as everyone eventually will), they have had a difficult time recovering and returning to their past greatness.

I love how Coach Butler talks about the fulfillment of playing competitive sports. She helps her student-athletes grasp the unlimited developmental values of athletic participation outside of simply winning, and thereby creating more fulfillment. As she stated, student-athletes should look forward to lacing up their shoes to play or practice because of their awareness and appreciation for the many intrinsic rewards of sports other than simply winning or losing and the zero-sum game.

---

[119] When I discuss the concept of "playing down" to lesser competition, I am referring to the conscious decision of coaches or parents to choose competitions where their teams or athletes have a better chance to win. Most elite-level athletes whom I have spoken with over the years deliberately chose to do the opposite, which was to "play up" against tougher and even older competition in order to rise to a higher level of development and ability. In my family over the past two generations, we have emphasized "playing up" in every opportunity possible, rather than playing down for fear of losing.

CV #23 Winning (How to Win the Right Way): Activities and Drills to increase Retention/Assessment:

- o At this mastery level of participation in sports, student-athletes should have a stronghold on the many values of winning. Typically, however, there is now more on the line for these student-athletes. They have scholarships and even professional contract offers looming. An important message from coaches and parents is to share real-life examples on the importance of demonstrating self-control, respect for the talents of their opponents, focus, etc.

- o Another important message for student-athletes at this advanced level is consistency. They are now at a stage where it is no longer as much about who has the most talent, but rather, who can consistently demonstrate mastery during the heat of the battle. Those who can remain focused, unfazed, and unintimidated by the competition and the magnitude of the event are the ones who will perform to their highest potential.

- o Give each of your student-athletes a small bound journal with the logo of your team on it. Have them write a short reflection after each practice or game about what they learned that day. Rather than have them simply dwell on winning or losing, have them focus on what they learned during the heat of the battle. Over time, they will start to realize that, through their reflections, they are learning a great deal more through the tough times of struggle. Eventually, they will begin to embrace the growth that comes from adversity and this will help them understand how to **win the right way** in sports and in life.

<u>Character Values (23-25):</u>

23. *Winning (How to Win the Right Way)*

24. *Servant Leadership*

25. *Legacy (Impact on Others Now and in the Future)*

BUILDING BLOCK #24: **Servant Leadership**

*"The **servant-leader** is servant first. It begins with the natural feeling that one wants to serve, to serve first. Then conscious choice brings one to aspire to lead. The difference manifests itself in the care taken by the servant - first to make sure that other people's needs are being served."*

—John Greenleaf, Founder of the term "Servant Leadership"

Servant leadership has become a common term over the past decade or so, however, it is one thing to talk about **servant leadership** and quite another to act and lead in such a manner.

My first contributor in this section is an expert and EdD[120] on this topic of servant leadership, **Dr. Lee Ellis** *(Long-Time College Coach/Athletic Director)*. Dr. Ellis shared the following statement with me regarding servant leadership:

*   **Servant leadership** is about serving the needs of others. Serving is first, and leading is an outcome of the serving. Coaches who are **servant leaders** succeed by developing their players. Empowered players make achieving team objectives possible. Empowered players, in turn, embrace serving others.*

---

[120] An EdD refers to an individual who holds a Doctoral Degree in Education.

What behaviors will you model? Your behaviors are expressed in your approach to the game, to the craft of coaching, the way you view opponents and the rules, the way you treat players, parents, other coaches--how you treat people generally. Will you have the courage to stand against those who will challenge this approach to leading? (Those who obsess over a win-at-all-cost mentality, those who understand only the control style of leadership, and those who wrap themselves in adultist attitudes that devalue the needs and desires of kids: these are the types who challenge servant leaders.)

As a fellow youth coach, I have two more questions...are you with us? Will you actually practice SL? Our youth need and deserve your example!

While writing this book, I came across some excellent coaches and mentors who continue to answer Dr. Ellis' call with a resounding "yes" that they are on board with the concept of servant leadership, and their daily actions attest to this fact.

From the first day that I entered **Master Boon Brown's** dojo at Ancient Ways Martial Arts Academy, it was highly evident to me that **servant leadership** is not just a priority there, but a way of life. During my sit-down interview with Master Brown, he never attempted to tout his own accomplishments, but rather, he was quick to point out the admiration, respect, and successes of his students. Self-promoting in the sports world, and in the business world, is a very common occurrence that many feel is a necessity these days. However, despite my repeated attempts to bring notice to all of the good that Master Brown has done, and continues to do, in his community, not once did he toot his own horn. Instead, he chose to rave about his students.

Master Brown is a highly skilled martial artist and one of the best youth mentors that I have met. He has been making a lasting impact in the lives of our youth and adults for more than 30 years. It was refreshingly energizing to see this big, strong man get a bit choked up at times thinking back on the accomplishments and growth of current and past students. He shared a moving story of one of his students from 20-years prior (an ex-Vietnam veteran) who became a martial arts student of his after serving our country for many years. This individual had passed away and a few days after the funeral this man's son showed up at the dojo and said that his dad wanted Master Brown to have his black belt. *"It is hanging in my office to this day,"* Master Brown told me. That is what coaching and mentoring are all about—making a difference in people's lives in a positive way.

Master Brown proceeded to reference students, one after another, who had successfully come through his program over the years. Many of those students were individuals who fought through adversity and supposed limitations in order to earn their black belts. He also referenced some who did not quite make it all the way to earning their black belt. But, for every student who did not get there, he wanted to help the next one and continue to learn to motivate and better enrich the lives of all who enter his studio. He remarked, *"Obviously, you cannot lead them all there, but I am always looking at new students as a second chance."*

I asked Master Brown about the intrinsic rewards that come from his mentorship. Here he provides an example of one of his students:

> *I had a young lady, Kayla, in the studio last night. Now, Kayla is one of the top martial artists in the country, but she's got humility and she will never show off. And she hates it when I make her show off here; she is just amazing. But, the best part about watching her is not watching her as a martial artist, but watching her as a human being and watching her grow and gain that confidence. No matter where she goes, whether it is a board room, or a back alley, she is going to be able to handle it. I look around the room and I see all these young kids that have been with us for six years or even more and I watch how they have grown and changed.*

> *Equally rewarding for me is seeing the adults change. The old adage is that you cannot teach an old dog new tricks. And that can be true much of the time, but when it is not true, it is absolutely mind-boggling.*

Throughout my interview and other conversations and interactions with Master Brown, it is always apparent that he is about serving and providing for others through his leadership. His purpose and incentive as a coach/mentor is a wonderful example of **servant leadership**, and his care and concern for others are leaving a lasting legacy!

BJ Bedford-Miller *(Olympic Gold Medalist and Mentor)* has learned to embrace the concept of **servant leadership** through sports. During our interview, this is what she shared with me:

I learned about the importance of [servant leadership] *while I was at UT. As a freshman, I swam the 100 butterfly. I didn't get to swim my best event because I did what the team needed. You see this a lot in football where these elite athletes at the college level are able to adapt and adjust in changing positions in order to play in the NFL. Versatility is so important in life. In talking about* **servant leadership***, it is about knowing what the team needs to do to work collectively toward a common goal to win—and sports teaches that very well.*

The willingness of young student-athletes to sacrifice their own personal goals and ego in order to help their team win the right way is a lost art for much of our youth and amateur athletes today. An overriding cause of this is rooted in parents' insistence that their child play the premier position on the field, or swim/run the high profile race at all times. I see and hear about this incessant demand time and time again. Many parents go to the extreme of pulling their child from a team if their demands—that "young Johnny" plays every inning of every game at his chosen position—are not met. These are the "character illiterate" individuals that I speak of throughout this book who just do not get it. They feel as if their son or daughter is being cheated out of their rightful college scholarship, or professional contract, if their demands are not met. In essence, they are shopping their child around from team to team, offering them out to the highest bidder. Such behavior is counterintuitive to the true intent of athletic participation and effective human behavior and growth.

Servant leadership is a highly advanced character value, and an approach that needs to be trained and developed. It is not going to happen overnight. This **CV** cannot be instilled unless student-athletes first learn the foundational level **CVs** such as respect, care and appreciation for others, integrity, sacrifice, etc. When one comprehends, retains, and practices **servant leadership**, that is when a legacy is established of **winning the right way**.

<u>CV #24 **Servant Leadership:**</u> <u>Activities and Drills to increase Retention/Assessment:</u>

- o At this point in their development as student-athletes, the individuals on your teams should have a firm handle on what character in sports looks like. Sharing stories from the news and media from all aspects of life (sports, business, politics, etc.) about positive and negative examples are excellent ways to bring emphasis to **servant leadership,** and other CVs. A good weekly team assignment could be to give a different player each week the task of doing a little research and finding a story in the news regarding an act of **servant leadership**, either good or bad (or any other CV). They would then begin practice (potentially during the early stretch period) by sharing the story that they found and then relating it to the team. This is a great way for your players to demonstrate their retention and application of these vital developmental character values. Once again, it is another great way for them to practice public speaking and the presentation and articulation of ideas.

o Have the players think about why it would be important for them to be able to play multiple positions on the team, or be versatile in their abilities to swim/run multiple races. Share the story of BJ Bedford-Miller in this section and her experience at UT. There are many similar examples of this that I have mentioned previously. If you have not already shared this scenario with your players, it could be a great time when discussing servant leadership:

Scenario:

There are two All-American student-athletes. One is a high school All-American graduating senior shortstop, and the other is a college All-American rising junior shortstop. They both enter their next season at the top college program in the country.

Ask them who they think is most likely to be given the nod to start at shortstop, the freshman or the returning junior? The junior has already proven herself/himself at that level while the freshman has not. They all know the answer. However, I emphasize to them that if they are willing and able to effectively play another position, they will have a good chance of earning playing time as a freshman. If they have never been humble enough to learn another position or role, and they refuse to try to do so in college, they will inevitably find themselves buried on the bench, or worse off, find themselves cut from the team. Coaches and employers, alike, are looking for team players who find ways to make the team or the organization as a whole more productive and successful.

CHARACTER
LOVES
COMPANY

<u>Character Values (23-25):</u>

23. *Winning (How to Win the Right Way)*

24. *Servant Leadership*

25. **Legacy (Impact on Others Now and in the Future)**

BUILDING BLOCK #25: Legacy
(Impact on Others Now and in the Future)

With permission from the Studenmund family, I want to begin this final section building block with a tribute to **Scott Studenmund**, an American hero, whose **legacy** continues in all whose lives he touched. In addition to his parents, I was able to reach out to four of Scott's coaches from his youth in order for them to share some of his lasting character values that are forever ingrained in their hearts and memories.

(Photo provided by The Studenmund Family)

SSG Scott Studenmund

KIA 9, JUNE 14, GAZA VALLEY, AFGHANISTAN

B/1/5TH SFG (A), DE OPPRESSO LIBER

At the time of his death on June 9, 2014, that job was complex. His team was participating in a multiple-day, high-priority mission in the Gaza Valley, Zabul Province, Afghanistan. The mission was nearing completion when the team came under fire by enemy forces in large numbers. Field reports about the mission had been highly positive; Scott died knowing that his final mission had been a tremendous success. —From Scott's Memorial Biography

Scott is a hero to me and to all who knew him. He earned just about every award and decoration for the highest honors given to a member of our great country's military: the Purple Heart, Bronze Star Medal, Meritorious Service Medal, and Expert Infantry Badge (which in the Army is known as "The Mark of a Man"). He was a Green Beret and a Special Forces instructor. When Scott was deployed to Afghanistan in January of 2014, he carried the rank of Staff Sergeant with the 1st Battalion of the 5th Special Forces Group, Bravo Company, at Fort Campbell, Kentucky.

"He loved what he did," said his mother, Jaynie Studenmund, of her son's service in the military. *"When people said, 'Scott, you can do anything you want to,' he'd say, 'I feel like it's a calling.' The last thing he shared with his band of brothers, high school friends, before his January deployment was that he wanted each of them to do something important with their lives,"* she added.

-John Paciorek (Scott's Physical Education Coach from first grade through sixth grade):

As I read Scottie's memorial biography, I could barely keep my eyes from watering. I surely miss his physical presence, but the memory and tangible essence of his enduring spirit will forever be implanted within my 'Mind's-eye' view – with the help from his fifth grade picture that I have on constant display on my office bulletin board.

Scottie was an outstanding person and athlete. He was alert and patient, and he always listened carefully and followed directions intently. No matter what the activity was in P.E., he would always participate wholeheartedly. When the signal to begin any activity was given, I could expect him to display genuine enthusiasm and thoughtful purpose, from start to finish.

Scottie loved playing all sports, especially Pass-Ball.[121] As in football, although not large in physical stature, he was a fast and powerful runner. He was always moving at full-speed, looking for 'day-light' and charging through an open hole. If there was no opening, he

---

[121] Pass-Ball is a game similar to traditional American football, but with more continuous motion and player interaction.

wasn't hesitant nor afraid to make one himself, but never with the intention of hurting anyone. He would always show respect and humility if he hurt someone or knocked them over, and offer to help them up.

Scottie was truly a joy to have in class and any of my other sports programs. He always set the highest example of Athleticism as well as Sportsmanship.

-Glen Beattie (High School Assistant Football Coach/Science Teacher):

"Football is where Scott found the ultimate test for himself; where he found out whether he could match up with players bigger than himself. Football taught him to never be afraid to challenge himself to be the best."

-Perry Skaggs (High School Head Football Coach):

During Scott's six years at Prep, he touched many with his love for life by challenging himself to be the best that he could be for others. Every coach I have talked to about Scott makes some reference to an individual who played bigger than he was. They all shared the various qualities of his character that allowed him to do so: tenacity, focus, toughness, and discipline. All his coaches remember Scott as an inspiration to the younger players. The ultimate compliment, in my mind, about Scott, is that he will be remembered by everyone who knew him as someone who always did things the right way, with integrity and honor.

-Alex Rivera (30+ year Athletic Director; Scott's Coach in Junior High and High School):

There are so many beautiful memories that I have of Scott. I'd be giving a motivational talk and look down and there would be Scott staring you right in the eyes getting psyched up. He played for his school, his team, and friends.

One of my favorite stories of Scott occurred during a seventh and eighth grade home baseball game. I gave a pre-game pep-talk about Darin Erstad, a MLB player for the Los Angeles Angels, who played the game with heart, passion, no fear of mistakes, and he always had fun. That day, Scott had a deep fly ball hit way over his head towards the trees in left field, and there was no way was he going to catch this ball. Most players would have stopped as they neared the tree line and raise their arms in the air indicating a ground rule double. Not Scott, he ran and ran, and disappeared into the trees as he dove for the ball. Moments later, he came out from the trees and brush after catching the ball for the final out of the game. He came sprinting into the dugout with a huge smile. Since that day, I now tell the motivational pep-talk to my students about Scott Studenmund: the young man who played with passion, love for life, and never with fear when it came to challenging himself to the next level; being the best for his teammates, family, and country!

As these coaches each stated, Scott Studenmund's **legacy for greatness** continues to thrive in the hearts and souls of all those who were fortunate to have met him. He has been an inspiration and motivation to us all. That is a life well-lived in the service and protection of mankind and of our country. There is no greater **legacy** than that!

I return to another individual who both inspires and motivates those with whom he comes in contact. **David Prince** *(Paralympian and World Record Holder in the 200M and 400M)* reminds me of Scottie Studenmund, as he is equally concerned with serving others through his words and actions. I know that David would have a difficult time comparing himself to a decorated American military hero who gave his life to his great country, but the **legacy** that he is working to create through his consistency of goodwill to others draws many parallels.

In spending a good deal of time discussing character in sports with David, he is equally excited about and concerned with helping our youth through his story than he is about his own performance. It is obvious that, for him, being an elite athlete is not going to consume and define who he is and what he can accomplish outside of the world of sports. David is definitely looking at the long-term and how he can influence others' attitudes about the many character values that can be fostered through sports participation. David stated:

I have met so many young athletes who build everything around winning. I have competed with some people who were truly good people inside and out. Then they started to win, and it changed who they were, and it is very sad to watch. It changes how they care about and treat others…When I am done, I want to train someone to break all of my records.

The way I see it, there is a slight difference between inspiration and motivation, and I want to both inspire and motivate. To inspire is short term and can last merely a few seconds, but motivation is more long lasting. I want to impact people in a way that gets them to break through limitations and work and challenge themselves to accomplish more. I want to both motivate and inspire others to see that they have no excuses.

David is not only training to compete and make his mark in athletic competition, but he is also working to leave a lasting footprint that far outlasts his performance on the track. For five years now, David has set out to bring equality for future Paralympic athletes who follow him. There is a central issue going on under the radar involving the equity and fairness of unilateral amputees[122] and bilateral amputees[123] competing in the Paralympics. This dilemma involves David's livelihood (and that of all unilateral amputees involved in competition) and what he has poured his heart and soul into for the past decade.

David holds the World Record in the 200 and 400M in track and field for a single (unilateral) amputee. Using advances in technology, bilateral amputees can, and are, adjusting the lengths of the blades in order to increase their stature in terms of height and stride length. This allows for notably faster times. Unilateral amputees are unable to capitalize on such a competitive advantage for the simple fact that they have a sound leg that cannot be altered or adjusted. In essence, this is significantly distancing bilateral Paralympic track and field athletes from the unilateral runners in the field.

The unfairness and inequality noted above is in no way an attack on bilateral Paralympic athletes. However, for David, and a large number of unilateral Paralympic hopefuls (as well as for people like me), this is a cause that needs to be addressed. David Prince knows that this is an important cause and he is leading the charge to effectuate positive change for future generations head on. The medals, though important, do not fuel him, rather it is the opportunity to compete at the World level.

Because single amputees are being pushed out due to exponentially faster qualifying times, there should be separate classifications for unilateral and bilateral competitors. According to David, there are more than enough singles[124] to compete. As I stated, double amputees can increase the length of their blades to increase height, stride

---

[122] A unilateral amputee refers to an individual who has one natural functioning leg along with a prosthetic leg, or blade, in the running world.
[123] A bilateral amputee refers to an individual who has two prosthetic legs (technology has allowed both blades for running to be identical in function and strength to each other).
[124] "Singles" is short for single amputees in the running world.

length, and ultimately, speed. Singles cannot because their sound leg has to keep up. What is simply amazing to me is that David can and does still compete. He will be on the Paralympic stage in Rio de Janeiro in September, 2016, but he will be one in a diminishing group of unilateral runners. Whether or not he makes the medal stand, David Prince is making a difference in the lives of future generations. Here is what David told me prior to departing for Rio de Janeiro:

> *As I have progressed through my career as an athlete, I have realized more and more that it's not about how much money I make or how 'famous' I become while competing to try to win a Gold medal. It's about the impact I can leave on future athletes and the sport as a whole. That is the only thing someone like me, in my position, can do.*
>
> *I can leave a negative impact by crying, 'It's not fair,' do nothing about it, and live with resentment for the rest of my life. Or, I can do something about it, using patience, foresight, understanding and proper planning; asking for help from anyone willing to give input in the best course of action.*
>
> *I'm figuring that out right now and with the help of my friends, we will change things. We will leave the sport better than we found it.*
>
> *As things develop, since I have the attitude of, 'I'm not losing, I'm learning,' I know that my future is secure. No matter what happens from here, I've already won by having the right attitude. Great things are coming!*

Now, that is another true example of what it means to leave a **lasting legacy**. For more information on David Prince and to learn more about what he is doing, follow him @runwithhim on Twitter, as well as the footnoted links listed below.[125]

Jeremy Peterson *(Former United States Army Ranger; Youth Mentor)* shares this passion for **legacy** and leaving a lasting imprint on the world through his service and care for others. Mr. Jeremy had a rough upbringing but he knows just how fortunate he was to have a strong mentor in his grandmother while growing up. His grandmother created a **legacy** through her love and care for him that is being carried on through him

---

[125] http://www.unation.com/runwithhim; https://m.facebook.com/runwithhim; and https://www.youtube.com/watch?v=saJVdquePYQ&feature=youtube_gdata_player

to others. He stated, *"My grandma was my go-to. She always had a way of keeping my spirits up and helping me to feel powerful and important—and every kid needs that."*

Mr. Jeremy is all about paying that forward and extending that **legacy** of mentoring and teaching life lessons to our youth. He remarked:

I love service to others. I want to feel like I am making a difference, and I get to see this difference in the young people who I train in martial arts. I get to see them demonstrate discipline and commitment and hard work each day. It has happened a few times when walking through the grocery store with my Captain America shirt [who happens to be Mr. Jeremy's favorite super hero] *and one of my young students yells out 'Hey, is that Mr. Jeremy?' And to see the joy on their faces; that is unbelievably rewarding.* [You should see this big, muscular former Army Ranger empower the young children (Wee Warriors, as they are called) that he trains in karate at Ancient Ways Martial Arts Academy. He has a way of bringing out the best in these young aspiring martial artists].

I love working with kids of all ages, but one of my biggest triumphs has been working with kids with autism and working with them in martial arts.

Mr. Jeremy's brother is a high school teacher in Texas working in special education. I could tell by the tone in his voice, and the look in his eyes, just how proud Mr. Jeremy is of what his brother is doing working with young children and making a real difference in their lives. Despite their differences and the fact that they have drifted apart, Mr. Jeremy recognizes the connection and interdependence between him and his brother, and the burning passion in their hearts for helping others (especially the underdog and the underserved).

He told me candidly, *"I'd love to sit down with my brother when the time is right to share how much our lives have in common and what we do with youth."* Mr. Jeremy's purpose is to mentor and make a difference in the lives of others. In doing so, he is making a big difference and leaving a lasting **legacy**.

Dr. Michael Sagas *(Founder & CEO of Twinnor, a non-profit for underserved children, UF Professor and Department Chair)* also places a high value on the potential **legacy** that each and every student-athlete has the power to create and the importance of this vital final character value. Here is what Dr. Sagas had to say about the concept of leaving a **lasting legacy** through his non-profit, Twinnor, as a way to enhance the lives of others:

*When looking at the concept of **legacy**, our kids need empathy and other life skills and they don't get that concept about caring about others a whole lot. Twinning[126] is one way to make that connection, but they have to have some 'skin in the game.'[127] Parents cannot simply write a check and say, 'Hey, here is enough money for a whole team over in a third-world country.' That will not help our youth really gain an appreciation of sacrifice for our fellow humankind.*

If only our young people could say 'I will raise 1% of the money my family provides for me each year or season.' This could be through tutoring, mowing lawns, birthday checks, mentoring, giving lessons, etc. And, maybe it is not about raising money for a 'twin' match; maybe it is about being a mentor for someone in need, or giving them one free lesson every week in whatever sport they play?

There was an obvious sense of pride and excitement that came over Dr. Sagas as he talked about his own daughter's experience "Twinning" with young underserved athletes in Guatemala:

When my daughter goes to Guatemala and gets to help and provide support for young soccer players over there, it is special for sure. However, it is not a life skill unless you can transfer it to someone or something else, for example, transferring it to the board room and making good decisions that are ethical and have a positive impact on others. Twinning is about teaching and training these necessary life skills.

Ultimately, as coaches, you have not accomplished anything unless your players can apply it to life outside of sports. You are a mentor and you embody either the good or the bad! We have all seen the coach who gets in his or her players' faces yelling and screaming and belittling them. That doesn't teach our youth how to treat a woman, or how to treat a man.

Youth [and amateur] sports are an opportunity to create awareness in these areas, but for it to transfer and stick, it needs to be more consistently delivered!

---

[126] Twinning is the act of giving to others (either through financial donations, or the donation of time and energy) who are less fortunate or underserved.

[127] "Skin in the game" refers to a child's need to personally invest one's own sweat, blood, and hard work into raising the financial or human resources to provide support for another. Too many parents of overserved children simply give their son or daughter the donation money, thinking that somehow their child will reap the rewards of giving to others with money that they did not earn. Though well-intentioned, this is only cheating their child out of an opportunity to grow.

Rafael Perez *(Director of Major League Baseball, Dominican Republic Operations; son of legendary Youth Coach/Mentor for 50 years)* adheres to the same principles as Dr. Sagas in stating:

> *I have tried to live my life following the lessons I have learned from my father. I have been blessed to know other people along the way who have also left their print on my character through sports. The game of baseball has shaped me into the man I am today and I hope to shape the character of my kids in the same way.*

The **legacy** and impact that a great coach, mentor, or parent can have in our children's lives is truly amazing. Our youth and amateur student-athletes need positive adult figures in their lives. To effectuate positive change in the lives of our youth, we need to embrace and own our roles as mentors. It is imperative for us to model the behavior that we wish to see in our student-athletes. Far too many adult figures, who hold positions of influence with impressionable youth and amateur student-athletes, choose to live by the mantra of "do as I say, and not as I do."

This takes me back to the first six words of this guidebook by the great Coach Wooden, *"What we emphasize gets improved upon."* It is an honor to wear the title of coach and one that should not be taken for granted. With such an honor comes great responsibility, as youth and amateur athletes of all ages are paying attention to their coach's every move, because actions speak much louder and truer than words.

As coaches, parents, and mentors of youth and amateur student-athletes, when we understand how to put character literacy development **CLD** first, in both word and action, that is when we will create a legacy of greatness in our youth.

CV #25 Legacy: Activities and Drills to increase Retention/Assessment:

- o At this final stage of **CLD**, all of our student-athletes should be true ambassadors for what athletic competition is all about. As I make note of in the next chapter, the student-athletes who remain involved in sports up to this advanced mastery level have the an extremely high chance of coaching the youth of future generations. They have accrued some good "sweat equity," as Dr. Michael Sagas *(Founder of Twinnor, Professor and Department Chair at UF)* likes to say. What behaviors have we, as coaches, modeled for these up-and-coming coaches? Think about the **legacy** that you are leaving behind through your words and actions as a coach/mentor. This could be a great conversation with your team at this advanced level. Let them know that many of them will coach and mentor the next generation. Ask them to think about what type of coach they want to emulate. Who knows, it may even be you.

○ Have each of your players take five or ten minutes during the start of a practice to write a hand-written letter to a coach or teacher or mentor who has made a positive impact in their life. Perhaps they taught them an important message that has stuck with them and influenced them in a positive way. Be sure to have envelopes with stamps and have them address and seal the letters for you to mail out after practice.

○ A great take home assignment for your team is to have them each write their own coaching philosophy. Break the group up into five sections, to match the five levels of **CLD** (i.e. if you have 15 players, three players for each CLD section). Have them each write a one-page, single-spaced coaching philosophy statement tailored specifically to the level of student-athlete that you assign to them. Give them a good week to work on this. Match them up at the start of practice with the others who were assigned the same level and have them first share with the others in their select group. This will allow them to fine tune and tweak their own coaching statements. After which, have them each present to the team. *Have the team vote on the top coaching philosophy at each level. If you feel so inclined, please send the top ones to me to use during my junior high and high school **CLD** curricula.

○ Lastly, have each of your student-athletes think about and write down the ten qualities or values that they would hope that their teammates and friends would say about them as individuals. Ask them to put one's athletic ability on the side, and focus more on one's character. Tell them that these will be kept confidential. Collect each of these as the coach to keep in a file for their next player evaluation. This list will provide you, as the coach, with some terrific talking points, as well as allow them to reflect on whether or not they have been working to demonstrate high character. This is a great spring board to analyze and improve the **legacy** that they are leaving behind.

Part III:

The Application, Retention, and Assessment of

Character Literacy Development (CLD)

CHARACTER
LOVES
COMPANY

APPENDIX—Essays on Important Topics for the Future of Youth Sports

This chapter will focus on topics that will promote more *deliberate* and *intentional* character growth in youth and amateur athletics. This section provides three different essays that I wrote as a graduate student at the University of Florida, after a nine-year professional baseball career, followed by 15 years as a head coach at the high school and collegiate levels. These essays are intended to spark introspection and deliberation over some controversial topics that have seemed to be untouchable concepts or practices prevalent in the hyper-masculine win-at-all-costs world of sports.

While we (as a society) frown with great disdain at the actions and behaviors of some of the past few generations of youth, we have not come up with a way to work together as adults to better encourage their development and character. We want our children to grow up with high ethical values, but at times many of us feel as if we are in this daunting fight alone. We have all heard the wise ancient proverb that it "takes a village" to raise a child. We can do this, but it is going to take a collective effort from parents, coaches, teachers, and administrators pulling from the rope in the same direction, like any good team, culture, or organization has done since the beginning of time.

Essay Topics:

1) Bridging the Great Divide Between Parents and Coaches: The Need to Unify a Common Message

2) Coaching the Next Generation of Coaches: What Type of Behaviors and Values Are We Modeling?

3) Cleaning up the "Locker Room" Talk: We Cannot Continue to Turn a Blind Eye

Essay #1: Bridging the Great Divide Between Parents and Coaches (The Need to Unify a Common Message)

My hope through this essay, as well as the focus of my guidebook, is to get all who are involved in the development of our youth through sports in America on the same page working toward a common goal. Once this begins to occur more frequently and all constituents begin to actively adhere to the foundational principles of this guidebook, as well as other books and programs on character development, then we will find that there is much more common ground in our intent and purpose. The end result of this systematic curriculum on our rising generations will be better respect, appreciation, and demonstration for character literacy development **CLD**, rather than the zero-sum score concept that is being peddled in the minds of youth and amateur student-athletes today.

Rather than working together, as parents and coaches, toward a common goal that both of these vital constituents can agree upon when it comes to the growth and development of our youth, I have witnessed a wider divide, or rift, than ever before between these most highly influential figures in the lives of our rising generations. Why is this? The answer is rooted in a lack of trust, a lack of communication, and lack of respect for the vital role of the collaborative efforts of a team working toward a common goal.

Teamwork and working toward a common goal is CV #8 and an important foundational life lesson that should be learned at the early stages of one's development. The best way for adults to teach this vital life skill is by living it through demonstration. Rather than always trying to play the hero or star role, it is time for coaches and parents alike to share the spotlight by complimenting each other and working hand in hand. Often, I will witness or hear about coaches who will talk down on the parents of their student-athletes instead of emphasizing all the hard work and sacrifice that it takes for a parent to provide for their children.

On the flip side of the coin, parents often return insult for insult, blow for blow, as if it is a heavyweight fight to earn the respect and approval of their child. Rather than supporting a coach's decision on playing time or positional choice, parents are often quick to negatively critique and condemn the coaching decision. This rift between coaches and parents is at a seemingly all-time high and the end result is far from a desirable outcome. This is why my approach to **CLD** can help to bridge this wide gap and bring coaches and parents together in an effort to emphasize and instill the 25 CVs that I present in this guidebook. The shared goal should be to progressively help our children and student-athletes to **identify, promote, develop,** and **assess** their own **Character Literacy Development** through sports.

In discussing ways to bridge this gap with coaches and administrators who have been successfully doing so for many years, I have concluded that the only effective approach is grounded in effective communication. This does not mean that the parents have a say in the practice plans or game lineups, etc. What it does mean is that coaches communicate effectively through appropriate on-field behavior and mannerisms, as well as potentially through written communication on weekly focal points and goals.

Master Boon Brown (*35+ year Instructor/Mentor; Owner of Ancient Ways Martial Arts Academy*) is excellent at this. He sends out weekly electronic newsletters to parents, similar to those that academic educators at the younger levels rely on to keep parents in the know about important learning activities. These e-newsletters are packed with expert advice about various life skills, as well as technical and tactical knowledge that Master Brown and his staff are teaching their students. This is a communication practice that I, too, have used with my teams and parents, even at the varsity and collegiate levels of sports. This is an excellent way to help parents realize the many values that they may be overlooking when they become absorbed by a hyper-focus on end results, and in the case of many team sports, winning-at-all-costs.

I am an expert coach who has been around great coaches and mentors my entire life. Despite this fact, I always look forward to Master Brown's e-Newsletter each week. There is always at least one pearl of wisdom that I can take from his parent letter, and often more than one perspective that I had not previously thought of. I am not at all surprised that most of Master Brown's families get it when it comes to character unfoldment and working together as parents and coaches pulling the rope in the same direction.

My own personal newsletter updates to parents typically take me 30-minutes leading in to each week, but what a powerful outreach and bridge this effective communication channel is in building a sense of trust and unity between coaches and parents. The price of investing 30 minutes each week on effective electronic communication, as well as other forms of communication, is well worth the time and effort.

Essay #2: Coaching the Next Generation of Coaches
(What Type of Behaviors and Values Are We Modeling?)

Over the past 10 years, I have scoured countless books and research studies on youth athletic participation that portray how impressionable student-athletes are. Parents, coaches, and teachers are the most influential role models in the lives of American youth today, either for good or for bad. As a coach, I have grown to realize that my players watch my every move and they hang on to and dissect my every word and action. When you think that they are not watching, they are. I am not perfect, and I have made plenty of mistakes as a coach, but the key is to realize that we are role models and to learn from our own mistakes in order to "own our role."

I humbly admit that one of the worst coaching/mentoring mistakes that I made was when I once snapped a plastic clipboard in the dugout in response to a poor play in the field. Though my intent was to get my team to focus, instead it was an act that was out of my normal behavior and demeanor, and it actually proved to be more of a distraction in the big game than anything else. It was not my style, nor should it be anyone's style as it does not provide the type of role modeling and example that any coach should want his or her players to model. Sports should be teaching messages that emphasize what one has control over: dominion, focus, positive energy, and respect (including equipment), etc.

My response that day with student-athletes at the advanced mastery level (Level 5) of sport was out of character, and not in tune with the character values that I want to instill in those who I am fortunate to get to coach and mentor. Student-athletes at this advanced mastery level of sports should be learning how to **win the right way, servant leadership,** and **legacy**. When we do make mistakes as coaches, the most important thing that we can do is to have the humility to apologize and admit our faults. That is what I was able to point out that night after a tough semi-final loss under the lights at

California State University, Fullerton. This was not just a lesson learned for me, but hopefully for my players as well.

Student-athletes who progress to the Advancing and Mastery Levels of Sport have the highest likelihood of becoming coaches during their lifetime, either as an occupation, or as a volunteer coach at the youth recreational level (which I have explained to be such a vital role in the development of our youth). My hope for the future of youth and amateur sports is that by the time all athletes reach the varsity level of high school, as well as collegiate level (which is a privilege and not a right), they will represent a community of student-athletes with strong moral fiber. The character values that have been discussed in my guidebook will have been nurtured and developed throughout the years of youth sport participation on up.

I have created a character literacy **CL** test that I have labeled the C-SALT "Student-Athlete (Character) Literacy Test."[128] Developing strong character is at the heart and center of this test. Whether it is the varsity level of high school, community college level, NAIA, or any of the three levels of the NCAA, my focus and vision is for all student-athletes who reach these advanced mastery levels of sports to have a firm foundation of all of the 25 character values within my **CLD** curriculum. My hope is that all high school and collegiate athletic directors and coaches will require all of their varsity level student-athletes to take the C-SALT test. All graduating sports participants (including players, team managers) would not only have to complete this **CL** test, but they will also need to demonstrate aptitude, retention, and application of these 25 values. In each successive year (i.e. four years NCAA/NAIA or two years for community college), the student-athletes will be required to re-test with the head coach present. The head coach's presence is vital to assure that the players and team buy in and commit to the purpose and values of character development and how they transcend the athletic arena in life after sports. Even though the head coach is to be present during the C-SALT testing, the seniors, or leaders on the team should be the ones to open up the discussion and administer the test.

---

[128] My C-SALT test is presented in the supplemental coaches' guide at the end of this book. It provides a link to a 15-minute activity where student-athletes are asked to think about the various CVs that should be developed through sport participation. While the C-SALT test is valuable in and of itself, the true worth is in the discussions that coaches, team captains, and all players can initiate and develop from the activity.

What is the **C-SALT**? The C-SALT is the exact survey that more than 125+ elite level coaches across the country, from all levels of sports, completed for my UF-IRB Research Study 2 (as mentioned in Chapter 5). This research study laid the character foundation on age-specific character values to promote **CLD**. The supplemental coaches' guide provides a link to that survey for all coaches at the advanced mastery levels to use for their teams. See Figure 13[129] below, which provides a screenshot of the electronic survey from my research study. Coaches were asked to identify which of the seven boxes provided was the most appropriate age grouping to introduce the particular character values of focus. They would then simply click on and drag each **CV** to the appropriate age category. Many of the expert coaches who completed my research survey, some of whom have coached for over 40 years, commented afterward on how much the simple activity made them think about character and what they value and emphasize as a coach.

Figure 13 below:

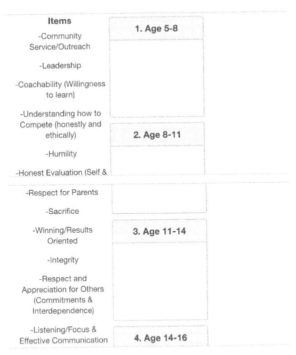

-Process Oriented	
-Sportsmanship	
-Discipline	
-Timeliness	
-Respect for opponents, officials/umpires/rules	**5. Age 16-19**
Legacy (Impact on others now and in future)	
-Confidence without being cocky	
-Work Ethic/Sense of Accomplishment	
-Body Language awareness	**6. Age 19-23**
-Concept of Working to a common goal (Teamwork)	
-Gratitude (love of sport/fitness and opportunities)	
-Servant Leadership	**7. Non-recommended**
-Handling	
-Servant Leadership	**7. Non-recommended Values**
-Handling Adversity/Struggle/Resilience	

While the hope is that coaches will use this same character building activity with their teams, it is important that they make it their own. However, I have provided easy directions for coaches to follow in administering the test. When the college coach, or high school coach for that matter, administers the C-SALT, he or she simply instructs the players to read over the 25 character values and then write each of the 25 character values in the box that they find most appropriate. In order to best facilitate the test, the seniors on the team are to have prepared a short personal reflection highlighting a character value development moment that changed their life from their youth to current day and share it with the rest of the team. This is a great opportunity to empower them in a leadership position, which will relay to the incoming freshmen and rising players that character development is something that the team, program, and athletic department highly value.

This is yet another means of dispelling the fallacy that somehow talking about character and emphasizing character is for the weak. I know this might sound like wishful thinking and a perfect world scenario, but to take it a bit further, I would require all the seniors to type their reflections of character out in a page or less and email it over to me as the head coach. The head coach could then catalog all of these character value moments. Hold on to them in a file and mail them out to each alumna or alumnus ten years later when most of them will have a family and children of their own. That is how you create a **legacy**.

Essay #3: Cleaning up the "Locker Room" Talk
(We Cannot Continue to Turn a Blind Eye)

Sexual assault and domestic violence are endemic problems that face our country today. Here, I draw a correlation between the fact that one in four homes in America are without fathers, and one in four girls/women in America are sexually assaulted in their lifetime. Sexual assault is the most horrifying act that one human being could commit on another, and domestic violence, which occurs even more frequently, is equally intolerable. As I have referenced earlier in this guidebook, there have been numerous reports and substantial evidence and testimony over the recent years from young girls and boys who have been sexually molested and assaulted by their own coaches.[130]

These sick and deranged coaches who exploit their positions of influence should be locked away for life. As a society of caring parents, coaches, and administrators, we need to be more present and aware of the coach to player relationships at our sports facilities. Proactive policies and guidelines need to be established and adhered to, such as always having another coach in a confined space or enclosed room with a student-athlete, without exception! Should a coach ever be confronted by a student-athlete with no one else around, that coach should be trained to immediately walk to a public area where others are present. Such policies and procedures would go a long way to eradicate the violent and deplorable actions against our young children involved in sports.

However, we need to take this conversation to a much deeper level where I believe young men are proliferating a hyper-sexual objectification and dominance of

---

[130] In a *Sports Illustrated* article from August 5, 2016 by Michael Rosenberg entitled: "It's Time for USOC to step up after USA Gymnastics sex abuse scandal." This article is similar to many reports related to sexual assault involving coaches tied to USA Swimming. Also, see Whiteside, K. (2014) and her *USA TODAY Sports* article entitled: "Citing sex abuse cases, swimmers protest Hall of Fame induction."

women. I believe there is a correlation between how adult males in our country talk about and even demean the opposite sex, and the vantage point and perspective of younger and highly impressionable males who look up to them as role models. If coaches and adult mentors of rising young boys and men would become more deliberate and aware of the power of their words, actions, and references to women, I believe these atrocities on the human rights of women would be lessened significantly. As men and women of influence, we need to join together to take a firm stand here.

As it relates to the content of this guidebook on character development, when coaches and adult males begin to model appropriate behavior toward women, then the next generation will follow suit and the true heroic sportsmen will re-emerge. However, if such behavior is not modeled by the coaches and parents of our youth then who is going to care enough to do it? If we want to eradicate the negative actions being witnessed on a daily basis in the media, we need to be that mirrored image of change.

I have heard all the excuses for why it is more difficult than ever before to have a real influence on our youth today; much of it rooted in kids' accessibility, nowadays, to anything and everything on the Internet. This may be the case as there is an endless array of inappropriate electronic garbage at the click of a mouse. However, in the world of sports, we, as coaches, administrators, and parents, have a powerful voice when it comes to influence. As I mentioned in my first essay on "Bridging the Great Divide Between Parents and Coaches," the only way that we can increase the character literacy of our children is if we unify and do it together.

The locker room, team room, or clubhouse is a sacred place in the world of sports. This is where teams are built and trust is formed. This does not mean that humanity is thrown out the window, as if there is a secret society that does not have to adhere to the norms of behavior. The term "locker room" talk has become an accepted and even expected practice or display of communication. Often, this is a place where it is okay to use violent, disrespectful, demeaning, and degrading language and gestures towards women. As someone who was a professional athlete and who grew up in and around sports locker rooms, such behavior tends to be taken for granted, or dismissed, as simply "joking around." However, we learn to behave from infancy up through adolescence and into early adulthood, based on what we see and hear from those whom we look up to.

For many coaches reading this short essay contribution on "Cleaning up the Locker Room," you may have never sat and analyzed the many adverse effects that such "locker room" talk or behavior could have on your young and impressionable student-athletes. My challenge for you, as a coach and mentor, is to think a little bit deeper about the impact that words and actions have on the growth of our youth. I realize that the locker room is often the players' place. However, you, as the coach and leader of the team, have a duty to establish rules and standards for them to follow. You have the power to influence your student-athletes who inevitably look up to you as a mentor. They will follow your lead and listen to your words more than you may know. The next time you overhear a few of your players using degrading language toward each other, or the opposite sex, seize that teachable moment. As the coach, you may not be seen as cool at the time, but your message on respect for others and human rights may be the most important mark that you leave on their future lives.

SUPPLEMENTAL "CLD" COACH-MENTOR GUIDE:

✓ Team Activities & Assignments from **CLD** Guidebook for each of the **25 CVs**

✓ Important Tables, Charts, and Graphs

✓ Link to **C-SALT** Student-athlete (Character) Literacy Test

✓ Contact Information for author—Coach Pete Paciorek (to share stories/ideas that I can use with future curricula)

Team Activities & Assignments from **CLD** Guidebook
for each of the **25 CV Building Blocks**:

CV #1 Respect for Parents: Activities and Drills to increase Retention/Assessment:

*Though my original intent was to provide drills that were applicable to the age-specific range of focus, some of these coach-initiated activities that I have provided at the end of each **CV** section (and in the **Supplemental Coaches' Guide** at the end of the book) may be a little advanced. This is deliberate on my part as I realize that coaches will be utilizing these **Foundational Level CVs** as character starting points for all levels from youth up through the amateur levels of collegiate athletics. The 8-week **CLD** curriculum that I facilitated this past summer in Pasadena, California was with high school students and we started at this foundational level. Please modify any and all of these drills to the age-range that you are working with.

o The best way to get respect is to show respect and care for others. The best way to teach your players at this young age to respect and value their parents is to constantly make it a point of emphasis.

o Have your players think about all the sacrifices that their parents/guardians make for them to be out there playing the sports that they love. Remind your young players to thank their parents on the car ride home from practices or games, as well as during various moments during each week. A simple thank you goes a long way and our players are never too young to learn this important gesture of gratitude.

o Within the first few weeks of practice and the season, bring a notepad of paper, enough pens or pencils for all of your players, along with stamps and envelopes. Have your players brainstorm a bit on the topic of respect for parents and what they are appreciative of. Then have them take 10 minutes at the end of practice on their own to write a hand-written note to mom or dad, or to their guardian. When they are finished, give them each an envelope with a stamp on it, and have them address it and seal it with the letter inside. Gather up all the letters and on your way home after that practice or game simply drop the letters in the mail.

o Depending on the age of your players, another great team activity is to have them stand up for 30 seconds and talk about someone who has been influential in their life (such as a parent). This not only works on their public speaking skills, but it also enhances the activity's effectiveness by having them articulate their respect and appreciation for the influential people in their lives.

CV #2 Sportspersonship: Activities and Drills to increase Retention/Assessment:

o Share with your team the story above from www.values.com where Mallory Holtman and Liz Wallace demonstrated great sportspersonship to their opponent in the NCAA softball regional. Go over the rules stating that her own teammate could not help her around the bases. What are your players' thoughts on this gesture of carrying a seriously injured opponent around the bases for a homerun? Help guide them to the side of sportsmanship vs. what many coaches/parents are teaching, the idea of gamesmanship. When it comes down to winning or losing, I know many coaches who would not have endorsed such a gesture. What is fair and right within the rules may not necessarily be correct, as sportspersonship goes beyond doing what the rules dictate to what is actually the right thing to do.

o Have your players work in groups of two or three, and ask each group to think about a recent event in the media where an individual, or team, demonstrated either negative or positive sportsmanship. Have each group present the story that they came up with to the rest of the team for discussion.

- Additional questions for teams to consider:
  - What external forces influence poor sportspersonship? How do you, as a coach, counter that?
  - Do your student-athletes think that as they get older it is more important to display good sportspersonship?
  - How does sportspersonship affect all aspects of life, not only sports?

CV #3 Respect for Opponents, etc.: Activities and Drills to increase Retention/Assessment:

- When focusing on respecting those on the field with your team, such as opponents, officials, etc., it is very important for a coach to emphasize that young student-athletes can be respectful and still play with a passion, edge, and desire to compete to win. I think about college football, or even professional football, which can be a ferocious and aggressive sport. Despite the fact that these players are going back and forth all game long, I always appreciate how, after a hard-fought battle, you oftentimes see players stick around on the field afterward for a group prayer or to give their opponent a "man-hug" out of respect (win or lose). Another occasion where you see this extension of respect after a hard-fought competition is in the boxing ring. Those are my favorite moments to witness in the athletic arena.
- If you have a road trip with your team, rent the movie *Chariots of Fire* which I discussed in the early going of this section for **CV #3**. Pick out a couple of specific scenes that highlight respect for opponents, rules, etc. and have your student-athlete reflect in a journal about what they took from those scenes as it relates to them and your team. You could follow up on this during the team breakfast which would get the players up on their feet doing a bit of public speaking.
- Another good clip to show your teams occurs each year in the Army-Navy Football game. After each game, both teams meet up and go to the other team's sideline and lock arms while respectfully saluting each other while listening to each band play that school's fight song.

- An excellent team activity is to have your players think about the scenario that Dr. Lee Ellis presented above regarding how to handle a "blow out." When your team is superior to the other team, you still want your student-athletes to compete with full focus and effort. Have them come up with a way to still do so as a team, but not to disrespectfully "run up the score" or demoralize their opponents. This can be hard for young, or even more mature Student-athletes. They can be so focused on their own statistics, the opportunity to get selected for "All Stars," or the looming college scholarship, that it can be difficult for them to buy in. More often than not, it is the parents who do not get the importance of building character through sports, who at times seem to care less about character and more about domination and accolades. If you have parents like that on your team, please give them a copy of my book.

CV #4 Gratitude (Joy of Sport/Fitness & Opportunity): Activities and Drills to increase Retention/Assessment:

- As a team homework assignment, ask your players to think about and write down on a notecard three things that they value about being able to participate in sports. This could be something that you collect at the next practice or game and keep in your coaching bag. When a player is struggling or facing adversity, you could remind them of what they value about the sport and their true purpose and intent for playing.
- One of my favorite activities related to gratitude is to get young student-athletes to better appreciate their opponents. All too often it is about crushing one's opponent, and while I am all for striving with all one's effort to win within the rules, I want our young student-athlete to realize the value of their opponent. Ask your team to think about the following questions: What if the other team decided not to show up? What if the opponent decided not to try? Would that make for a fun experience? In the next section, I discuss in more detail the idea of interconnectedness, or interdependence, which ties in closely to this CV on **gratitude and appreciation for one's opportunities.**
- An excellent team activity is to have your players get into pairs and have them think about how fortunate they are to be able to be a member of a team. Ask

them to think about the sacrifices that their parents make to allow them to get to practice and games on time each week.

CV #5 Appreciation/Care for Others (Interdependence and Commitment):

Activities and Drills to increase Retention/Assessment:

- o Towards the mid-way point of the season, have your players take 10 minutes to jot down a positive quality that they admire or respect about each of their teammates. Be sure that they write the teammate's name next to each quality. Collect each of these sheets and take that weekend to type out the result for each player from their peers. This is a great drill to get your players to highlight and notice the positive qualities in one another. It is so easy nowadays to only see and dwell on the negatives, or what they do not like. The following practice, give each player a laminated notecard of the responses from each of their peers. You can decide whether to include the players' names who made the positive comment or not. You can also include a quality that you value about each one of them. This could be something that you hand out at the end of practice. I can guarantee that these positive comments from their peers will lift them up. Who knows, it may be something that they keep with them for the rest of their lives.
- o If you are working with slightly older student-athletes, perhaps in the 13+ age range, take a rain delay, traffic jam, or other period of lengthy time to burn and start a discussion on the transferable skills of sports to the business-world, friendships, parenthood, or life in general.
- o The next team activity on interconnectedness and interdependence is one that I did with my first CLD curriculum in Southern California with a group of high school freshmen through seniors. This activity may take a bit more preparation, as I had them use the Internet and present their findings. I had them get into a couple groups of four or five people. I then handed them each a topic and asked them to brainstorm, research, and analyze how their topic related to baseball. The topics each involved everyday processes that occur in nature that involve an interconnectedness of many moving parts to function. A few good topics were: the various roles and responsibilities of an ant colony, the inner workings of bees, and a more creative one, the process of photosynthesis. It was amazing to

watch the creativity of these young student-athletes' minds at work in drawing the correlation between these topics and the importance of teamwork and interdependence in the sport(s) that they love.

CV #6 Coachability (Willingness to Learn): Activities and Drills to increase Retention/Assessment:

- o According to Peterson & Seligman (2004, pg. 163) in their 800-page book entitled *Character Strengths and Virtues: A Handbook and Classification*, the authors state the following:

  It is likely that people with love of learning as a general strength would strongly endorse statements such as the following:

  - *I can't do this task now, but I think I will be able to do it in the future.*
  - *I like to learn new things.*
  - *I will do whatever it takes in order to do a task correctly.*
  - *Learning is a positive experience.*
  - *I care more about doing a thorough job than whether I receive a good grade.*

  *The works of Peterson and Seligman (2004) provide a terrific resource from which to initiate a starting point for a team conversation on the topic of being **coachable** and having a **willingness to learn** through a growth mindset. For bullet point three above, I would potentially adjust the wording away from "whatever it takes" when discussing this idea with young children, as in their minds "whatever it takes" could become fuzzy and potentially encourage cheating within the realm of the statement. Perhaps "by all ethical means" would be a more appropriate statement as it relates to youth sports. The point here is that we, as coaches and parents of youth sports participants, need to be very *deliberate* and *intentional* about our messages. For the fifth and final bullet, the end statement of "receiving a good grade" could easily be replaced with "receiving a trophy or award or D1 scholarship."

- o Reference the definition of a "fixed mindset" vs. a "growth mindset" that Carol Dweck discusses in her works. Have your players think about and actively choose to be an individual with a growth mindset.

- o A fun activity is to take 36 cones and line them up in six rows of six. Chart out a path in your mind from the first cone to the 36th cone. Explain to the players that this is a game that takes the collective effort of all the players working together and learning from each other's mistakes. In the end, they will win if they stick together. The basic rules are that they cannot go backward. The first person steps up and tries to go from cone one to the next cone. If his or her step to cone two is correct, you say "yes." If their path is incorrect, you say "no" and then the next teammate steps up and tries a new path starting from the beginning. The next person always has to start from the beginning, but the emphasis is on paying attention to when their teammate went the correct way and followed their lead, while avoiding the wrong path (or cone) that they chose. What I especially love about this game is the **willingness to learn** from each other, but also the fact that no one can have an ego and simply do it all by themselves. When they figure it out in the end, the entire group should be excited about it. Sure, they all want to be that last person to complete the whole maze, but sports are about teamwork and continuing to grow and learn.

CV #7 Integrity and Honor: Activities and Drills to increase Retention/Assessment:

- o When discussing the **CV** of **integrity** and **honor** with your team or young student-athletes at this developmental stage of **CLD,** ask them if they would endorse the following statements on **integrity** as presented by Dr. Peterson and Dr. Seligman (2004):
  - It is more important to be myself than to be popular.
  - When people keep telling the truth, things work out.
  - I would never lie just to get something I wanted from someone.
  - My life is guided and given meaning by my code of values.
  - It is important to me to be open and honest about my feelings.
  - I always follow through on my commitments, even when it costs me.
- o Relate these statements/questions now to sport-specific situations. This could be a way to create core team values about appropriate behavior. Examples of questions could be:
  - When our team loses a game, we will still show respect to our opponent by shaking their hand and telling them "good game."

- When a teammate makes a mistake, we will not look down on them, but rather pick them up and support them.
- When the official/umpire/judge makes what seems to be a bad call or decision, I will respect his/her call and move on.
- If we have the opportunity to cheat in order to win, we will choose to do the right thing.

○ Bring in a guest speaker, before or after practice, to talk with your team about a certain character value that you are working to emphasize with your players. I did this when I was discussing the concept of leadership with my group of young student-athletes, who were part of our youth development company BAT 1000 in Pasadena, California. I invited out a friend and mentor of mine, **Fred Claire** (past-GM of the Los Angeles Dodgers when they last won the World Series in 1988), and he spoke with the boys about what it takes to be a leader. The young student-athletes talked about their takeaways with Mr. Claire throughout the summer. Similarly, in the way that many young student-athletes want to do it all themselves and be the hero, oftentimes coaches do the same thing. There are many wonderfully successful individuals in our communities throughout the country who would jump at the idea to impart some of their knowledge for 15-20 minutes with the rising generations. You would be surprised by how many such individuals would be honored to jump on the opportunity.

○ In discussing **integrity** and **honor** with student-athletes at this level of their development, ask your players to come up with a succinct and concise purpose statement that will help guide them when they are faced with adversity or a crossroads in life. I gave a group of high school student-athletes 30 seconds to think about it and write down their statement, and I was blown away by the clarity in many of their responses. Here are a few to note:

- "Integrity is doing the right thing when no one is looking."
- "Integrity is taking responsibility for one's actions, and acting with honor."
- "Integrity is being honest regardless of the personal consequences."

CV #8 Concept of Working to a Common Goal (Teamwork): Activities and Drills to increase Retention/Assessment:

- o The team activity with the 36 cones and figuring out the path to victory as a team applies to this concept of teamwork and working to a common goal as well. Another version of this activity is to blindfold the person whose turn it is to go, and have the rest of the team guide them through the maze. Trusting in one another is an important component in working to a common goal.

- o Have your players come up with a team motto, similar to Coach Amanda Butler's team at the University of Florida with "TLC" (Trust, Loyalty, and Commitment). Ask them what three characteristics or qualities they want to embody each time they come together as a team, whether it be practice or games. When a teammate gets off track, it is very easy for you as the coach, or for a player, to simply remind each other of the team's motto or focus.

- o Coach Butler also talked about "energy givers" and "energy suckers." While this message could be a team message for everyone to hear, it could also be a great heart-to-heart with a player whose body language and demeanor needs an adjustment. This meaningful message will not only pay dividends for the team's culture, but more importantly help that individual in all areas of life.

CV #9 Listening and Focus: Activities and Drills to increase Retention/Assessment: This CV on **listening** and **focus** is directly correlated to CV #6 being coachable. You simply cannot have one without the other. Listening and paying attention to directions are vitally important; coaches must find ways to engage our student-athletes and make learning relevant and fun.

- o While we as coaches understand the need for our student-athletes to listen well to instructions, we also have to realize that we need to be brief with our messages. There are coaches who will keep their teams after games for 30 minutes to an hour in effort to really try to drive home a message. Some will even punish their teams with sprints until exhaustion. While there is some value from that, we (as coaches) have to realize that we may have their full focus for as long as 30 seconds. Yes, 30 seconds. Then, they will inevitably zone out. Obviously, with varying levels of SAs, we have increased concentration and focus and the message can be longer and more complex. However, at certain times, when explaining the directives for a certain drill, I have found that actually getting into the drill and having players try it and catch on to the flow of the drill is the best way for them to learn. It is more engaging and taps into the fact that we are all very visual as human beings in the way that we learn and retain information. Try a 30-second approach to messages of great importance. With longer explanations, try to limit it to three minutes. When this does happen, try to engage your team with questions and get them to speak and contribute.

- One of my favorite team activities of all time is "blind dodgeball." Be sure to locate soft snowball type balls and enough blind-folds (bandanas) for half of the players on your team. Section off an 80 foot by 80-foot area of grass free of danger (i.e. sprinkler heads and holes.) Assign pairs to work together. One is to wear the blindfold and the other is to stand behind them and act as their eyes. A side note: I usually have the players throw the ball with their opposite hand to avoid injury, as well as make for more comedic relief. During this activity, the duos quickly realize how important focus, teamwork, listening, and clear directives are. Your teams will love the activity and want to play it far longer than time will permit. However, be sure to save 10 minutes at the end of the activity for player reflections on their takeaways from the activity.

- I have a simple **listening** and **focus** batting practice routine that can be adjusted and applied to any sport. I have the players say out loud after each pitch what the pitch was. If they cannot remember, they do not get that next swing. If they miss two, their round is over. Losing out on swings will get their attention. All of a sudden, the players who have focus problems in the athletic arena, or in the classroom, will suddenly find a way to lock it in very quickly. This is a concept that a few of my contributors discussed about youth and video games, and how kids can sit and play video games for hours on end with **razor sharp focus**. Obviously, the more we can bring the "fun" back into sports the better. However, working on the process that it takes to improve one's craft is extremely fun and rewarding.

- o One thing that I have learned is that when it is a game, they lock it in. When it is a drill, they zone out. Simple phrases can draw them in, or freeze them out. It is true for all of us. Now, at the younger levels, the research discussed the importance of deliberate play (meaning more fun focus) as the primary mode of sport delivery. However, as kids grow older, they do not shy away from drills as they begin to become a bit more **process-oriented,** which is **CV #19** in Chapter 9.

- o In baseball, basketball, football, and many other sports, student-athletes loathe running, or conditioning. As a baseball coach, it is very common to end practice by running the bases. Next time you have your players run from home plate to first base, take out your stop watch and record their times. When they cross first base, yell out their times. I can guarantee you that they will ask if they can do it again. Use that competitive edge that resides in all of us to make practice more fun and rewarding.

CV #10 Understanding How to Compete (Honestly & Ethically): Activities and Drills to increase Retention/Assessment:

- o Share the example from above with Andy Roddick in the Rome Open. He was honest to the line judge about a missed call. It ended up costing him the tennis match in the long run, as well as potentially $100,000 or more. However, in a day and age when greed for money and the win-at-all-costs mentality is raging, Roddick showed the world that you cannot put a price tag on one's integrity. Ask your players how they would have handled that situation if the Little League World Series, High School championship, or College National Title was on the line? It is one thing to say that we would act a certain way, and quite another to actually follow through with it. By having this conversation, there is a much better chance that when a similar situation arises, your student-athletes will have at least broached the topic.

- o Go ahead and play out some scenarios (there are scores of different temptations that can and do arise in each sport). Break your team up into smaller working groups, and give each group a different scenario to play out. After five minutes, have each group get up and present their case. Once again, this is a terrific way to work in a little public speaking and confidence building with their voices.

o Share the story that Olympic gold medalist **BJ Bedford-Miller** provided in this chapter regarding how to compete the correct way. This could be a great message leading up to the championship game, in order for your student-athletes to have a better perspective of what it takes to win with class and lose with dignity. As **David Prince** stated in CV #6 on coachability, there really is no such thing as losing because, when we lose on the scoreboard, we learn and grow more from it than when we win.

CV #11 Discipline: Activities and Drills to increase Retention/Assessment:

o While we want kids to keep fun first and foremost in sports, this mid-level developing stage is where we want to begin to emphasize the **discipline** that it takes to develop true skills. This is where the power of a short thematic story or parable can give the student-athletes something to relate to. Below I have provided a few great messages of success that came about through strong discipline and commitment toward a certain goal. The following list will give you as a coach some talking points that you can research further and make your own. The key to remember, especially at this age, is to keep it brief and to the point, and try to stimulate team involvement and players' perspectives and insights. This will increase their comprehension and retention. Potential topics:

- Going back to the story of **Olympic gold medalist Betsy Mitchell** waking up at 4:30am on her own. If they found something that they were passionate about, do they think that they could do that? What would it take for you to rise up out of bed that early? Would they have to sacrifice something on the other end (at night) in order to be more productive in the mornings?

- Ask them about the quote at the beginning of this section by one of our Founding Fathers and the 1st President of the United States of America, George Washington, *"Discipline is the soul of an Army."*

Ask your players what that means to them and how it relates to sports and the concept of team.

- Favorite video game? What do they love about it? When they first played that game, were they good at it? How did they become good at it? Wasn't the challenge of learning how to play the game well a big part of the fun? Did it take discipline to sit there and get beaten by their friends over and over until they figured it out?

- Ask them what they think about **Coach Ken Leavoy's** statement about how disciplined behavior leads to more disciplined behavior, which ultimately leads to building highly effective habits? Does this work both ways as it relates to establishing potentially bad habits?

- Come up with a team goal to increase their discipline. Tell them that you will do it as well. Perhaps it could be making their beds each morning when they rise. That simple act, first thing in the morning, will be their test that could trigger the tone for their willingness to be disciplined with their actions that day.

o Once you have covered this topic of the importance of discipline in their lives, make a call to action. Ask them about an area of their lives that they know would benefit greatly from becoming more disciplined. We all have areas to improve upon. After a few minutes of reflection, if you are willing, share an area of your life that you are working to become more disciplined in. Your leadership and humility will help break the ice for your team. When I did this exercise for the first time with a group of high school baseball players, I was amazed by the thoughtfulness in their responses, as well as their willingness to share.

CV #12 Timeliness (Time Management/Preparation): Activities and Drills to increase Retention/Assessment:

o Present the following quote with your team. Have them discuss what they think it means. Begin to explain to them that this is the stage when they need to start taking a bit more ownership in their endeavors. Their parents should no longer have to lay out their uniform, carry their sport's bag, or backpack, nor remind them about what time practice starts. This is where timeliness and time management begin to develop in our youth. *"Tardiness often robs us opportunity, and the dispatch of our forces."* –Niccolo Machiavelli

- o Rainy Day Chalk Ideas:
    - Why do we ever cancel practice due to rain or weather? Unless it is unsafe to drive, if a coach can find a covered, sheltered and safe place indoors, there is much to be taught and learned regarding **CLD.** Practice is on!
- o Top 10 List:
    - Give each member of your team a notecard and a pencil (every coach should have a small box of golf pencils for team activities such as these). Have them take one minute only to quickly come up with the top 10 qualities of a good teammate, or captain. I can guarantee that the discipline needed to be consistent and show up on time will make many top 10 lists. After they spend one minute individually, have them partner up for two minutes and ask them to circle their overlapping responses. Then have the duo present in 30 seconds their findings to the entire team. This is a terrific way to get them up in front of the group sharing important ideas and leading the charge on character development. It is important that we empower them to use their voices and take an active role in their development and retention of **CLD.**
- o Similar to Coach Wooden's quote: *"Be quick, but don't hurry,"* have your team come up with a team slogan. Come up with a team slogan or philosophy regarding a team commitment to outwork the opponent while maintaining control and poise.

CV #13 Humility: Activities and Drills to increase Retention/Assessment:

- o There are many different ways to help young student-athletes, and children in general appreciate and learn to be humble. However, the most important approach is to model such behavior as a coach or parent. Are you demonstrating humility as a coach and mentor for your student-athletes?

○ A post-game tradition that my brother Mack (who has been a successful high school head baseball coach for the past decade) does is to begin by pointing out what a great performance the obvious star of that game had. His point is that everyone was there, and they all witnessed the great accomplishments from that individual. It is traditionally not the extraordinary acts that make the difference in the end result, but rather the sum of all the smaller, less noticeable contributions all coming together towards a common goal. What Mack does, and what I have started to do, is to have the obvious star individual pick someone else to "brag on" for their contribution to the team's success. This is a way to not only get your team to comprehend the importance of the power of the entire unit, but it also minimizes some of the ego-centrism that we see in youth, amateur, and professional sports. Try it out for yourself with your team.

○ A team activity that I learned from one of my previous players is called the "Three Snaps Game." At the heart of this fun game is the necessity of members of a team working to get in unison with each other. The most effective teams and organizations have cohesion and continuity. Have your players get into pairs with a cone in between them. They are to snap three times and after the third snap say whatever word is in their head (be sure they are mindful and respectful with their words). Without giving each other any kind of secret signal, they are to work to eventually say the same word. After each turn, they should think for a second or two about what word they want to say next based on the feedback from their partner. Then they do their three snaps and say their next word. This is a good way to get players to adapt and adjust, as well as realize that if they want to succeed, they have to be on the same page as their teammates, and not living on an island all by themselves.

(A hint as the coach is to come up with topics for them such as: sports, movies, music, etc.)

- o Another terrific activity that I mentioned in a previous section is to work with your student-athletes on their interviews/meetings with potential future high school or college coaches. Sit down with each of them and ask them the tough questions that seek to gain information about their ability as athletes to adapt to difficult situations; how to be good team players; whether they are concerned with the team's ultimate success rather than simply personal accolades. In the end, coaches want players with confidence in themselves, but more importantly, they want student-athletes who can be humble and who have an understanding of the power of a team all pulling in the same direction.

CV #14 Work Ethic/Sense of Accomplishment: Activities and Drills to increase Retention/Assessment:

- o This is a perfect opportunity as a coach or a parent at home to encourage young student-athletes to put in some conscientious effort outside of practice time working to improve their abilities. No one ever became great at anything by accident. Over the years, I have seen some of the best athletes in the world train first hand, and it was not an accident that they became great.

- o Give each of your players a note card and have them write their favorite athlete's name down on the card. Ask them to go on the Internet and do some research on this individual. Have them try to find out the secret to their favorite athlete's success. My guess is that hard work and passion will be at the root of what most of them find. Have them write their findings on the back of the card to share with their teammates. Unless you have a rain delay or long bus/van trip, you will most likely not have time to get through all of them but you will be surprised by how many of them actually look forward to volunteering to educate their teammates on what they found out.

- o Regarding Michael Jordan's quote at the beginning of this section on making things happen vs. waiting or hoping for things to happen, ask your players whether they want, wish, or are willing to work to make their dreams become a reality? Talk and mentor them about what it takes to accomplish something great.

CV #15 Leadership (Mentoring): Activities and Drills to increase Retention/Assessment:

- o Building Team Culture: Ask your student-athletes what it takes to be a great leader. Have them think of situations when it would be tough to be a leader. For instance, can a leader just simply coast and go along with the crowd?
- o Homework exercise for your players prior to the next practice or game: Ask them to come up with a good captain/leader in professional sports, and why he or she is an effective leader.
- o As a coach, come up with your own Top 10 Qualities of a good Team Captain. Share your list with your players. Ask them if they possess what it takes to be a true captain of the team? Are they willing to make the sacrifice and stand up for the high standards and principles that you demand? There are many wonderful captain and leadership training books for young student-athletes at the high school and college levels. As a coach over the past two decades, I have been guided and inspired by many such books. I have come up with and used what I call my "Top 10" essentials of an effective captain. I am not one who takes "captainship" lightly, nor one who automatically rewards an upper-classman with the title and honor. The right to be a captain has to be earned at all times. During my coaching career, I have gone a year without a player-captain. I have also relinquished two players of their title of captain, one of whom earned it back. I have also been fortunate to coach some of the most gifted and natural leaders and captains in youth and amateur sports.

In my mind, the team captain (or captains) is someone who will always lead by example, despite the consequences or backlash that he or she may receive from their teammates, or the media. A captain is no higher than his or her teammates, and a true captain would never want to be regarded as so. A player-captain is someone who acts as a liaison, or link, between the players and the coaches. Two absolute characteristics that such a captain must possess are trustworthiness and respect.

CV #16 Confidence without being Cocky: Activities and Drills to increase Retention/Assessment:

- This is the perfect age in which to take the time to emphasize the difference between confidence and cockiness. Come up with your own definitions, or borrow from my ideas as laid out in this chapter. The key is to help your young student-athletes discern between the two dichotomous terms.
- Have your players practice walking from the on-deck circle to the batter's box, or likewise stepping up to the free throw line, starting blocks, etc., with the entire team watching. Every elite-level performer has a routine that allows them to embrace the situation with confidence. Have them work on their own routines of confidence in preparation for competition.
- Ask your student-athletes to go home and think about their fears. Do any of those fears get in the way of their short-term, or ultimate goals? If they do, ask them to challenge themselves to be confident in addressing challenges head on. After all, they don't want to miss out on something due to fear or lack of confidence.
- When your student-athletes break through a limitation, or address a challenge head on, be sure to highlight that. A simple, "*I see you working*" goes a long way.
- In CV #20 on **Body Language Awareness**, I will share some activities or exercises to improve your student-athletes' non-verbal communication which, in turn, affects their outward and inward appearance.

CV #17 Sacrifice: Activities and Drills to increase Retention/Assessment:

- Have the players think about sports other than the one that you are coaching them in currently, and try to think of where sacrifice for the team goal is necessary (i.e. bunting in baseball, the extra pass in basketball, participating in a certain event in swimming or track and field). Perhaps the sacrifice itself is not the player's best event or skill, but that person is simply the best woman or man for the job. When sacrificing for the betterment of the team, there exists a willingness to put the interest of others above one's self.

- On a similar note above, instead of applying the importance of sacrifice to sports, have your team think about how **sacrifice** relates to success in business, or family life.

- Share the exact scenario that I presented above about the high school All-American and the NCAA All-American. Ask them to think about who the coach is going to play at shortstop, or whatever the preferred position is in your sport. At this point in their **CLD**, they should all have the requisite character values to answer and acknowledge the validity of this analogy as it pertains to their need to learn to play multiple positions, and run or swim a variety of events.

- Another great team activity for a rain delay is to have the players on your team think about sacrifices that they are going to have to make in life, and perhaps even sacrifices that they have already begun to make in order to be a dedicated and successful student-athlete.

- If you have access to a projector screen and Internet access at a hotel on the road, get your team together and have them view what I feel is one of the most inspiring commencement addresses of all time. Naval Admiral William H. McRaven, 9th Commander of U.S. Special Operations Command, gave the 2014 commencement speech at the University of Texas. He covers many of the CVs that I discuss in this guidebook, and one that really stood out to me was the **CV** on **sacrifice**. You can find a transcription of the speech at: www.news.utexas.edu as well as find the 20-minute video on YouTube.

CV #18 Handling Adversity/Resilience (Toughness): Activities and Drills to increase Retention/Assessment:

- Here, again, is another terrific opportunity to open up a dialogue with your players or children about the overlapping values between sports and life. The message could be as simple and powerful as never "quit" something in the middle of a season. When things get tough, or they don't get along with all the teammates, they need to learn to persevere and battle through them. (Now, there are extenuating circumstances when safety or physical/emotional harm trumps the loyalty and stick-to-it-tiveness). In a job, they may not like their boss, or a co-worker, but they need to find a way to work together despite differences in opinion or taste.

○ I recently heard about and watched the **Invictus Games** that took place in May of 2016 in Orlando, Florida. The Invictus Games were created by Great Britain's Prince Henry as an international event to honor, celebrate, and support the athletic pursuits of excellence by injured war veterans. I recommend that any coach and his or her team stayed tuned in for the next Invictus Games in order to witness the honor, bravery, **perseverance**, and **grit** on display by true heroes.

○ Share the example that I provided to start this CV on Rockefeller's **grit.**

○ Share an example of the way life works in nature. For example, a tree curves, contours, and adapts in order to stretch toward the light. It is constantly bending and reaching outward. That is what we as human beings need to do.

○ Talk about the **resilience** that it took for President Lincoln to become the President of the United States, and all that he was able to accomplish in his tenure.

○ When your players think that they have had to endure some tough times to get to where they are in sports, share the story of **grit** and determination from Malaika Underwood to follow her dreams.

○ Life will oftentimes throw us curveballs. The more that your teams and student-athletes learn to adjust and adapt, while continuing to move forward, the better. A fun and care-free activity to play with your team is the "Adjustment Game." This is a game that I learned from my brother Mack, whom I mentioned earlier is a youth coach as well. I actually play this in my public speaking classes to help get my students out of their shells a bit, and to tap into their creative minds. The way it works is that you have a player/student come to the front of group. You then ask them a question, such as: "Tell us all about your favorite vacation." As the individual is telling his or her story, you are confirming with a "yes" throughout. However, as he/she gets rolling, you interject a "no." For every "no," they now have to adjust their story without getting flustered, and simply go with the flow. It is fun to hear how creative they become, and how they are able to react on the fly. Try it, as it is always entertaining.

CV #19 Process Oriented: <u>Activities and Drills to increase Retention/Assessment:</u>

- o Ask your players to think about the quote by Aristotle at the outset of this chapter: *"Excellence is not an act, but a habit."* Have them write in their journals for a few minutes on what that statement means to them and how it relates to their **process** of improvement in their sport? A good follow-up question is to ask them to think about the progress that they have seen during this season, as well as what areas they will improve most if they keep "**trusting the process**"?

- o A good take-home activity in terms of **trusting the process** is to have your student-athletes do some research on "watering the bamboo." In order for bamboo to show signs of life and growth, one has to water it every day for two years. There is typically no growth for a full two years. This is a great analogy and lesson for growth in sports, as well as in life. This will teach our rising generation about the importance of reaping what you sow.

- o As Paralympian and World Record Holder in the 200M and 400M, David Prince, points out, kids do know how to **work the process**. They do it every day, sometimes for hours, as they play video games. Though I am not a big proponent of video games, I have observed in amazement as some of my players sat locked in like a fighter pilot, conquering stage by stage, paying attention to the fine details that it takes to learn and adapt in order to conquer the game. Because many young people love playing video games, we need to tap into that passion and find ways to use a **process oriented** approach in the athletic arena or classroom.

- o A valuable activity at this level is to practice the "college coach: player interview" with each player individually at this 14-16-year-old range and above. Help them gain a better understanding of what college coaches are looking for in recruits. This is a great activity, as student-athletes will get better and better at this with practice and from your coaching tips. The biggest mistake that I have seen parents make is that they try to do all of the talking for their son or daughter with the college coaches. This stunts the process of growth for student-athletes who are aspiring to play in college. College coaches are turned off by the recruit who cannot speak for themselves. However, this takes repetitive practice. I have heard parents tell me that they feel that they cannot resist the urge to speak for their son or daughter because they are much better at saying all the right things. Well, actually, that could not be further from the truth. Such parents could also do their son or daughter's science project for them, but in the end, how does that prepare their child for success in life?

o If you are a junior high or high school coach, you could devise a decal reward system based on whichever measurements you find to be important. As Coach Wooden says, what we emphasize gets improved upon. You could do what I did when I was a DIII head baseball coach trying to motivate my players to "buy in" to the team concept. I created an 11x17 laminated card stock board for each player. My assistant coaches and I then put them up on the outside of their lockers (obviously, they each did not have their own helmet as football players do). I then came up with 10 different decals for big plays such as: "SAC" for a sacrifice bunt or sacrifice fly; a lightning bolt for sparking a rally, or a "GC" for a game-changing play. As a coach, you can have fun with it, but from a **CLD** standpoint, there has to be a character/teamwork component to the decals. For instance, in football, to emphasize **integrity**, or **compassion,** a player could be rewarded a decal for a big-time crushing tackle followed by the same player helping his opponent back up off the turf after the end of the play. Such a sign of **sportspersonship** could be rewarded with a decal. There is nothing "soft" or "weak" about a linebacker lighting up an opposing ball carrier and then showing respect for his opponent by helping him back up in order to line up and have the challenge of doing it again on the next play.

o To add more buy in from your student-athletes on the **process** of doing things the correct way, or team way, have them work in pairs to each come up with a specific decal, and then have the duo present their idea to the team. They could then take it a step further and ask them to go home and design the artwork for the decals. The cost is very minimal for the internal rewards of seeing your players begin to see how paying attention to the minor details of the game leads to better overall performance over the long haul.

o Emphasize to your student-athletes that at this age-range the current "best" players can have a tendency to become content with their abilities and, thus, they stop working the **process** of getting better. The player who is driven by a purpose of improving a little bit each day oftentimes surpasses those early bloomers. Take Michael Jordan, who in my mind is the greatest basketball player of all time. We all know the story. He was cut from his team in high school as a freshman. Imagine if he would have stopped working the process?

CV #20 Body Language Awareness: Activities and Drills to increase

Retention/Assessment:

- o Start with an effective activity in "Power Stance & Statement" building. Lead a team activity where each member of the team has to come up with a 30-second confidence building game plan filled with reminders for strong body language and positive self-talk.

- o The best activity for emphasis and retention of the message of effective body language and awareness is by recording your student-athletes live during pivotal moments in games. Film them just before an event, race, at-bat, free throw, penalty kick, etc. Ask them to critique themselves. Do not allow them to beat themselves up too much, as we can easily become our own worst critics. As Dr. Angus Mugford and the research by Dr. Amy Cuddy emphasized, one's body language (good or bad) will impact not only how others view that person, but how that person views themselves.

  *In order to do this activity, first gain permission from the parents of your student-athletes. It is always critical for parents and coaches to be on the same team, and this would be an excellent way to join forces in emphasizing this important life skill development.

- o Another activity that will help young student-athletes to become more conscious of their body language is to have an assistant coach tell a story and pick a few players to watch your mannerisms while sitting on the bench or huddle amongst the other players. The coach will tell the same story three times. The first time you will show mannerisms of the disengaged SA (or player who is too cool to listen). The second time you will portray the rude and bored SA (yawning and checking phone). The third time you will impersonate the SA who is coachable, attentive and fully engaged. Ask the three players standing to notate to the rest of the team who they would want as a player. This drill is both educational, and eye opening for many young SAs.

CV #21 Community Service/Outreach: Activities and Drills to increase Retention/Assessment:

- o The most important approach with **Community Service** and **Outreach** is to get your teams out in the community serving others
- o Charitable Events for student-athletes of all ages:
  - • Local Challenger Leagues
  - • Miracle League
  - • Make a Wish Foundation
  - • Canned food drive for Homeless
- o As Student-Athletes get older and more mature"
  - • Homeless Shelters
  - • Children's hospitals
  - • Big Brothers & Big Sisters
  - • Animal Shelters
  - • Offer sports/tutoring lessons for younger kids
  - • Volunteer to umpire (if you want to give your players some perspective)
  - • Volunteer to help at B&G Club or YMCA as a coach/mentor
- o Team Outreach Concepts that take more Planning on Coach or Parents
  - • Take a team trip in HS or College to the Dominican Republic (play three or four games with the local talent, but, more importantly, help build a house through Habitat for Humanity, help with youth camps like I did—one of the top five life-changing events in my life, after getting married and having children--It was an inspiration.
  - • Something that my brothers and I do with our BAT1000 youth sports development programs is to fundraise to provide for

three homeless children from the Union Rescue Mission to take part in our weekend activities in Southern California.

- Twinning (The student-athletes need to raise the money themselves—maybe through a team car wash to raise $200 for equipment and fees to sponsor a team in Guatemala, for example). Parents cannot simply buy it for them—the message needs to be taught on the intrinsic rewards of sacrificing something (as a team, or individual) and accruing "sweat equity" to provide for others in need. Go to www.twinnor.org to find out more.

CV #22 Honest Evaluation (Self & Peer): Activities and Drills to increase Retention/Assessment:

- o Honest evaluation can be a difficult thing for any dedicated student-athlete. However, at this advanced stage of sport development honest and fair assessment is vital.

  What I have found at this level is that a written assessment to accompany a post-season face-to-face evaluation is the most effective approach to allow for growth in each student-athlete. It is typically a good idea to have your assistant coach in the room with you to give additional insights, but also to combat any potential disagreements.

- o Give your players 10-15 minutes after a practice towards the end of the season write a self-evaluation in their player journals. Be sure that they are not simply evaluating the physical performance on the field but all areas of their lives: Athletically, socially, family, relationship with peers, character, and leadership.

- o It can be very easy for young student-athletes to fall into the trap of only caring and focusing on their own improvements and development. When you are having your post-game meeting, ask each of the players to think about something about a teammate that has impressed you. Give them a few minutes to think about the person to their left or right. It is a rewarding activity to hear and see each of these young SA's complimenting one another.

- o At the mid-way point of the season, have your student-athletes identify their three biggest strengths related to the sport of focus, as well as their three biggest areas for improvement. Perhaps you can give them a print out for them to fill out prior to the next practice or game.

- o For my end-of-the-season player evaluation, I usually give the players a blank copy of my evaluation form and ask that they fill it out to the best of their ability prior to our meeting. Prior to disclosing my assessment, I ask the student-athletes to rate themselves followed by my assessment, line by line. This is an excellent way to highlight any incongruities and help them to be more realistic in areas of needed improvement, or for some, unrecognized strengths. The players typically appreciate this approach, though they may not like the honest feedback. An important note: At this point, you have hopefully been able to get to know your players well enough and together you have earned a mutual respect that would invite honest and constructive feedback. There is a fine line between constructive criticism and demoralizing a player, but at this stage, student-athletes need to be given honest feedback in order to move forward.

CV #23 Winning (How to Win the Right Way): Activities and Drills to increase Retention/Assessment:

- o At this advanced-mastery level of participation in sports, student-athletes should have a stronghold on the many values of winning. Typically, however, there is now more on the line for these student-athletes. They have scholarships and even professional contract offers looming. An important message from coaches and parents is to share real-life examples in the importance of demonstrating self-control, respect for the talents of their opponents, focus, etc.

- o An important message for student-athletes at this advanced level is consistency. They are now at a stage where it is no longer as much about who has the most talent, but rather who can consistently demonstrate mastery during the heat of the battle. Those who can remain focused, unfazed, and unintimidated by the competition and the magnitude of the event are the ones who will perform to their highest potential.

- o Give each of your student-athletes a small bound journal with the logo of your team on it. Have them write a short reflection after each practice or game about what they learned that day. Rather than have them simply dwell on winning or losing, have them focus on what they learned during the heat of the battle. Over time, they will start to realize that, through their reflections, they are learning a great deal more through the tough times of struggle. Eventually, they will begin to embrace the rewards and growth that comes from adversity and this will help them understand how to **win the right way** in sports and in life.

CV #24 Servant Leadership: Activities and Drills to increase Retention/Assessment:

- o At this point in their development as student-athletes, the individuals on your teams should have a firm handle on what character in sports looks like. Sharing stories from the news and media from all aspects of life (sports, business, politics, etc.) about positive and negative examples are excellent ways to bring emphasis to **servant leadership,** and other CVs. A good weekly team assignment could be to give a different player each week the task of doing a little research and finding a story in the news regarding an act of **servant leadership**, either good or bad (or any other CV). They would then begin practice (potentially during the early stretch period) by sharing the story that they found and then relating it to the team. This is a great way for your players to demonstrate their retention and application of these vital developmental character values. Once again, it is another great way for them to practice public speaking and the presentation and articulation of ideas.
- o Have the players think about why it would be important for them to be able to play multiple positions on the team, or be versatile in their abilities to swim/run multiple races. Share the story of BJ Bedford-

Miller in this section and her experience at UT. There are many similar examples of this that I have mentioned previously. If you have not already shared this scenario with your players, it could be a great time when discussing servant leadership:

Scenario:

There are two All-American student-athletes. One is a high school All-American graduating senior shortstop, and the other is a college All-America rising junior shortstop. They both enter their next season at the top college program in the country. I asked them who is going to get to play shortstop, the freshman or the returning junior? The junior has already proven herself/himself at that level while the freshman has not. They all know the answer. However, I emphasize to them that if they are willing and able to effectively play another position, they will have a good chance of earning playing time as a freshman. If they have never been humble enough to learn another position or role, and they refuse to try to do so in college, they will inevitably find themselves buried on the bench, or worse off find themselves cut from the team. Coaches and employers, alike, are looking for team players who find ways to make the team or the organization as a whole more productive and successful.

CV #25 Legacy: Activities and Drills to increase Retention/Assessment:

- o At this final stage of **CLD**, all of our student-athletes should be true ambassadors for what athletic competition is all about. As I make note of in the next chapter, the student-athletes who remain involved in sports up to this advanced mastery level have the an extremely high chance of coaching the youth of future generations. They have accrued some good "sweat equity," as Dr. Michael Sagas (founder of Twinnor; Professor and Department Chair at UF) likes to say. What behaviors have we, as coaches, modeled for these up-and-coming coaches? Think about the **legacy** that you are leaving behind through your words and actions as a coach/mentor. This could be a great conversation with your team at this advanced level. Let them know that many of them will coach and mentor the next generation. Ask them to think about what type of coach they want to emulate? Who knows, it may even be you.

o   Have each of your players take 10 minutes during the start of a practice to write a hand-written letter to a coach or teacher or mentor who has made a positive impact in their life. Perhaps they taught them an important message that has stuck with them and influenced them in a positive way. Be sure to have envelopes with stamps and have them address and seal the letters after which you mail them off after practice.

o   A great take home assignment for your team is to have them each write their own coaching philosophy. Break the group up into five sections, to match the five levels of **CLD** (i.e. if you have 15 players, three players for each CLD section). Have them each write a one page, single-spaced coaching philosophy statement tailored specifically to the level of student-athlete that you assign to them. Give them a good week to work on this. Match them up at the start of practice with the others who were assigned the same level and have them first share with the others in their select group. This will allow them to fine tune and tweak their own coaching statements. After which, have them each present to the team. *Have the team vote on the top coaching philosophy at each level. If you feel so inclined, please send the top ones to me to use during my junior high and high school **CLD** curricula.

o   Lastly, have each of your student-athletes think about and write down the ten qualities or values that they would hope that their teammates and friends would say about them as individuals. Ask them to put one's athletic ability on the side, and focus more on one's character. Tell them that these will be kept confidential. Collect each of these as the coach to keep in a file for their next player evaluation. This list will provide you, as the coach, with some terrific talking points, as well as allow them to reflect on whether or not they have been working to demonstrate high character. This is a great spring board to analyze and improve the **legacy** that they are leaving behind.

Paciorek UF-IRB Study 2--Character Lit Age Appropriate Curriculum

Figures 8-12 (25 Character Values Developed Through Sports--Best Age to Initiate Emphasis on Character Value—The Line Charts provided below show a noticeable bell curve that develops around the age grouping of CVs)

Y-Axis=Number of Respondents/X-Axis=Age Range to Best Initiate CVs

Figure 8 Highest Character Values for the 5-7-Year-Old Range (Line Chart 2)

CVs: *Respect for Parents, Interdependence (Care for Others), Sportspersonship, Respect for Coaches & Rules, Gratitude (Joy)*

QID5 - Groups

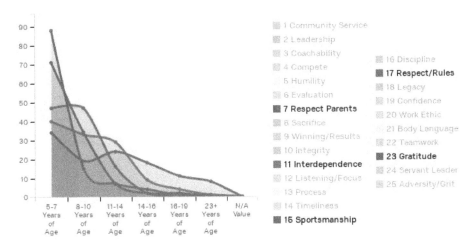

Figure 9 Highest Character Values for the 8-10-Year-Old Range (Line Chart 3)

<u>CVs:</u> *Coachability, Competition (Honest & Ethical), Integrity & Honor, Listening/Focus, Teamwork*

QID5 - Groups

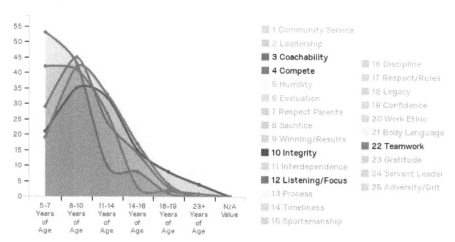

Fig. 10 Highest Character Values for the 11-14-Year-Old Range (Line Chart 4)

<u>CVs:</u> *Leadership, Humility, Timeliness, Discipline, Confidence not Cockiness, Work Ethic/Sense of Accomplishment*

QID5 - Groups

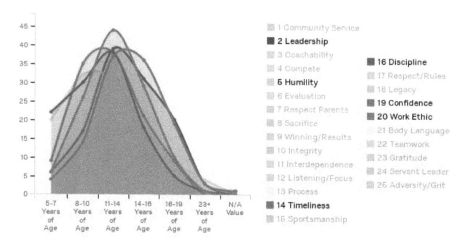

Fig. 11 Highest Character Values for the 14-16-Year-Old Range (Line Chart 5)

<u>CVs:</u> *Community Service/Outreach, Honest Evaluation (Self & Peers), Sacrifice, Process Oriented, Body Language, Handling Adversity/Grit*

QID5 - Groups

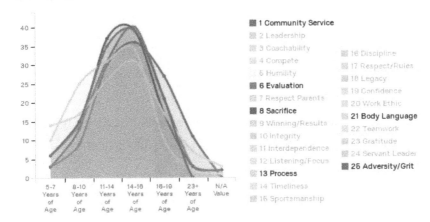

Fig. 12 Highest CVs for 16-19 & 19-23+ Year-Old Range (Line Chart 6)

<u>CVs:</u> *Winning (The Right Way), Legacy, Servant Leadership*

QID5 - Groups

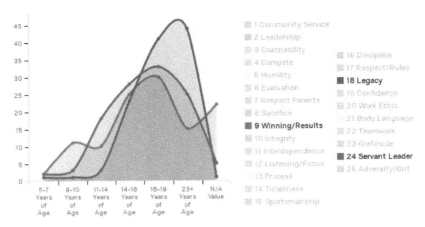

INFORMATION ABOUT PACIOREK C-SALT TEST

The C-SALT Test is designed for input from coaches, administrators, parents, and a higher age range of advanced student-athletes. This test is a replica version taken directly from my UF-IRB Research Study (Paciorek UF-IRB Study 2—Character Lit Age Appropriate Curriculum) that has been taken by some of our country's most experienced coaches. While there is no right or wrong answer, or official score for the C-SALT Test, the point is to get our young coaches, as well as sport management professionals, and even veteran coaches to contemplate the many values of character that can be developed through sports, if delivered appropriately and effectively. If you are a youth or amateur coach of at least five years and you would like to participate and have your data included in my ongoing research study, you can contact me using the information provided below. If you would like a version of the C-SALT Test to use with your advanced level teams or captains, I can also provide you with a separate version of the test.

CONTACT INFORMATION

How to get in contact with me, Coach Pete Paciorek, to share your stories of character, or lack of character, in sports to incorporate into my CLD curricula.

Website: www.characterlovescompany.org

Twitter page: @CharacterLovesCompany

Facebook Page: facebook.com/characterlovescompany

Blog Page: characterlovescompany.org/blog

Email: info@characterlovescompany.org

characterlovescompany@gmail.com

CHARACTER
LOVES
COMPANY

ADDENDUM—Contributing Research and Literature
in the Field of Character in Sports

Over the past 50 years, character development has been in and out of the spotlight in modern society, though its roots go back to ancient western civilization and the days of Socrates, Plato, and Aristotle.[131] According to Kohlberg (1973) in his article: "The Claim to Moral Adequacy of a Highest Stage of Moral Judgment," he depicted six different stages of moral development in human beings from birth to adulthood. Each of these successive stages was built on the previous one, as Kohlberg attempted to codify each of these stages into age specific groupings from which human beings advance morally and ethically. These six stages were divided into three sections: pre-conventional, Conventional, and Post-Conventional with each section having two stages. The premise of each of these stages is that a certain degree of mental maturity is requisite in order to comprehend the various advancing stages. Though accepted by many, Kohlberg's studies were critiqued and advanced by Gilligan (1982).[132] Whereas Kohlberg's findings were based on studies of males, Gilligan took more of a female approach to moral development.

These works by Kohlberg and Gilligan gave rise to more recent books and theories which have proven to be germane to my study of character development in our youth up through adulthood. Though not directly related to sports, the following three books helped frame my **CLD** curriculum: *Character Strengths and Virtues: A Handbook and*

---

[131] *Nicomachean Ethics* by Aristotle (originally published 350 BC, and *Introduction to Virtue Ethics Insights of the Ancient Greeks* (Devettere, 2002).
[132] Carol Gilligan's work was entitled: *In a Different Voice: Women's Conceptions of Self and Morality*

Classification (2004),[133] *Character and Moral Education: A Reader* (2011),[134] and *Leadership: Theory and Practice* (2015).[135] All three books descriptively blend in great detail the theoretical with real life application of moral and character development in everyday lives. Two of the more salient reads that I would highly recommend on building character in our youth on up are: *How Children Succeed: Grit, Curiosity, and the Hidden Power of Character* (2012),[136] and *Resilience* (2015).[137]

In narrowing the broad scope of ethics and virtue down the funnel as it relates to my two great passions, character and athletics, let's now turn to the pertinent literature in the world of youth and amateur sports. As a coach by profession and a graduate student on each of the bookends of the last ten years, I have devoured hundreds of excellent books and articles on character development in and through sports participation. From a coaching standpoint, at the pinnacle of this mountain of manuscripts, shining like a guiding light for all coaches and parents seeking to develop our youth through sports, will always be Coach Wooden's *Pyramid of Success Playbook* (2005).[138] Despite the fact that Coach Wooden's exceptional formula for coaching and mentoring in sports and the game of life, was not actually published for the first time until 2005, he had been relying on the content of his masterful template of success long before that. Many decades before Kohlberg and Gulligan presented and published their studies on mankind's moral development, Coach Wooden was already laying the foundation for successful moral development through sports both on and off the court.

---

[133] *Character Strengths and Virtues: A Handbook and Classification* is a nearly **800**-page book written by Christopher Peterson and Martin E.P. Seligman. Peterson and Seligman are highly respected PhD's and professors in the field of positive psychology at the University of Michigan and University of Pennsylvania, respectively. Together, they analyzed **24** strengths in the development of human character and virtue.

[134] *Character and Moral Education: A Reader* is a compilation of works and articles on character development from **33** contributors who are some of the top experts in the fields of Education, Humanities, Philosophy, Public Policy, Environmental Studies and other such topics relevant to the development of higher ethics, decision making, and virtue. This book is edited by Joseph L. DeVitis and Tianlong Yu.

[135] *Leadership: Theory and Practice* by Peter Northouse "…reviews and analyzes a selected number of leadership theories, giving special attention to how each theoretical approach could be applied in real-world organizations."

[136] *How Children Succeed* is a great read on the power of character, written by Paul Tough.

[137] *Resilience* is an excellent book, written by ex-Navy Seal Eric Greitens, about finding the inner-warrior.

[138] *Coach Wooden's Pyramid of Success Playbook* presents a foundation of building blocks for all coaches to follow. Though Wooden wrote numerous books disclosing the secrets to his success as a coach and mentor, the *Pyramid of Success Playbook* was written along with Jay Carty and published for the first time in 2005.

Even after his passing in 2009, Coach Wooden's *Pyramid of Success*[139] remains one of the most frequently cited and revered approaches for guaranteed success in sports, business, and most importantly, in life.

Similar to Coach Wooden's work and impact on society as a whole, there have been dozens, if not hundreds, of best sellers that have influenced my life, and, more specifically, the impetus for my guidebook. The following books on youth character development in sports were all written by long-term expert coaches who have been in the field of youth, amateur, or professional sports for the bulk of their professional lives (Hutslar, 1985,[140] Thompson, 1995; Clifford & Feezell, 1997; Ehrmann, 2011; Thornton, Champion Jr. & Ruddell, 2011; Summit, 2013; and Matheny, 2015). From a spiritual or religious lens, there have been many remarkable reads (Osborne, 1999, Dungy,[141] 2007; Gibbs, 2009; and Dungy, 2011) that have provided a focus on actively enhancing one's morals and virtues in the game of life. As someone with strong religious beliefs, I want to be clear to emphasize the importance of strong character and morals, irrespective of being religious. Character is not defined by one's religious affiliation, though I do believe that religion and church involvement can help promote strong character.

With a single-mindedness to character development in our youth, I have been highly influenced by the works and examples of the extraordinary coaches and mentors included in this book. Despite the proof that sports can have a positive societal impact, I could not precisely put my finger on why such a vast divide continued to manifest itself between the knowledge or theory and the actual demonstration of character in sports. I continued to dig into the literature on sports and I found that character development is indeed a focus. However, from a sport-focused perspective the implementation of character has typically been a "grab bag"[142] approach. Teaching character through the vehicle of sports is not easy and we have taken this vital task for granted for far too long.

---

[139] The components or building blocks that comprise Coach Wooden's *Pyramid of Success* is provided in a for the reader on the following website: www.coachwooden.com

[140] Jack Hutslar was way ahead of his time with as the title of his book indicates: *Beyond X's and O's, What Generic Parents, Volunteer Coaches, and Teachers Can Learn about Generic Kids and All the Sports They Play.* Though I provide a different delivery style and more modern perspective, the absolute truths of high morals and character remain unchanged.

[141] Tony Dungy, prior Super Bowl Champion NFL coach, wrote two of my favorite books (*Quiet Strength* in 2007 and *Uncommon* in 2011) about what it means to truly be a man in the hyper-competitive, aggressive, and seemingly cutthroat culture that we live in.

[142] I use the term "grab bag" because the approach of most coaches (though noble in their efforts to try to incorporate character) is sporadic and has no real consistency or sequence of progress checks.

I know that in my 15 years of coaching youth and amateur athletics I have been guilty of this "grab bag" approach to teaching character as well, but at least I can say that I was trying. As most of us have heard from a coach along the line, *"Anyone can try! I don't want you to simply try, I need you to do it* [whatever your task is] *correctly!"* It is time that we begin to emphasize youth character development through sports with a more *deliberate* and *intentional* purpose, rivaling the focus that we take to winning.

I have been dedicated to looking intently through the lens of the microscope, probing, and examining how we all (coaches, parents, administrators, and student-athletes) can be better at implementing character development. This became the basis of my **CLD** curriculum. The 25 character values create a foundational framework, or ladder, for the coach at all levels of youth and amateur sports to follow in order to effectively and consistently identify, promote, develop, and assess one's comprehension and retention of the immeasurable significance of character literacy development in our youth.

As I noted in Chapter 5, my "Aha moment" came as I was cross-researching Istvan Balyi and the previously referenced works of Coach Wooden's *Pyramid of Success*. Balyi is considered by much of the sports world as the founding father of the Long-Term Athlete Development Model (LTAD). The LTAD was originally created with the intent of maximizing the performance of elite-level athletes. Over the past decade, LTAD has sparked a whole new field of study at American universities in Kinesiology, Sport Management, and Human Performance Development programs. Leading experts in this field of performance development in sports, Balyi and Hamilton (2004) and Côté et al. (2007, 2009) have presented evidence that physical performance and growth could be maximized through age specific training regimens.

In Balyi and Hamilton's work (2004) they posit five clearly distinct stages from which to most effectively train and physically develop young athletes from six years old up through adolescence and into adulthood. These five stages paved the way for a more adaptable model for coaches to integrate based on the different ages they were coaching. Balyi's conceptions crystallized the notion that a youth coach working with children in his first stage: FUNdamentals (6-9 for boys and 6-8 for girls) would not necessarily be well-suited in assimilating the coaching practices that John Wooden had used while working with elite-level athletes at UCLA. Balyi is praised for bringing an awareness to creating appropriate practice/game plans and coaching philosophy for the requisite level of one's athletes. This type of logic had existed and been applied for decades, if not longer than that, but Balyi is credited for advancing this notion through empirical research on how the human body and brain develops.

Balyi's five stages are: **Stage 1** (age 6-9 boys and 6-8 girls) which emphasizes making physical fitness fun for children, while teaching them the basic motor skills and proper techniques. **Stage 2** (age 9-12 boys and 8-11 in girls) works to teach athletes how to learn to train through broad sport movements. **Stage 3** (age 12-16 boys and 11-15 girls) teaches athletes to know how to train, which is more serious and committed than the previous stage. **Stage 4** (age 16-18 boys and 15-17 girls) turns to high levels of competition to demonstrate acumen and competency in sport. **Stage 5** is the final stage from the higher levels of high school and beyond where now the stakes are at the highest for one's performance and where the results matter the most. At this stage, college scholarships and financial incentives are on the line.

Studies by Côté et al. (1999, 2007, 2009) are in agreement with the position taken by Balyi of the existence of progressive stages of development as athletes move through life. However, Côté and his colleagues found much more overlap between the various age groupings than Balyi and his colleagues. Côté added much value to the conversation by turning the discussion to the ideas of "deliberate play" versus "deliberate practice," and how those two concepts could and should be applied to the LTAD model. He posited that deliberate play introduces children to a variety of sports, while at the same time not being so overly structured which would remove the creativity and fun from the sport for children at the lower levels. As children participating in sports begin to better understand the rules of the game and how to participate most effectively, they can advance into the next stage of deliberate practice. Still today, the differentiation between these two concepts is unrecognizable, for the most part, to the majority of youth coaches. Though these concepts are getting more support and attention from elite experts in the field of sport coaching, the tendency is for coaches and parents to skip over deliberate practice, or what Balyi referred to as the FUNdamentals, in an effort to specialize earlier in order to meet the 10,000-hour mark[143] sooner or other unrealistic

---

[143] The 10,000-hours rule is one that was first posited by KA Ericsson (1993), but the fame of the concept of 10,000 hours of deliberate practice came from its inclusion in the ever popular 2008 book by Malcolm Gladwell entitled: *Outliers*. Though Ericsson made it known that applying his theory to

benchmarks or goals for the common child (Gladwell, 2008; Coyle, 2009; Woods, 1997). The bypassing of this integral early stage of youth sport development is becoming more and more common and one of many potential reasons why children at the lowest levels of sport are opting out. As masterfully depicted by ESPN columnist Tom Farrey (2008), the fun and excitement of youth sports from yesteryear are almost unrecognizable as the childlike enthusiasm and joy of sports has become an endangered occurrence.

The meaningful takeaway for the establishment of my **CLD** in regards to Balyi, Côté, and many other experts involved in physical development is precisely that their field of study on performance maximization is lightyears ahead of the field of character development in sports that I have chosen to focus on. Coach Wooden has provided the sports' world with 15 key components to becoming successful in life. However, the lack of application across all levels of coaching (both from a talent and age level) makes it difficult to consistently apply in a sequential and progressive order. My inquiry into the crossover between the underlying principles of Balyi's age specific LTAD and Wooden's *Pyramid of Success* has resulted in the creation of the **CLD** curriculum.

There are many studies on coaching efficacy[144] (Stones & Morris, 1972; Jones, Harris & Miles, 2009; Kavussanu et al., 2008; Chelladurai, 2007; Smith & Smoll, 1989) that analyzed the characteristics that make up an effective coach. Further studies (Barnett, Smoll, and Smith,1992; Nelson, Cushion and Potrac, 2006; Lemyre et al., 2007; Dieffenbach, Murray, & Zakrajsek, 2011; and Lynch and Mallett, 2006) discussed how important an expert or seasoned coach is in the retention and satisfaction of student-athlete participants. I found other valuable studies (Gilbert & Trudel 2001; Farres, 2001; Gilbert, Gallimore & Trudel, 2009; & Côté & Gilbert, 2009) that focused on the reflective approach to coaching. This approach is constantly looking back on each day and analyzing how it went. The reflective approach then attempts to apply the empirical data with current community of practices, which blends a variety approaches to maximize effectiveness with team and players. Farres (2001) lists five key elements of reflective practice; identification, self-awareness, critical assessment, experimentation, and evaluation of themselves as coaches constantly which provides a daily feedback loop.

---

sports was not the intent and is not a viable application, the term 10,000 hours has set the Tiger moms and dads ablaze in the world of youth sports.
[144] Coaching efficacy programs focus on finding the most effective approaches in order to assure coaching success through retention and respect of student-athletes.

While the above-mentioned studies provide valuable research about the need for coaching expertise to teach the tactical needs for training, I believe excellence in coaching has to marry character development with the physical development. These referenced studies are vital to a more comprehensive development in coaching effectiveness. I agree wholeheartedly that until more of our youth coaches have a higher level of sport acumen, we are going to keep losing kids who feel they are not getting better but actually getting worse. However, while we are in the process of looking for ways to teach coaches the skills and tactics for the game let's not wait another 20 years to incorporate or infuse an equally comprehensive **CLD** curriculum such as mine. I have mentioned many times that children want to see applicability between sport and the world and teaching character moments brings relevance to their lives.

There have been numerous organizations that place a premium on championing the development of character through sports. These organizations helped crystallize my concentration on **CL** and **CLD.** I would be remiss to think that I am the only one seeking answers to the inquiry of how we (coaches, parents, administrators, and student-athletes) can develop stronger and more lasting character in our youth through sports participation. I am honored that my non-profit organization, 501(c)(3), **Character Loves Company**, is wearing the same uniform as some truly inspiring and impactful youth development organizations across the United States of America: UF's LAADR program,[145] Arizona Sports Summit Accord,[146] Positive Coaching Alliance,[147] The Aspen Institute: Project Play: Reimagining Youth Sports in America,[148] True Competition,[149]

---

[145] LAADR was founded by a leader in the field of youth sports, Michael Sagas, and his team with the TRSM program at the University of Florida. http://laadr.hhp.ufl.edu/

[146] Arizona Sports Summit Accord was formed in 1999, and it seeks to recognize the highest potential of sports through "Six Pillars of Character." http://sports.josephsoninstitute.org

[147] PCA is an organization founded by Jim Thompson, who has written numerous books on the topic of character in sports. PCA has been focused on developing character in youth through the vehicle of sports for decades, and they have many branches throughout the country. PCA originated in Palo Alto, CA. http://www.positivecoach.org/

[148] The Aspen Institute: Project Play: Reimagining Youth Sports in America has teamed up with many experts in the field of youth and amateur sports to create a better tomorrow for our youth. http://www.aspenprojectplay.org/

[149] http://www.TrueCompetition.org was founded, and is operated, by three key contributors to the field, David Shields Ph.D., Brenda Bredemeier Ph.D., and Christopher Funk. Their mission is "Reclaiming competition for ethics, excellence, and enjoyment."

Coach Across America,[150] What Drives Winning,[151] BAT1000.[152] It is encouraging and reassuring to know that we are not alone in our quest and passion for developing character during these most formative years of our rising generations.

Most coaches would agree with the great John Wooden, who preached that what you emphasize most improves the most. However, looking at how our society trains our athletes from childhood through college it is ever apparent by the length of time spent on character development that it is simply a box to check off, as if to say, "Done that."

The time is now for character development and **CLD** to become a priority in youth and amateur sports. For far too long, character has been seen as a lesser component to the greater good in the pursuit of athletic excellence. I have a different stance as I view character as something that needs to be coached and nourished with the same intensity and regularity as the physical component of athlete training. I see the physical athlete development and character literacy development **CLD** as co-partners in the journey through the world of sports. I sincerely hope that through reading this guidebook on **CLD** that you, as Coach/Mentor or Parent, will choose to be *intentional* and *deliberate* in your emphasis on character development with the young and impressionable student-athletes whom you have the fortune of mentoring and leading!

---

[150] http://www.up2us.org Coach Across America's (CAA) mission is to help train, educate, and empower coaches to makes a difference in the lives of their student-athletes.
[151] http://whatdriveswinning.com/ Author Brett Ledbetter's book, *What Drives Winning*, provides some excellent tools for better performance through increased performance.
[152] BAT1000 is the company that my family started in Southern California based on the premise of going 3-3 in life (Student/Athlete/Character-Leader). http://www.bat1000.net/ & http://www.b1collegetours.us/

REFERENCES

Anderson, E. (2010). *Sport, theory, and social problems: A critical introduction*. London: Routledge.

Barnett, N. P., Smoll, F. L., & Smith, R. E. (1992). Effects of enhancing coach-athlete relationships on youth sport attrition. *Sport Psychologist, 6*(2).

Bass, B. M., & Riggio, R. E. (2006). *Transformational leadership*. Psychology Press.

Balyi, I., & Hamilton, A. (2004). Long-term athlete development: Trainability in childhood and adolescence. Windows of opportunity. Optimal trainability. *Victoria: National Coaching Institute British Columbia & Advanced Training and Performance Ltd*, 194.

Bear, L. C. (2016). The NFL's New Domestic Violence Policy Is a Joke. Retrieved June 10, 2016, from http://www.vocativ.com/283111/the-nfls-new-domestic-violence-policy-is-a-joke/

Beatty and Fawyer (2013). "Project Play" Research Briefs. Retrieved November 15, 2015, http://sparc.hhp.ufl.edu/index.php/research/publications/project-play-research-briefs/

Borland, J. F., Burton, L. J., & Kane, G. M. (2014). *Sport Leadership in the 21st Century*. Jones & Bartlett Publishers.

Branta, C. F. (2010). Sport specialization: Developmental and learning issues. *Journal of Physical Education, Recreation & Dance, 81*(8), 19-28.

Bronson, P., & Merryman, A. (2013). *Top dog: The science of winning and losing*. New York: Twelve.

Burgess, D.J., & Naughton, G.A. (2010). Talent development in adolescent team sports: A review. *International Journal of Sports Physiology and Performance, 5*, 103-116.

Chelladurai, P. (2007). Leadership in sports. *Handbook of Sport Psychology, Third Edition*, 111-135.

Clifford, C., & Feezell, R. M. (1997). Coaching for character. *Human Kinetics*. Champagne, IL.

Collins, J. C. (2001). *Good to great: Why some companies make the leap...and others don't*. Random House.

Conger, J. A. (1999). Charismatic and transformational leadership in organizations: An insider's perspective on these developing streams of research. *The Leadership Quarterly, 10*(2), 145-179.

Côté, J. (1999). The influence of the family in the development of talent in sport. *The sport psychologist, 13*(4), 395-417.

Côté, J., & Gilbert, W. (2009). An integrative definition of coaching effectiveness and expertise.

Côté, J., Lidor, R., & Hackfort, D. (2009). ISSP position stand: To sample or to specialize? *International Journal of Sport and Exercise Psychology, 9*, 717.

Côté, J., Baker, J., & Abernethy, B. (2007). Practice to play in the development of sport expertise. Eklund, R., & Tenenbaum, G. (Eds.), *Handbook of Sport Psychology,* (pp. 184-202). Hoboken, NJ: Wiley.

Côté, J. & Fraser-Thomas (2008). Play, practice, and athlete development. Farrow, D., Baker, J., & MacMahon, C. (Eds.), *Developing Sport Expertise* (pp. 17-28). New York: Taylor and Francis.

Coyle, D. (2009). *The talent code: Greatness isn't born: It's grown, here's how.* New York: Bantam Books.

Cuddy, A. (2015). *Presence: Bringing your boldest self to your biggest challenges.* New York: Little, Brown and Company.

Cuddy, A. (2012). *Amy Cuddy: Your body language shapes who you are.* [Video file]. Retrieved March 8, 2016 from, https://www.ted.com/talks/amy_cuddy_your_body_language_shapes_who_yo u_are?language=en

Dieffenbach, K. D., Murray, M., & Zakrajsek, R. (2011). The coach education internship experience: An exploratory study. *International Journal of Coaching Science, 5*(1), 3-25.

Dungy, T. (2007). *Quiet strength: a memoir.* Tyndale House Publishers, Inc.

Dungy, T. (2011). *Uncommon: Finding Your Path to Significance.* Tyndale House Publishers, Inc.

Dweck, C. S. (2006). Mindset: The new psychology of success. New York: Random House.

Dweck, C. S. (2012). Mindset: How You Can Fulfill Your Potential. Constable & Robinson Limited.

Eagle Palm Requirements. (n.d.). Retrieved July 15, 2016, from
http://usscouts.org/advance/boyscout/bsrank8.asp

Ehrmann, J., & Jordan, G. (2011). *InsideOut coaching: How sports can transform lives*. Simon and Schuster.

Elliott, R. (2014). *Everything you need to know about the Ray Rice case*. Retrieved February 2, 2016, from http://time.com/3329351/ray-rice-timeline/

Farres, L. G. (2001). Becoming a better coach through reflective practice. *Perspective, 6*, 10-11.

Farrey, T. (2008). *Game on: The all-American race to make champions of our children*. New York: ESPN Books.

Fatherhood Data & Statistics. (n.d.). Retrieved January 2, 2016, from
http://www.fatherhood.org/fatherhood-data-statistics

Fraser-Thomas, J. L., Côté, J., & Deakin, J. (2005). Youth sport programs: An avenue to foster positive youth development. *Physical Education & Sport Pedagogy, 10*(1), 19-40.

Gibbs, J. (2011). *Game Plan for Life: Your Personal Playbook for Success*. Tyndale House Publishers, Inc.

Gibson, M. (Director), Gibson, M. (Producer), & Wallace, R. (Writer). (1995). *Braveheart* [Video file].

Gilbert, W. D., & Trudel, P. (2001). Learning to coach through experience: Reflection in model youth sport coaches. *Journal of teaching in physical education, 21*(1), 16-34.

Gilbert, W., Gallimore, R., & Trudel, P. (2009). A learning community approach to coach development in youth sport. *Journal of coaching education, 2*(2), 1-21.

Gilligan, C. (1982). *In a different voice*. Harvard University Press.

Gould, D., Udry, E., Tuffey, S. and Loehr, J. (1996). Burnout in competitive junior tennis player: A quantitative psychological assessment. *The Sport Psychologist, 10*, 322-340.

Gladwell, M. (2008). *Outliers: The story of success*. Hachette UK.

Greitens, E. (2015). *Resilience: Hard-won Wisdom for Living a Better Life*. Houghton Mifflin, Harcourt.

Grenoble , R. (2014). Florida State Suspends Star Quarterback Jameis Winston for Jumping On Table, Yelling Obscenity. Retrieved February 11, 2016, from http://www.huffingtonpost.com/2014/09/17/florida-state-jameis-winston-obscenity_n_5836616.html

Hall, J., Johnson, S., Wysocki, A., & Kepner, K. (2002). Transformational leadership: The transformation of managers and associates. *University of Florida IFAS Extension.*

Hill, A., & Wooden, J. (2002). *Be Quick-But Don't Hurry: Finding Success in the Teachings of a Lifetime.* Simon and Schuster.

Horton, S. (2012). Environmental influences on early development in sports experts. Baker, J., Cobley, S., & Schorer, J., (Eds), *Talent Identification and Development in Sport: International Perspectives:* New York: Routledge.

Hutslar, J. (1985). *Beyond X's and O's: what generic parents, volunteer coaches and teachers can learn about generic kids and all of the sports they play.* Wooten.

Jacobs, P. (2014). Navy SEAL Commander Tells Students To Make Their Beds Every Morning In Incredible Commencement Speech. Retrieved June 17, 2016, from http://www.businessinsider.com/bill-mcraven-commencement-speech-at-ut-2014-5

Jayanthi, N. (December, 2012). Injury risks of sports specialization and training in junior tennis players: A clinical study. Paper presented at the Society for Tennis and Medicine Science North American Regional Conference, Atlanta, GA

Johnny Manziel is the NFL's first domestic violence case in 2016. He won't be the last. (2016). Retrieved June 10, 2016, from https://www.washingtonpost.com/news/wonk/wp/2016/02/09/johnny-manziel-is-the-nfls-first-domestic-violence-case-in-2016-he-wont-be-the-last/

Jones, R. L., Harris, R., & Miles, A. (2009). Mentoring in sports coaching: A review of the literature. *Physical Education and Sport Pedagogy, 14*(3), 267-284.

Jose Reyes Suspended Through May 31 Under Domestic Violence Policy. (2016). Retrieved June 7, 2016, from http://www.mlbtraderumors.com/2016/05/jose-reyes-suspended-through-may-31.html

Kavussanu, M., Boardley, I. D., Jutkiewicz, N., Vincent, S., & Ring, C. (2008). Coaching efficacy and coaching effectiveness: Examining their predictors and comparing coaches' and athletes' reports. *The Sport Psychologist, 22*(4), 383-404.

Kohlberg, L. (1973). *Continuities in childhood and adult moral development revisited.* Moral Education Research Foundation.

Kuhnert, K. W., & Lewis, P. (1987). Transactional and transformational leadership: A constructive/developmental analysis. *Academy of Management review, 12*(4), 648-657.

Lee, M. J., Whitehead, J., & Balchin, N. (2000). The measurement of values in youth sport: Development of the Youth Sport Values Questionnaire. *Journal of sport and exercise psychology, 22*(4), 307-326.

Lee, M. J., Whitehead, J., Ntoumanis, N., & Hatzigeorgiadis, A. (2008). Relationships among values, achievement orientations, and attitudes in youth sport. *Journal of sport and exercise psychology, 30*(5), 581-610.

Lemyre, F., Trudel, P., & Durand-Bush, N. (2007). How youth-sport coaches learn to coach. *Sport psychologist, 21*(2), 191.

Loehr, J. (2008). *The power of story: change your story, change your destiny in business and in life.* Simon and Schuster.

Loehr, J., & Schwartz, T. (2003). The Power of Full Engagement: Managing Energy. *Not Time, is the Key to High Performance and Personal Renewal,* Simon and Schuster.

Loehr, J. E. (2012). *The only way to win: How building character helps you achieve more and find greater fulfillment in business and life.* Hyperion: New York.

MacLuhan, M., Fiore, Q., & Agel, J. (1967). *The medium is the massage.* Penguin Books.

Mallett, C., & Lynch, M. (2006). Becoming a successful high performance track and field coach. *Modern Athlete and Coach, 44*(2), 15-20.

Manziel's HS coach: 'I really don't know that guy' (2016). Retrieved July 01, 2016, from http://www.msn.com/en-us/sports/nfl/manziels-hs-coach-i-really-dont-know-that-guy/ar-BBsPYc7?li=BBnb7Kz

Matheny, M., & Jenkins, J. B. (2015). *The Matheny Manifesto: A young manager's old school views on success in sports and life.*

McLaughlin, E. & Lett, C. (2015). *CNN.* "Texas coach accused of ordering player to hit referee resigns". Retrieved February 20, 2016, from http://www.cnn.com/2015/09/24/us/high-school-players-hit-texas-football-official-hearing/

Nelson, L., Cushion, C., & Potrac, P. (2006). Formal, nonformal and informal coach learning: A holistic conceptualisation. *International Journal of Sports Science and Coaching, 1*(3), 247-259.

Nelson Mandela speech that changed the world. (2000). Retrieved January 25, 2016, from https://www.laureus.com/content/nelson-mandela-speech-changed-world

Newman, M. (2015). MLB set to introduce domestic violence policy. Retrieved May 21, 2016, from http://m.mlb.com/news/article/138225204/mlb-set-to-introduce-domestic-violence-policy

Northouse, P. G. (2015). *Leadership: Theory and practice*. Sage publications.

Opinionator The Power of Positive Coaching Comments: http://opinionator.blogs.nytimes.com/2011/10/20/the-power-of-positive-coaching/

Osborne, T. (1999). *Faith in the game: Lessons on football, work, and life*. New York: Broadway Books.

Penn State Could Face Claims From Six More Alleged Jerry Sandusky Victims. (n.d.). Retrieved May 25, 2016, from http://www.nbcnews.com/news/us-news/penn-state-could-face-claims-six-more-alleged-jerry-sandusky-n469766

Peterson, C., & Seligman, M. E. (2004). *Character strengths and virtues: A handbook and classification*. Oxford University Press.

Pope Francis sees sports as a world changer. (2016). Retrieved April 16, 2016, from http://www.sportsbusinessdaily.com/Journal/Issues/2016/01/25/Sports-in-Society/Pope-Francis.aspx?hl=pope

Rankings. (n.d.). Retrieved May 23, 2016, from http://www.usssa.com/baseball/Rank1/#/?gdSport=1

Red Hot Sox: 5/26/16. (2016). Retrieved June 30, 2016, from http://podtail.com/podcast/baseballtonight-with-buster-olney/red-hot-sox-5-26-16/

Rosenberg, M. (August, 2016). *Sports Illustrated*. "It's Time for USOC to Step up after USA Gymnastics Sex Abuse Scandal." Web. 05 Aug. 2016. Retrieved August 5, 2016, from http://www.msn.com/en-us/sports/olympics/it%e2%80%99s-time-for-usoc-to-step-up-after-usa-gymnastics-sex-abuse-scandal/ar-BBvhwiv#image=1

Sagas, M., & Wigley, B. J. (2014). Gray Area Ethical Leadership in the NCAA: The Ethics of Doing the Wrong Things Right. *Journal of Intercollegiate Sport JIS, 7*(1), 40-57.

See the Sportsmanship Billboard of a Team that Helped Injured Opponent Values.com. (n.d.). Retrieved April 30, 2016, from http://www.values.com/inspirational-sayings-billboards/42-sportsmanship

Shields, D. L., & Bredemeier, B. L. (2007). Advances in sport morality research.

Shields, D. L., LaVoi, N. M., Bredemeier, B. L., & Power, F. C. (2007). Predictors of poor sportspersonship in youth sports: Personal attitudes and social influences. *Journal of Sport and Exercise Psychology, 29*(6), 747.

Sivers, D. (2013). *Derek Sivers' TED Talk: "How to Start a Movement"*. [Video File]. Retrieved February 13, 2016, from https://www.youtube.com/watch?v=RXMnDG3QzxE

Smoll, F. L., & Smith, R. E. (1989). Leadership Behaviors in Sport: A Theoretical Model and Research Paradigm1. *Journal of Applied Social Psychology, 19*(18), 1522-1551.

Sports Illustrated (2015). *UFC's Ronda Rousey is world's most dominant athlete*. [Video file]. Retrieved May 30, 2016, from http://www.si.com/mma/2015/05/12/ronda-rousey-ufc-mma-fighter-armbar

Stoltz, P. G. (2015). *Grit: The new science of what it takes to persevere, flourish, succeed*.

Stones, E., & Morris, S. (1972). The assessment of practical teaching. *Educational Research, 14*(2), 110-119.

Subotnik, R.F., Olszewski-Kubilius, P., & Worrell, F.C. (2011). Rethinking giftedness and gifted education: A proposed direction forward based on psychological science. *Psychological Science in the Public Interest, 12*, 3-54.

Summitt, P. H., & Jenkins, S. (2013). *Sum it up: 1,098 victories, a couple of irrelevant losses, and a life in perspective*.

Thompson, J. (1995). *Positive coaching: Building character and self-esteem through sports*. Warde Publishers.

Thornton, P. K., Champion, W. T., Ruddell, L. S., & Ruddell, L. (2011). *Sports ethics for sports management professionals*. Jones & Bartlett Publishers.

Tough, P. (2013). *How children succeed*. Random House.

USATODAY.com - Roddick's honesty turns out costly at Rome Masters. (2005).
Retrieved February 17, 2016, from
http://usatoday30.usatoday.com/sports/tennis/2005-05-05-rome-
masters_x.htm

Vadrevu, S. (2012). Character and moral education: A reader. *Asia Pacific Journal of
Education, 32*(4), 518-519.

Vergara, A. (2016). Johnny Manziel's dad: 'My son is a druggie and he needs help'.
Retrieved July 15, 2016, from http://www.foxsports.com/nfl/story/johnny-
manziel-dad-my-son-is-a-druggie-and-he-needs-help-062416

Wagner, S. K. (2014). *Perfect: The rise and fall of John Paciorek, baseball's greatest one-game
wonder.*

Weirsma, L.D. (2000). Risks and benefits of youth sport specialization: Perspectives and
recommendations. *Pediatric Exercise Science,* 12, 13-22.

Whiteside, K. (2014). *USA TODAY Sports.* Citing sex abuse cases, swimmers protest Hall
of Fame induction. Retrieved March 29, 2016, from
http://www.usatoday.com/story/sports/olympics/2014/05/29/swimming-hall-
of-fame-induction-protest/9738737/

Wooden, J., & Carty, J. (2005). *Coach Wooden's Pyramid of Success Playbook.* Revell.

Wooden, J. (n.d.). Retrieved August 1, 2015, from BrainyQuote.com Web site:
http://www.brainyquote.com/quotes/quotes/j/johnwooden163015.html

Woods, E., & McDaniel, P. (1997). *Training a Tiger: A father's guide to raising a winner in both
golf and life.* New York: HarperCollins.

Website Links for Effective Youth Development Through Sports:

http://www.characterlovescompany.org

http://laadr.hhp.ufl.edu/

http://sports.josephsoninstitute.org

http://www.positivecoach.org/

http://www.aspenprojectplay.org/

http://www.TrueCompetition.org

http://www.up2us.org

http://whatdriveswinning.com/

http://www.bat1000.net/

ACKNOWLEDGEMENTS

This guidebook on character literacy development **CLD** has been a steady undertaking for the past year and a half. However, the impetus for the content and emphasis of **CLD** has been forming in my mind for more than 20 years. I have wrestled with the true purpose of athletic competition for much of my life coming from a family legacy of student-athletes and professional athletes. I have been blessed by the many coaches and mentors who have positively influenced the development of my character, and I am grateful to all of them. While certain individuals played a more direct and impactful role, other coaches and teachers have played smaller (but no less vital) roles.

Life is about positive influence. Though my mom passed away when I was only 11-years-old, she has been one of the most influential people in my life, and I am extremely grateful for those early foundational years. My dad, whom I reference quite often in this guidebook, has been a youth coach for five decades and I credit him for molding the approach to coaching that I have today.

I want to thank all of my contributors who are listed in the table of contents. Their interviews, in person and on the phone, were both inspiring and motivating. They all share a burning passion for competition in sports and what I refer to as "winning the right way." However, the most notable characteristic that they all possess is a genuine and true concern for the well-being of others. They are all strong leaders who are leaving a positive footprint on their communities through their legacy. I am also grateful to the more than 125 expert coaches who contributed to both of my UF-IRB Research studies.

I want to thank all of my graduate school professors, both at the University of Florida for my M.S. in Sport Management, as well as my professors at California State University, Los Angeles for my M.A. in Communications. These incredible educators have dedicated their lives to research and to the development of young, earnest thinkers. In the classrooms and lecture halls with these great minds was where my inspiration to respond to the need for a more intentional and deliberate approach to character development in sports was sharpened and refined. It was apropos that my first graduate school class at the University of Florida was a course in Sports Ethics. In this class, Dr. Alyssa Tavormina challenged all of the young (or in my case, older), up-and-coming sports managers to re-evaluate the current landscape of amateur sports in America from an ethical vantage point. I am grateful to Dr. Tavormina for her commitment to taking a firm stance on the value of ethics in sports.

I especially want to thank Dr. Michael Sagas, Professor and Chair of the Department of Tourism, Recreation, and Sport Management at the University of Florida, for his leadership and commitment to improving the plight of youth and amateur sports. It was his specific article entitled, "Gray Area Ethical Leadership in the NCAA: The Ethics of Doing the Wrong Things Right" that helped to crystallize the various components of this guidebook that were scattered about in my mind. Dr. Sagas has become a strong mentor of mine ever since, and I cannot thank him enough for his guidance and support during the process of writing this book.

I want to thank Mr. Fred Claire, who has been a most reliable mentor to me for the past 10 years dating back to my previous master's degree and thesis dissertation on leadership from CSULA. I have never met someone who embodies leadership more so than Mr. Claire. I have found that each conversation or correspondence that I have had the fortune to have with him is a learning opportunity. Mr. Claire will never give me the answers or the silver bullet, but rather, he always empowers me to think bigger and to be bolder with my vision, intent, and purpose.

I want to give thanks to my sister Amy for her terrific artwork on the cover depicting my message, as well as to Jocelyn Greene at Green Girl Design for creating the cover and logo design.

Most importantly, I want to thank my wife (who was also my high school sweetheart), Sara, who knowing her humility would not want me to include her in my acknowledgements section. She and our three children are the greatest blessings in my life. No one has influenced my perspective on life more so than she has!

Pete—The Player

Pete—The Coach
(Photo courtesy of Kit Carlson Photography)

Pete—The Mentor

Pete with mentor, Mr. Fred Claire (draft of Pete's guidebook in hand)

Pete with mentor, Dr. Michael Sagas (working in the UF Lab)

www.characterlovescompany.org